To Susie,

With very best
wishes,

Brian

March 2010

TERRIBLE EXILE

Sir Brian Unwin studied at the universities of Oxford and Yale. After a career in the civil service in Whitehall he became President of the European Investment Bank. He has a long-standing interest in the Napoleonic period and Napoleon's captivity on St Helena and in 2007 visited the island in pursuit of his research into Napoleon's captivity there.

TERRIBLE EXILE

*The Last Days
of Napoleon on
St Helena*

BRIAN UNWIN

I.B. TAURIS

LONDON · NEW YORK

Published in 2010 by I.B.Tauris & Co Ltd
6 Salem Road, London W2 4BU
175 Fifth Avenue, New York NY 10010
www.ibtauris.com

Distributed in the United States and Canada Exclusively by Palgrave Macmillan,
175 Fifth Avenue, New York NY 10010

ISBN 978 1 84885 287 7

A full CIP record for this book is available from the British Library
A full CIP record is available from the Library of Congress

Library of Congress Catalog Card Number: available

Typeset by JCS Publishing Services Ltd, www.jcs-publishing.co.uk
Printed and bound in Great Britain by CPI Antony Rowe, Chippenham

CONTENTS

~~~

ILLUSTRATIONS

~~~

~~~

to Diana

~~~

MAP OF ST HELENA

5 km

N

Sugarloaf Point
Flagstaff Bay
Prosperous Bay
Rupert's Bay
James Bay
Flagstaff Hill
The Barn
Sugarloaf
Stone Top Bay
Jamestown
Deadwood Plain
Boer Camp
Bertrands' Cottage
Stone Top
Lemon Valley Bay
Ladder Hill
Devil's Punch Bowl
Alarm House
Longwood House
Napoleon's Tomb
(Geranium Valley)
The Briars
Lemon Valley
Plantation House
Hutt's Gate
Diana's Peak
Sandy Bay
Mount Pleasant
South-West Point

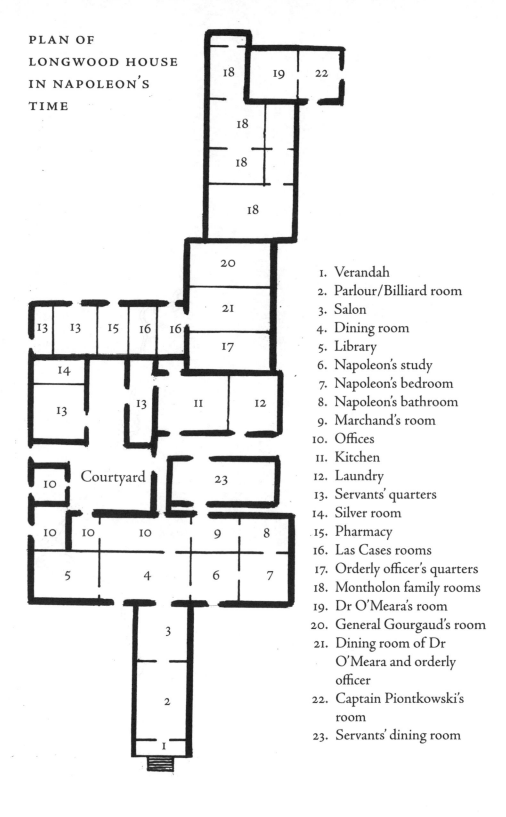

PLAN OF
LONGWOOD HOUSE
IN NAPOLEON'S
TIME

18   19   22
18
18
18
20
21
13   13   15   16   16
17
14
13   13   11   12
10   Courtyard   23
10   10   10   9   8
5   4   6   7
3
2
1

1. Verandah
2. Parlour/Billiard room
3. Salon
4. Dining room
5. Library
6. Napoleon's study
7. Napoleon's bedroom
8. Napoleon's bathroom
9. Marchand's room
10. Offices
11. Kitchen
12. Laundry
13. Servants' quarters
14. Silver room
15. Pharmacy
16. Las Cases rooms
17. Orderly officer's quarters
18. Montholon family rooms
19. Dr O'Meara's room
20. General Gourgaud's room
21. Dining room of Dr
    O'Meara and orderly
    officer
22. Captain Piontkowski's
    room
23. Servants' dining room

PREFACE

~~~

My first hero was the Duke of Wellington. He was a public servant of the utmost dedication and integrity – a 'nimmukwallah', who served the King 'with unfailing zeal and cheerfulness' as long as he ate the King's salt – and probably the finest general Britain has ever had. He never lost a battle. I avidly collected books about his great final victory, thanks to Blücher and the Prussians, at Waterloo and often tramped over the battlefield when I could escape from my own battles over the European budget in the Council and Commission meeting rooms in Brussels.

The more I studied Waterloo, however, the more curious I became about the fate of the defeated Napoleon. With some feeling of guilt at deserting my first hero the emphasis of my research switched from the Duke to the Emperor and I began to devour the memoirs of those who had shared or witnessed his captivity on St Helena. My interest became an obsession and I felt compelled to write about it, moved partly by the fact that although there are thousands of books about Napoleon, there is relatively little detailed coverage, at least in English, of this final period of his life.

The heart of the St Helena drama is the confrontation between Napoleon and the British Governor, General Sir Hudson Lowe, who was sent out with over 2,000 troops to ensure he did not escape. Although Andrew Roberts in his *Napoleon and Wellington* dismisses the rows between Napoleon and Lowe as no more than a 'footnote to a footnote to history', it is a fascinating story. History has, however, been hard on Lowe. The French tradition casts him as an out and out villain – a brutal jailor, who cruelly persecuted his prisoner – and much of the British tradition is little kinder. I therefore set out to judge how fair this verdict is and whether Lowe's reputation could be rehabilitated. I found it hard to do so entirely, but I came to believe that for all his faults the balance should be struck more evenly in his favour.

My obsession became such that I had to visit St Helena to see the place of Napoleon's prison for myself. My wife and I accordingly went to the island in December 2007. It was an amazing adventure and I was able to visit Longwood House, the Briars, Napoleon's tomb in Geranium Valley, and even Mount Pleasant House, where Napoleon made his last excursion from Longwood in October 1820. I am most grateful to J.J. Smith, Trevor Magellan and Rebecca Cairns-Smith for facilitating our visits to Longwood, the Briars and Mount Pleasant respectively; and also for the kind hospitality of the Governor, Andrew Gurr, and Jean Gurr which allowed us to explore his official residence, Plantation House, which Lowe had occupied. As we walked through the corridors I could almost feel the presence of Lowe's aide de camp (ADC), Major Gideon Gorrequer, as he sat alone in his small room each evening scribbling by candle light his extraordinarily bitter diary of each day's events. But the most dramatic moment of the visit was our first sighting of the island from the good ship RMS *St Helena*, as the distant dot on the horizon gradually transformed into a mass of high, jagged, volcanic cliffs, like prison walls. I could just begin to imagine Napoleon's horrified feelings as he saw it for the first time from the deck of the *Northumberland* on 15 October 1815.

Many people have helped and encouraged me, above all my wife, Diana. In addition to the photographs she took on St Helena she read each chapter as it emerged, making many valuable corrections and suggestions; she gave particular help in compiling the notes and the index; but above all tolerated patiently my incessant chatter about Napoleon, who somehow crept into every conversation both at home and with friends. I also benefited greatly from the professional advice and help of our eldest son, Michael, a talented author, artist and editor himself, whose chapter heading illustrations adorn this book. My sister-in-law, Dr Elspeth Adams, kindly gave me valuable advice on Napoleon's illness; and I was much helped by the librarian of the Reform Club, Simon Blundell, who allowed me a long lease of crucial 19th-century texts. Finally, I owe a great debt to my editor, Liz Friend-Smith, for her faith in this project and her ever perceptive and constructive advice when it came to organizing and licking it into shape; and also to Jessica Cuthbert-Smith and copy-editor Steve Williamson for their expert help in the final stages. Needless to say, however, any errors or failings of fact or judgement are entirely mine.

I hope this book will be an interesting and enjoyable read and that, while seeking to portray sympathetically the appalling circumstances in which Napoleon ended his career, it will also correct the historical balance a little more in Sir Hudson Lowe's favour. He certainly did not merit the shabby treatment he received from the British Government after he returned from St Helena 'mission accomplished'. As Napoleon's companion, General Gourgaud, remarked: 'Even if an angel had been sent out as Governor, it would have been all the same.'

PRINCIPAL
CHARACTERS ON
ST HELENA

~~~

Abell, Mrs Elizabeth: see Balcombe, Betsy.

Ali, Mameluke (1788–1856): Napoleon's second valet, whose real name was Louis-Etienne St-Denis. He entered Napoleon's service in 1806 and on being made 'Second Mameluke' in December 1811 (an appointment dating back to Napoleon's 1798 Egyptian expedition) became known as Ali. He served Napoleon on many campaigns, including Russia and Waterloo, and accompanied him in exile on both Elba and St Helena, where he remained until Napoleon's death one of his most loyal and trusted servants. His memoirs, published for the first time in 1926, form a touching account of his service. He was a member of the party sent to bring Napoleon's body back to France in 1840.

Antommarchi, Dr Francisco (1789–1838): a Corsican doctor who was sent to St Helena in July 1820 by Napoleon's mother, Madame Mère, and his uncle, Cardinal Fesch. Although a skilled anatomist, who had studied at Pisa and Florence, he had little experience of general practice and no credibility with Napoleon. He nevertheless performed the autopsy on Napoleon but, in a dispute with the English doctors present, refused to sign the official report. He published his memoirs of that time in 1825 in *Les Derniers Moments de Napoléon*.

Archambault, Achille Thomas L'Union, and Joseph Olivier: brothers, who were coachman and groom respectively to Napoleon on St Helena. Achille remained until Napoleon's death and returned in 1840 for the exhumation. Joseph was expelled by Sir Hudson Lowe in October 1816 but later found service with Napoleon's elder brother, Joseph, in the United States.

Arnott, Dr Archibald (1771–1855): surgeon to the 20th foot regiment, he came to St Helena in April 1819 and paid his first professional call on Napoleon in April 1821, shortly before his death. They quickly established a good rapport and he attended Napoleon until his death and was present at the autopsy. In 1822 he published *An Account of the Last Illness of Napoleon*, which upset Sir Hudson Lowe.

Balcombe, Betsy (1802–71): Betsy was the younger daughter of William and Jane Balcombe and became a great favourite of Napoleon during his stay at the Briars. Under her married name, Mrs Abell, she published in 1844 *To Befriend an Emperor*, a delightfully fresh and lively account of her relationship with Napoleon.

Balcombe, William (1779–1829): superintendent of public sales for the East India Company on St Helena and official purveyor to Longwood. He went to St Helena in 1807 and he and his wife, Jane, established a cordial relationship with Napoleon during the latter's stay in a pavilion in the garden of the Briars, from October to December 1815. After Napoleon's move to Longwood they were frequent visitors there but Sir Hudson Lowe caused Balcombe to leave the island in March 1818 on suspicion of abetting Napoleon in clandestine correspondence and for other alleged irregularities. He was later rehabilitated and appointed Colonial Treasurer of New South Wales, where he died in 1829.

Balmain, Alexandre Antonovitch Ramsay, Count de (d.1848): the Russian Commissioner, who arrived on St Helena in June 1816 and left in May 1820, having married Sir Hudson Lowe's elder step-daughter. He was generally supportive of Lowe's policies and conduct.

Baxter, Dr Alexander (1771–1841): an army surgeon who had served in the Corsican Rangers with Sir Hudson Lowe and been with him at the surrender of Capri. At Lowe's request he accompanied him to St Helena as Deputy-Inspector of Hospitals and became closely involved in the politics of the medical treatment of Napoleon in the weeks prior to his death. After leaving St Helena he took a medical degree in Edinburgh and became Chief Medical Officer in Barbados.

Bertrand, General Henri Gratien, Count (1773–1844): a military engineer by training, Bertrand served with great distinction in many of Napoleon's campaigns and was appointed Grand Marshal of the Court in November 1814. He was with Napoleon in exile on Elba and present at Waterloo, and followed Napoleon to St Helena, where he was the senior member of the Longwood household and bore the brunt of Napoleon's fraught relations with Sir Hudson Lowe. Despite much provocation and pressure from his wife to return to Europe, he served Napoleon with touching loyalty until the end. He was a prominent member of the party sent to St Helena in 1840 to bring back Napoleon's remains to France.

Bertrand, Fanny, Countess: daughter of General Arthur Dillon, an Irish refugee, and well connected in London, she accompanied her husband, under protest, to St Helena. A feisty character, she incurred Napoleon's displeasure by insisting on living separately from Longwood (initially at Hutt's Gate and later in a newly built cottage opposite Longwood). She took three children with her and had a fourth on the island.

Bingham, Brigadier-General Sir George Ridout (1776–1833): having served with distinction in the Peninsular War he was appointed to command the troops on St Helena and travelled there on the *Northumberland* with Napoleon and his party. He remained on the island until May 1820 and enjoyed a friendly relationship with Napoleon.

Buonavita, Abbé Antonio (b.1753): he was sent out in September 1820 by Napoleon's uncle, Cardinal Fesch, to serve as his priest. He was, however, elderly and infirm, and after a miserable and unproductive time returned to Europe in March 1821.

Cipriani (d.1818): his full name was Cipriani Franchesci but he was always known only by his first name. He served as maître d'hôtel at Longwood and as a fellow Corsican was particularly close to Napoleon. He died mysteriously on 26 February 1818 after developing severe stomach pains at a dinner a few days previously.

Cockburn, Rear-Admiral Sir George (1772–1853): a distinguished sailor who served in most theatres of the Napoleonic wars and was also involved in the burning of Washington. He was chosen to convey Napoleon to St Helena on the *Northumberland* in July 1815 and remained in command of the forces on the island until the arrival of the new Governor, Sir Hudson Lowe, in April 1816. He established good relations with Napoleon, who regretted that he did not become the Governor. He left St Helena in June 1816, was promoted vice-admiral in 1819, full admiral in 1837, and First Sea Lord in 1841.

Doveton, Sir William Webber (1753–1843): one of St Helena's grandees, and a member of the island Council. He was knighted for services to the East India Company and St Helena during a visit to England in 1818–19. On his last excursion from Longwood, on 4 October 1820, Napoleon visited Doveton's house, Mount Pleasant, overlooking Sandy Bay, and had breakfast with the family on the lawn.

Gorrequer, Major Gideon (1781–1841): Aide de Camp and acting Military Secretary to Sir Hudson Lowe, with whom he had served in Sicily and the Ionian Islands. Although not the most senior of Lowe's aides, he was the closest to him and the most influential. He resided with the Lowes at Plantation House throughout Napoleon's detention, returning to Britain with them in July 1821. Although a supporter of Lowe's policies, he nevertheless bitterly resented the way Lowe treated him and gave vent to his feelings in remarkably frank private diaries, which were not decoded and published until 1968.

Gentilini, Angelo: an Elban who was a footman at Longwood and left the island in October 1820.

Gourgaud, General Gaspard, Baron de (1783–1852): an artillery officer who served in many of Napoleon's campaigns, including Waterloo, and claimed to have saved his life on two occasions. He was Master of the Horse at Longwood and shared Napoleon's dictation duties with fellow 'evangelist', Count de Las Cases. He was, however, intensely jealous of his companions, even challenging General Montholon to a duel, and left St Helena in unhappy circumstances in March 1818. Promoted to lieutenant-general and aide de camp to King Louis-Philippe, he was a member of the exhumation party in 1840, which he described in detail in his memoir, *Le Retour des Cendres de l'Empereur Napoléon*.

Hodson, Major Charles Robert George (1799–1858): an officer in the St Helena Regiment and Judge Advocate of the island, known as 'Hercules' by Napoleon in view of his exceptional height. He was present at both the funeral and the 1840 exhumation of Napoleon.

Jackson, Lieutenant-Colonel Basil (1795–1889): he went to St Helena with Sir Hudson Lowe and was responsible for the repairs to Longwood and the building of the Bertrands' villa and Longwood New House. A French speaker, he was frequently at Longwood and widely suspected of an affair with Madame de Montholon. He left St Helena at the same time as her in July 1819 and in 1877 published an account of his time there in *Reminiscences of a Staff Officer*. When he died at the age of ninety-four he was the last survivor of those connected with Napoleon's captivity.

Lambert, Rear-Admiral Robert (1772–1836): in command of the St Helena naval station from July 1820 to September 1821, he played little part in the relationship between Sir Hudson Lowe and Napoleon and was never, unlike his predecessors, received by Napoleon.

Las Cases, Emmanuel-Auguste-Dieudonné-Marius-Joseph, Count de (1766–1842): in some ways the odd one out among Napoleon's four senior companions on St Helena. Of aristocratic background, his military service was confined to a junior rank in the royalist navy, but he was the author of the successful *Atlas Historique, Généalogique et Géographique*, which Napoleon admired. A refugee in England during the Revolution, he returned to France under an amnesty in 1802 and eventually became chamberlain in Napoleon's household. He accompanied him from Paris to St Helena in 1815 and, as Napoleon's principal amanuensis, became very close to him. He was expelled by Sir Hudson Lowe in November 1816 for conducting clandestine correspondence for Napoleon but earned great fame, and not a little reward, by publishing in 1823 the monumental *Mémorial de St Hélène*, which glorified the Napoleonic legend and is an important source on Napoleon's first year in captivity.

Lowe, Lieutenant-General Sir Hudson, (1769–1844): a soldier from his teens, Lowe served honourably in many campaigns and was responsible for raising and commanding the Corsican Rangers, a regiment of dissident Corsican rebels. In 1813 he was appointed liaison officer to the Russian and Prussian armies and was highly rated by Marshal Blücher. He was not present at Waterloo but in August 1815 he was selected by the British Government to become military governor of St Helena and Napoleon's jailor. He arrived there in April 1816 but his relationship with Napoleon, who despised him, quickly broke down and Napoleon refused to see him again after only their sixth meeting in August 1816. He nevertheless continued as Governor until Napoleon's death, and returned to London, mission accomplished. He was, however, treated shabbily by the British Government, who used him as a scapegoat for popular criticism of the treatment of Napoleon, and he was never again given an appointment commensurate with his rank and seniority.

Malcolm, Rear-Admiral Sir Pulteney (1768–1838): a distinguished sailor who had served throughout the Napoleonic wars, he arrived at St Helena on 17 June 1816 to succeed Admiral Cockburn as Commander of the St Helena Station. He made an immediately favourable impression on Napoleon and, with his wife – Clementina, a niece of Lord Keith – visited him often. Although loyal to Sir Hudson Lowe his relationship with Napoleon aroused Lowe's suspicion and jealousy and when he left the island in June 1817 they parted on strained terms. Lady Malcolm's diary, published in 1899, is an interesting account of their conversations with Napoleon.

Marchand, Louis-Joseph (1792–1876): Napoleon's first valet, who joined his household in 1811 and accompanied him throughout his campaigns and exile on Elba and on to St Helena. He was the devoted servant par excellence and before his death Napoleon made him an executor and beneficiary of his will and appointed him a count. He went with the 1840 expedition to recover Napoleon's remains and his memoirs are an important source on Napoleon and St Helena.

Montchenu, Claude Marin Henri, Count (1757–1831): the French Commissioner on St Helena, who arrived in June 1816 and left in July 1821 after Napoleon's death. A royalist of the old school, he was a somewhat comic figure, respected neither by Sir Hudson Lowe nor by Napoleon, whom he never met.

Montholon, General Charles Jean Tristan, Count de (1783–1853): following a modest military career he joined the Empress Josephine's household and, after switching allegiance to the restored Louis XVIII, returned to Napoleon after the escape from Elba and was promoted to general shortly before Waterloo. He accompanied Napoleon to St Helena, with his wife and son, Tristan, and remained until the end, becoming one of Napoleon's most trusted companions and principal executor of his will.

Following Napoleon's death he wrote his memoirs and, after involvement in Louis-Napoleon's abortive coup in 1840, ended his career as a deputy in the National Assembly.

Montholon, Albine-Hélène, Countess de (1770–1848): wife of Count de Montholon, she accompanied him to St Helena but left, with her recently born child, Napoléone-Joséphine, in July 1819. It is possible that she became Napoleon's mistress and that the child was his.

Noverazz, Jean Abram (1790–1849): third valet to Napoleon; he was at Longwood throughout the captivity and returned for the exhumation in 1840.

O'Meara, Dr Barry Edward (1782–1836): a native of County Cork, after service as an army doctor he became surgeon on the *Bellerophon*, quickly gaining Napoleon's confidence. With British permission he accepted the post of physician to Napoleon and established a close rapport with him at Longwood. Sir Hudson Lowe's suspicion of this relationship led to his removal from St Helena in July 1818. O'Meara had his revenge with the publication of his best-selling *A Voice from St Helena* in 1822, which seriously damaged Lowe's reputation. He subsequently became a founder member of the Reform Club in London.

Plampin, Rear-Admiral Robert (1762–1834): in July 1817 he succeeded Admiral Malcolm as Commander of the St Helena Station and remained until July 1820. He was a strong supporter of Sir Hudson Lowe's treatment of Napoleon and as such out of favour with the latter. He caused controversy on St Helena by bringing out to the island a lady to whom he was not married.

Poppleton, Captain Thomas William (1775–1827): of the 53rd regiment and the first orderly officer at Longwood (from December 1815 to July 1817).

Reade, Lieutenant-Colonel Sir Thomas (1785–1849): after service mainly in the Mediterranean he was chosen by Sir Hudson Lowe to accompany him as his Deputy Adjutant General to St Helena. A strong supporter of Lowe's policies towards Napoleon.

Stokoe, Dr John (1775–1852): surgeon to the Admiral's flagship *Conqueror*, he was called to attend Napoleon on 17 January 1819 and saw him on five occasions before 21 January. Sir Hudson Lowe accused him of breaking the rules on contact with Napoleon and had him court-martialled and dismissed from the service.

Stürmer, Barthelémy, Baron de (1787–1853): the Austrian Commissioner on St Helena who arrived in June 1816 and left in July 1818. Like the other two Commissioners he never met Napoleon.

Verling, Dr James Roche (1787–1858): Irish surgeon to the Royal Artillery on St Helena, he was appointed to reside at Longwood to give medical aid to Napoleon in August 1818. Napoleon refused to see him and he left the island in September 1819. His diaries are a useful insight into this period.

Vignali, Abbé Ange: a Corsican priest, of little education, sent out by Napoleon's uncle, Cardinal Fesch, in September 1819. He was of little use to Napoleon but conducted his funeral service and left St Helena on 27 May 1821.

Warden, Dr William (1777–1849): surgeon on the *Northumberland*, he remained at St Helena until 19 June 1816 and often visited Longwood. His *Letters* are an entertaining, if not wholly reliable, account of that time.

Wilks, Colonel Mark (1760–1831): the popular Governor of St Helena under the East India Company until Sir Hudson Lowe's arrival in April 1816.

Wynyard, Lieutenant-Colonel Edward Buckley (1780–1865): arriving in St Helena in May 1816, he served as Sir Hudson Lowe's military secretary, but did not play an important part in the relationship with Napoleon.

THE LION OR THE ASS?

Napoleon, wishing to learn English, procured some English books and among them Aesop's Fables was sent him. In one of the fables the sick lion, after submitting with fortitude to the insults of the many animals who came to exult over his fallen greatness, at last received a kick in the face from the ass. 'I could have borne everything but this', the lion said. Napoleon showed the wood-cut and added, 'It is me and your governor'.

Betsy Balcombe, *To Befriend an Emperor*[1]

AT ONE O'CLOCK IN the afternoon of Thursday 15 October 1840, a tired, wet, bedraggled group of veterans, soldiers and officials stood huddled apprehensively over a coffin placed on the ground in a tent in Geranium Valley, a lush, green, spring-fed vale deep in the interior of the isolated British Crown colony of St Helena. It had rained all the previous night and their vigil had been a long and tiring one. It was twenty-five years to the day since Napoleon and his small group of loyal companions had landed on the island to begin his five-and-a-half years of captivity there. The lid of the tin-plate coffin before them had already been prised open, and after a short debate on whether the final cover should be removed from the body in the coffin, the silk shroud that concealed it was slowly drawn back, from the feet upwards. It revealed the corpse of Napoleon Bonaparte, which had lain there since his death in May 1821. He was dressed in his favourite green uniform of the Chasseurs de la Garde, the insignia of his own Légion d'Honneur at his breast and his famous tricorn hat resting across the upper part of his thighs. Only its silk cockade had perished.

It was the face that gripped the astonished and overawed onlookers. Apart from a slight disfigurement of the nose where it had been pressed by the covering shroud, it appeared to be almost perfectly preserved. The features of the giant who had commanded the greatest European empire since the Romans were peaceful and at rest. In the view of some of the witnesses who had also been present at the burial nineteen years before, they were even more like their hero in his pomp, the living Emperor Napoleon, than the wasted and rambling invalid at the time of his agonizing death. There was no doubt in their view that this was the corpse of Napoleon and that there was no truth in the rumours that another body had been substituted for his by the British before the actual interment. The rest of his body was also virtually intact, almost as if mummified, the left arm lying just a little higher than the other where General Bertrand, who had remained in exile with him until the very end, had raised it to give it a final kiss before the coffin had been closed.

Around and over much of the body was what seemed to be a delicate white foam, emanating from the silk lining which had covered the inside of the coffin, so that parts of it appeared to be seen through a fine muslin gauze. At his feet were the silver vases containing his heart and stomach, which, at British insistence, had also been buried with him in the grave. The British did not want them to be preserved and displayed like saintly relics. After a few tense and tearful minutes, the silk cover was pulled carefully back over the body and the coffin sealed again, to minimize any further decomposition. Preparations then began to replace it within its outer covering of lead and wooden coffins and to transport it to the French frigate, *La Belle Poule*, which was waiting in Jamestown harbour to take it back home to France.

The negotiations within the French Government and between the British and French governments leading to the agreement to the exhumation had been slow and complicated. King Louis-Philippe was not initially enthusiastic – he was not an admirer of Napoleon – but had finally consented to the proposal and obtained authorization and the necessary funds from the French National Assembly. The British Government were approached and gave their consent, prompted by the Foreign Secretary, Lord Palmerston, who thought it would be wrong not to accede to the French request with good grace. The Government thought it right, however, to seek the views of Napoleon's conqueror, the by then septuagenarian Duke of Wellington. He in effect gave the all-clear in the following characteristic response:

> Field Marshal the Duke of Wellington presents his compliments to Her Majesty's Ministers. If they wish to know his opinion as a matter of public policy he must decline to give one. If, however, they wish only to consult him as a private individual he has no hesitation in saying that he does not care one twopenny damn what becomes of the ashes of Napoleon Bonaparte.[2]

This was perhaps a fair tit for tat given the uncomplimentary views that Napoleon normally expressed on the Duke.

The expedition to recover the body was nominally commanded by the King's third son, the Prince de Joinville, but it was effectively under the control of a senior diplomat with a part-British ancestry, Count Philippe de Rohan-Chabot. There is a suggestion that this was a ruse by the King to ensure that if there were a disaster the blame would not fall principally on the Crown. The party accordingly set sail in the frigate, *La Belle Poule*, accompanied by a small escorting flotilla, and arrived at St Helena on 9 October 1840. Included in the Prince's party, after much lobbying and place seeking, was a nucleus of those officers and servants who had accompanied Napoleon on St Helena during his captivity. Prominent among them was the most faithful and uncomplaining companion of all, General Henri Gratien Bertrand, the former Grand Marshal of Napoleon's imperial court, together with his son, Arthur, who had been born on the island during the captivity (the only French male, according to Bertrand's wife, the redoubtable Fanny Bertrand, to succeed in arriving there without the Governor's permission!). The other senior veteran present was General Gaspard Gourgaud, the 'fretful porcupine' of Lord Rosebery's 1900 study, *Napoleon, The Last Phase*, whose touchiness and fits of jealousy had irritated almost everyone in Napoleon's household during the captivity and who characteristically spent much of the expedition protesting about his order of precedence in the exhumation ceremonies. Others included Emmanuel de Las Cases, the son of the late Count Emmanuel de Las Cases, Napoleon's favourite interlocutor and amanuensis – both of whom had accompanied Napoleon to St Helena but had been expelled by the Governor on charges of spying in December 1816 – and a number of Napoleon's closest personal servants.

The difficult and laborious task of exhuming the body – a genuine engineering challenge – had begun thirteen hours previously, just after midnight. The damp and drizzly night was only redeemed by a glimmer of moonlight. In his short but vivid account of the expedition, *Le Retour des Cendres de L'Empereur Napoléon*,[3] General Gourgaud describes the long drawn-out proceedings, hour by hour. First it had been necessary to penetrate and clear away the layers of compacted earth and cement overlaying the huge iron-bound stones that covered the top of the three-metre-deep trench in which the coffin had been placed. Then the really hard work had begun. Determined that Napoleon should have no greater chance of escaping from the island in death than when he was alive in captivity, the Governor had had Napoleon enclosed, like a Russian doll, in no fewer than four strong coffins, each one fitting inside another. The outside one was made of tough mahogany, the next one of lead, the third one again of mahogany, and the innermost one of tin plate. This immensely heavy sarcophagus had then been lowered deep into the grave onto more large stone slabs placed at the bottom, and the walls of the grave also lined with stones to prevent the water from the nearby spring seeping in. Although the tomb was in theory to be a temporary resting place, prior to a further decision by the British authorities on a final destination, the Governor had made sure that any attempt to disinter Napoleon and let the 'Eagle' rise up once again to the open skies would not be an easy one.

By 3.30am the engineers had succeeded in removing the earth and concrete and the three iron-linked stones that sealed the surface of the tomb. The clashing and scraping of their picks and shovels as they struck the rock and metal, and the grunts of the sweating labourers, must have broken the almost holy silence of the vale. By 6.45am, now in the first daylight, they had reached the huge single stone slab that lay immediately over the coffins. By 9.40am, with the aid of two derricks erected over the trench on the spot, they had lifted this stone and revealed the coffins themselves. After prayers and the sprinkling of holy water by the expedition's priest, the Abbé Félix Coquereau – which was somewhat more practically supplemented, for health and safety reasons, with a scattering of chlorine by the attendant doctor– the coffins were hauled carefully out of the grave and carried to a tent pitched on the level ground some thirty paces away.

The process of opening the coffins then began. One by one they were levered open by brute force and the broken pieces of wood and metal, which were seized on later as souvenirs, if not holy relics, were set on one side. Finally, after thirteen hours of wearisome hard slog – wearisome not only for the engineers and workmen but also for Bertrand, Gourgaud and the other spectators who had stood and watched patiently but helplessly for so many hours – the inner tin-plate coffin was finally revealed. The corrosion of the screws and bolts was such that the lid had to be forced back open, rather like that of a huge sardine tin, so that the almost-intact body could be revealed. Gourgaud says that the atmosphere was oppressively heavy and electric and that time seemed to stand still for several moments. He nonetheless could not stop himself from crying out that it was indeed the Emperor and that there was no doubt of this.

After verification of the corpse by Gourgaud and Bertrand, which was also witnessed by the Governor of St Helena, Colonel George Mittlemore, who had shortly before arrived on the scene, the tin-plate coffin was quickly sealed again. It was then replaced in the lead coffin and both of them laid inside an ebony coffin that had been brought by the expedition for the purpose. By 4pm it had been lifted by the derricks onto a waiting carriage, dressed with a rich violet cloak and the imperial insignia, and a slow procession started back down the steep descent to the island's capital, Jamestown, and to the waiting frigate. The narrow twisting road is hazardous enough to negotiate even now. At that time it was unsurfaced and bounded for much of its winding way by a sheer drop into the depths of the seemingly bottomless valley known as the Devil's Punch Bowl. Fifty tough artillery men with ropes strained to prevent the overloaded vehicle from running away down the hill, and the cortège was led by troops of the 9th infantry regiment, with the drums beating and the band playing suitable funeral music, including the 'Dead March' from *Saul*.

The procession arrived in Jamestown at 4.30pm as the great guns high up on the overlooking High Knoll Fort, originally and ironically built to prevent Napoleon leaving the island, fired a thundering salvo every minute. As the cortège passed by the Castle, the Governor's administrative headquarters in Jamestown, and through the wide wooden gates leading to the landing stage and the sea, the sentries presented arms, and the troops lining the route stood to respectful attention, with rifles and swords reversed. Governor Mittlemore, too moved to articulate the official speech prepared for him fully or clearly, handed the coffin over formally on behalf of the British Government to the awaiting Prince de Joinville, and by 6.30pm it had been conveyed in a launch, steered by the Prince himself, to *La Belle Poule*. It was then, with difficulty, lifted on to the deck and placed under guard for that night in front of a temporary altar erected between the capstan and the mizzenmast.

After a service on board the next morning, followed by the removal of the coffin to below decks and various farewell ceremonies the day after – only marred once more by the petulant Gourgaud's continuing protestations about precedence and protocol, this time in relation to the official record of the exhumation proceedings – the frigate set sail on Sunday 18 October. By 5pm St Helena was out of sight. 'Je ne désire pas la revoir' (I don't want to see it again),[4] declared Gourgaud with a sigh of relief. Changeable of mood as ever, he had in fact enjoyed the surprisingly warm welcome he had received from many old friends on the island, but he never wanted to return again to the place that he had left in March 1818 – sick, discontented and after quarrelling with Napoleon and practically all his other colleagues.

Gourgaud's former colleagues surely echoed his final sentiments. General Bertrand in particular must have cast his mind back to Napoleon's funeral in May 1821,[5] when the sequence of events described above had more or less taken place in reverse. Napoleon died in the house where he had spent most of his captivity, Longwood House, in the late afternoon of 5 May, after weeks of distressing sickness and suffering, aggravated by the primitively incompetent medical care which he received. Following an autopsy conducted by his own doctor, Antommarchi, in the presence of several British military surgeons, and other necessary formalities, including a virtual lying in state for a whole day while the inhabitants of the island filed reverentially past, the funeral had been arranged for 9 May. A religious service was first held in the house, conducted by the young Corsican priest, the Abbé Vignali, whom Napoleon's uncle and mother had sent out to him the previous year; the funeral procession then left Longwood at about 11am.

Although it was probably the greatest ceremonial occasion, civil or military, that had ever taken place on St Helena, Napoleon's wishes were denied in two respects. First, he had always asked to be allowed to 'repose on the banks of the Seine in the midst of the French people I have loved so much'. The Governor, on instructions from London, refused this but agreed to Napoleon's fallback choice (that is, if he was not allowed to be buried away from the island), the peaceful Geranium or Sane Valley, under the willow trees, next to a little freshwater spring from which drinking water had been carried by Chinese labourers to Longwood nearly every day. Napoleon had become familiar with this tranquil spot by pausing there sometimes en route to visit the Bertrands when they lived for their first year on the island in a cottage at Hutt's Gate about a mile away from Longwood. Second, obedient again to the very last to his instructions, the Governor accorded only those funeral honours that were appropriate for an officer of general rank, not those prescribed with head-of-state pomp for an emperor.

Even so, by St Helena standards it had been a very grand affair. Twelve scarlet-coated grenadiers carried the enormously heavy multiple coffin on their shoulders out of Longwood House and placed it on a waiting hearse, which was drawn by four of Napoleon's horses, attended by two grooms dressed in full imperial livery. The coffin was covered by a blue velvet pall, on top of which General Bertrand solemnly placed Napoleon's sword and the cloak he had worn at the battle of Marengo, the crushing victory in June 1800 that had been a crucial turning point in his career. The tassels on the two forward corners of the pall were held by Napoleon's first valet, Louis-Joseph Marchand, and Bertrand's eldest son, Napoleon, and those at the rear by General Bertrand himself and the other senior officer who had remained with Napoleon to the end, General Montholon, marching along slowly at the side. They were followed by Napoleon's state horse, led by his groom, Archambault, and then by the other members of his Longwood household. Behind them, on horseback, came Napoleon's hated enemy, the Governor, Sir Hudson Lowe, in the full plumed-hat regalia and scarlet uniform of a British lieutenant-general, dutifully paying his final respects, but absolutely determined to see Napoleon securely buried. He was accompanied by a retinue of his civilian and military staff, including Rear-Admiral Lambert, the Commander in Chief of the South Atlantic Station, followed by leading dignitaries and notables of the island.

Almost the whole of St Helena turned out to witness the funeral. Some 2,000 soldiers, sailors and marines were on duty, lining the route from Longwood House to the intermediate point of Hutt's Gate, where the Governor's wife, Lady Lowe, also joined the procession in a carriage. As the cortège passed the silent soldiers, they filed in behind it and marched in slow order. The regimental bands played lugubrious funeral music and when the cortège reached the junction in the road where the specially cleared grassy path led steeply at a sharp angle down to the burial site in Geranium Valley the hills of the island echoed with the salvoes of fifteen rounds fired by the troops still standing to attention on the main road, and the repeated thuds of one round every minute from the guns of the British warships in the bay and on the coastal forts.

Although the willow trees have long since disappeared – there was a scramble to grab pieces of them as souvenirs as soon as Napoleon had been laid to rest, and the Governor had to erect a rail around the site and post sentries to keep the scavengers away – the burial site is still very much as it was nearly 200 years ago. The air is peaceful and the grass lush and green. The only sound is the repetitive musical croaking of hundreds of small unseen frogs in the damp undergrowth. The carefully tended flowers in the raised beds on top of the stone walls around the enclosure are a rich variety of reds, pinks, whites and yellows, and brilliantly white black-eyed fairy terns alternately hover above and perch delicately on the branches of the trees surrounding the site. The tomb still looks much as it did before Napoleon was taken away. It is protected by a strong iron railing and covered by a large, weathered, lichen-covered stone slab. The difference is that it is now eerily empty. It remains guarded reverentially, however, by an elderly attendant who still sits in the little sentry box at the entrance to the site; he looks as if he might have been on watch there since the day Napoleon was laid in the ground.

On the day of the funeral the whole company dismounted at the top of the grassy track and the heavy sarcophagus was carried slowly and laboriously down the slope on the shoulders of the straining grenadiers, relieved from time to time by marines and other soldiers. It was then lowered carefully into the grave and covered with the huge flat stones and layers of cement and earth. Napoleon was, it seemed, now condemned to rot slowly in perpetuity in the volcanic soil of this British colony, thousands of miles from his beloved France, never to disturb the peace of Europe again.

Even his tombstone remained unmarked and anonymous. The French had requested that it should carry a simple inscription, with just the name Napoleon on it, together with the dates and places of his birth and death. The Governor refused, insisting that the word Bonaparte should be added. So the French decided to leave the tombstone without any inscription, as it remains to this day.

With the exhumation nineteen years later, Napoleon returned to Europe to great pomp and circumstance. The legend of his glory years took wing again, not that it had ever really been forgotten during the Bourbon restoration and the reign of King Louis-Philippe. The Eagle that had been buried in the volcanic isolation of St Helena now soared high in the sky again. But how was it that the greatest general since Alexander the Great and Julius Caesar, the master of Europe for over a decade, who created kingdoms and princedoms, and before whom kings, princes and even emperors and the Pope trembled, came to such a sad and lonely end on a small rocky island in the middle of the Atlantic? How did the old lion, who had longed to found a lasting imperial dynasty, come to be kicked in the face by the ass? The rest of this book will tell the story.

ONE

FROM WATERLOO TO ROCHEFORT

THE STORY OF THE tragic final years of Napoleon's life begins on the battlefield of Waterloo, a few miles south of Brussels on the Charleroi road. By the evening of Sunday 18 June 1815, as the sun at last broke through to start drying the muddy, sodden fields of corn, beaten down by torrential rain and trampled by the feet and hooves of nearly 200,000 men and horses, Napoleon's Grande Armée of over 70,000 men was in headlong retreat. His dreams of reasserting French mastery over Europe were shattered. Over 50,000 men on both sides were dead, wounded or missing after nine hours of one of the bloodiest battles in history on a scrap of farming land near the village of Waterloo, barely five miles square. Mutilated bodies of men and horses littered the field of battle and it was impossible to cross it without stumbling over them. As dusk began to fall, silent groups of scavengers crept in among the fallen bodies to pursue their gruesome task of stripping the corpses of their uniforms and anything else of value, even gold teeth and fillings, and to finish off with a knife those of the wounded who showed any remaining signs of life.

Wellington's sodden and exhausted troops were a hastily assembled multinational army of British, Dutch, Belgians, Hanoverians, Brunswick-ians, Nassauvians and the German Legion, some of whom had not long since fought on Napoleon's side. The British element in fact comprised only just over a third of the force, but among them were the crack Cold-stream and other Guards regiments, including a nucleus of veterans who had fought with Wellington in the Peninsular War. They had grimly held the line under horrific artillery bombardment and infantry and cavalry onslaughts all day, and, despite having suffered fearful casualties, now gath-ered renewed heart and energy. At a raised-arm signal from the Duke, still mounted on his favourite chestnut stallion, Copenhagen, at the centre of their defensive position on the ridge at Mont St Jean, they poured down the slope in pursuit of the defeated enemy. However, their impetus was only temporary; they had reached the limits of their endurance. The Prus-sians, faithful to their undertaking to Wellington, had saved the day with their afternoon intervention on the Duke's left flank, and it was now left to them to continue the chase. The Prussian cavalry comprised hussars, with their sinister death's head insignia, dragoons and lancers, but the most feared of all were the dreaded uhlans with their dark uniforms, tall black shakos and wickedly long lances.

The Prussians were led by the indomitable septuagenarian, Marshal Gebhard Blücher, the Prince of Wahlstatt, who hated Napoleon and had nearly been killed in the heavy, but still indecisive, defeat of the Prussians by Napoleon at the battle of Ligny only three days earlier. For his attacking impetuosity, Blücher was known as Marshal 'Forwäerts' (Forwards) and Napoleon once said of him that he was 'like a bull who shuts his eyes and, seeing no danger, rushes on.'[1] He had certainly rushed on at Ligny on 16 June where he had been swept aside by French cavalry, crushed beneath his own horse – he had already had two horses shot under him during the battle – left for dead, and only revived by being rubbed all over with brandy. Not normally a man for fancy words, his laconic comment to Wellington when they met just after the battle near Napoleon's former headquarters at the inn, La Belle Alliance, was 'Mein liebe kamerad. Quelle affaire!'[2] – according to Wellington, these were just about the only words of French he knew. Blücher wrote to his wife later that evening: 'With my friend Wellington, I have put an end to Bonaparte's dancing. His army is in utter rout ... We shall be finished with Bonaparte shortly.'[3] For Wellington it was enough to say in typical laconic fashion, 'By God it was a good job I was there', and later more reflectively, 'I don't know what it is to lose a battle; but certainly nothing can be more painful than to gain one with the loss of so many friends.'[4] He then rode away slowly and reflectively back to his own headquarters in the village of Waterloo, to compose his immortal Waterloo dispatch, in deep sadness at the slaughter and death of so many dear comrades. Blücher wanted to call the battle that of La Belle Alliance. Wellington simply ignored this and called it the battle of Waterloo, the name by which it has been known ever since.

Napoleon had not expected defeat, nor did he ever understand or acknowledge the reasons for it. At breakfast on the morning of the battle he told his assembled marshals and generals that the odds were overwhelmingly on their side. After all, Wellington was no more than a 'sepoy general', who had won his reputation fighting against inferior native troops in India. 'We have ninety chances in our favour,' he claimed. 'Because you have been beaten by Wellington, you consider him a great general. And now I tell *you* that Wellington is a bad general, the English are bad troops, and this affair is nothing more than a picnic [a 'déjeuner']. We shall dine in Brussels tonight.'[5] Napoleon had some justification for his confidence. The astonishingly rapid movement of his army into Belgium had indeed caught Wellington by surprise. 'By God, he's humbugged me. He has gained 24 hours march on me,'[6] even Wellington himself admitted when the news was brought to him at the Duchess of Richmond's ball late in the evening of 15 June that Napoleon had crossed the River Sambre and was already marching on Brussels. Wellington had also allowed his own army to be separated from the Prussians and had chosen a defensive position that, with the Forêt de Soignes immediately to its rear, offered little chance of an orderly withdrawal should that be necessary. This was a fundamental departure from the strategy agreed with Blücher that they should keep their armies in close contact with each other and not allow Napoleon to drive a wedge between them and beat them separately. However, those of Napoleon's marshals and generals who had been beaten by Wellington time after time in the Peninsula were less certain of an easy victory. They knew that the British infantry, which, though in a minority, formed the core of Wellington's army, were formidably tenacious in holding a defensive position. Napoleon angrily dismissed their reservations. He was so sure of victory, or at least claimed to be, that he had already prepared victory proclamations for distribution to the Belgian people – somewhat like the Germans in August 1914 who were so certain of success under the Schlieffen plan that they had struck medals celebrating the entry into Paris in advance.

The disorganized French army, its morale utterly shattered by the retreat of the elite Imperial Guard, continued its chaotic flight past La Belle Alliance and the farmhouse some three kilometres further back at Le Caillou where Napoleon had spent the previous night. It carried on in disarray through the crossroads at Quatre Bras towards Genappe, Charleroi and the French frontier, but Napoleon still maintained his desperate self-delusion. He continued to give orders and make battle plans, even though there were no troops to carry them out, perhaps like the raving Hitler in the Berlin bunker as the Russians closed in. In his view he had outwitted Wellington and defeated the Prussians but had been let down by the incompetence of his marshals, in particular by Grouchy, who had ignored his admittedly somewhat ambiguous orders and spent the whole day marching his fresh troops aimlessly to and fro, like the grand old Duke of York, without ever coming near the battle. It never occurred to Napoleon that his own orders, transmitted through Marshal Soult – who at Waterloo had succeeded Napoleon's supreme Chief of Staff, Marshal Berthier – might have been less than clear. He later complained to Dr O'Meara, the British naval surgeon who was with him on St Helena, 'Had it not been for the imbecility of Grouchy, I would have won the day.'[7] There was also the brainlessness of Marshal Ney, the Prince of Moscow. Although he was the 'bravest of the brave', who had performed miracles of heroism in the retreat from Moscow, he had recklessly launched the finest cavalry, the flower of the Grande Armée, at Wellington's centre without infantry in support, so that they broke on the English squares, like waves on breakwaters. He was, according to Napoleon, despite his bravery 'toujours une pauvre tête' (always muddle-headed).[8] Nevertheless Napoleon claimed to O'Meara that even after the Prussian intervention he could still have won the battle if he had not been so let down.[9]

That Napoleon himself survived the defeat and subsequent rout was due to the one element of the French army that, at least for a time, held firm. As the rest of the panic-stricken columns poured past them in disarray, three infantry battalions of the Old Guard, and a battalion of the Middle Guard, which had constituted the French reserve second line, formed squares and began an orderly withdrawal, step by step. There were only some 2,000 of them, but they proudly maintained discipline and held their pursuers at bay and slowly covered the retreat south along the Charleroi road. Napoleon and a handful of his generals, including Bertrand and Gourgaud, his future companions on St Helena, took refuge inside a square of the 1st regiment of grenadiers. According to General Gourgaud, Napoleon still wanted to fight on and die on the spot with his beloved grenadiers.[10] But it was useless and does not sound very convincing, although it would perhaps have been better if he had died a soldier's death there and then, saving himself the long drawn-out years of Promethean suffering on St Helena, and the British Government and the hapless Governor, Sir Hudson Lowe, so much expense and trouble.

As the scattered columns neared the little town of Genappe even the Guard began to disintegrate and break away. Utter bedlam ensued as hundreds of men, horses and wagons, fighting, scrambling and trampling on each other, struggled through the enclosed cobbled streets to try to reach and cross the one narrow bridge over the river, even though the bridge itself was blocked with fleeing soldiers, animals and artillery wagons. The Prussian cavalry, taking no prisoners – at Le Caillou they had set fire to the farm and its adjacent barns, burning alive all the wounded French soldiers who were held there – were now almost on their backs. Their engineers were already clearing away the hasty barricade of wagons and cannons that the French had erected at the entrance to the village; Napoleon was obliged to abandon his carriage, which the Prussians soon afterwards captured and plundered, and take to horseback again. On reaching the crossroads at Quatre Bras, where Marshal Ney had fatally failed to press home his attack against Wellington's surprised, outnumbered and thinly spread allied troops on 15 and 16 June, he paused once more before hurrying on to cross the River Sambre back into France and on towards Paris, followed at some distance by about 10,000 men, the remnants of the army that had fought at Waterloo.

Napoleon was in Paris for three days and he decided to go straight to the Elysée Palace to confer with General Caulaincourt and other trusted ministers rather than to brazen it out immediately with the deputies in the Chamber. If he had done so, still wearing the dusty, sweaty, battle-stained uniform he had worn at Waterloo, he might just have carried the day. Instead he went home and ordered a long hot bath. Sinking into the warm steamy comfort of a deep hot bath increasingly became a way of passing the time and seeking physical and mental relief during the long boring days to come on St Helena. Thus soothed and at least temporarily physically restored he started to discuss with his ministers plans for national defence, and, most immediate and important, the defence of Paris itself. He still did not accept Waterloo as the final blow. So far as he was concerned, Grouchy still had under his command the 30,000 or so uncommitted troops that had now reached Laon and he claimed to his brother Joseph that it would quickly be possible, as in the old days, to raise another 300,000 troops to defend France through a levy of new conscripts, the National Guard and elements of the army scattered in the provinces.

Napoleon had, however, made a grave political misjudgement. He had gone one step too far. The political classes in both France and the rest of Europe wanted to be finished with him. They were tired of war and were in no mood for treating with him again, as they had done before he was sent away to rule the tiny island of Elba. They now regarded Napoleon as the only obstacle to peace and the future happiness of France. Accordingly the Chamber of Deputies – despite the emotional entreaties of Napoleon's younger brother Lucien, who had won them over in earlier days on Napoleon's behalf – would not listen to any of his proposals. France had already suffered too much. Tens of thousands of its young men already remained rotting under the earth in Spain, Russia, Germany and Belgium. The overwhelmingly superior allied armies were rapidly converging on Paris, with the victorious and now feared Wellington coming from the north, and France's territory was now reduced to even less than before Napoleon started his imperial adventures. There were loud cries in the Chamber urging him to abdicate. Lafayette in particular was prominent in turning the sentiment of the Chamber against him." They told Napoleon that he must either abdicate or be dethroned. They had no interest in his offer to stand down as Emperor and continue leading the surviving French armies against the advancing Wellington and Blücher in the simple role of a general of division (an interesting offer in view of his subsequent violent objection to being titled general by the British on St Helena).

Napoleon had little choice but to concede to their wishes. In his memoirs Napoleon's first valet, Louis-Joseph Marchand, claims that Napoleon was motivated only by the patriotic wish to avoid further bloodshed and civil strife, but the brutal reality was that he now had no realistic alternative to doing what they requested. The exhausted and war-weary French had had enough of him. They wanted him out of the way as soon as possible. He had entirely lost their confidence and support. Accordingly, shortly after midday on 22 June, Napoleon, looking hesitant and depressed, appeared before the Chamber and formally abdicated in favour of his infant son, the King of Rome, who was still in Vienna as a virtual prisoner with his mother, the Empress Marie-Louise. Napoleon had seen neither of them since he left them behind in Paris on 25 January 1814 to mount his last losing campaign against the invading allied armies.

On this second occasion the terms of his abdication differed from those of his abdication prior to Elba on 6 April 1814, when he had eventually renounced the throne both for himself and for his children. He was still desperately eager to establish an imperial dynasty. Despite all the kings and princes – mostly his brothers – whom he had appointed during his imperial pomp, his only legitimate son, the infant King of Rome, was now his only hope. This time he therefore stepped down in favour of his son. The Chamber of Deputies quickly accepted the abdication and even went to the Elysée to thank him for his act of patriotism. But they were not, however, prepared to go along with his dynastic pretensions. Emboldened by their success so far, to Napoleon's intense anger and disgust, they quickly rejected the claims of the putative Emperor Napoleon II, recognizing him nominally only for a couple of days – during which time, somewhat astonishingly, some low-value coins were issued with his image on them – and then switched their allegiance to the restored Bourbon king, Louis XVIII. They appointed a Commission of five members, under the chairmanship of the sinister survivor and duplicitous double dealer, the ubiquitous former Minister of Police, Joseph Fouché, to form a provisional government. Napoleon knew well that Fouché, whose previous service had allowed him to accumulate secret dossiers on everyone of consequence in Paris, including Napoleon himself, could not be trusted and was secretly using him as a bargaining pawn with the British. He had already dismissed Fouché once in June 1810 because he could no longer trust him and he must have bitterly regretted that he had not had him shot when there had been an opportunity to do so. Among his many grievances against Fouché was that the Minister had been among the first to press Napoleon to divorce

Josephine, and for several years he had been suspected of conducting secret negotiations with the English.

The new government immediately ordered Napoleon to leave Paris. After further hesitation and indecision, he finally did so at half an hour after midnight on 25 June, slipping out of the back entrance of the Elysée in the dark like a celebrity avoiding the paparazzi, even swapping carriages with General Bertrand so as to escape detection and intervention.[12] He drove directly to Malmaison, the mansion just outside Paris that was familiar to him as a frequent venue for councils and other meetings during the Consulate, and, perhaps more significantly, after the divorce he had given to his beloved first wife, Josephine. It was still haunted by the ghost of her presence. He had already asked Hortense Beauharnais to go ahead to Malmaison and prepare it for him. Hortense was Josephine's daughter and had been forced by Napoleon into an unhappy marriage with his youngest brother, Louis, whom he had made King of Holland. She was thus both Napoleon's sister-in-law and step-daughter. Despite the deep unhappiness of her marriage, and Napoleon's anger with her for remaining in or near Paris and consorting with the occupying allied commanders – including notably Tsar Alexander of Russia – while he was in exile in Elba, she still worshipped him. During the few days together at Malmaison their relationship became once more warm and intense, especially as they walked in the garden and talked of Josephine and the flowers she had so loved. Hortense had travelled to Malmaison the day before Napoleon's arrival there and had tactfully prepared and set aside for him the wing opposite the one Josephine had occupied.

Before he left Paris Napoleon had asked the provisional government to equip two frigates for him and to request the British Government to provide the necessary passports or documents of safe conduct to enable him to go into exile in America, where he expected to find sympathizers. It is quite clear from Hortense's memoirs that at this stage Napoleon was set on going to America. He had always been fascinated by the young American republic, which had already proved itself the equal of its former colonial master, Great Britain. He had ordered a collection of books about it and now dreamed, or at least toyed with the idea, of starting a completely new life in exile there. That was also the intention of his brother, Joseph, even though, according to Marchand, some of Napoleon's companions even at this stage were floating the possibility of surrendering voluntarily to the

British. Madame Bertrand, who had now joined them at Malmaison, was strongly in favour of this, although Hortense consistently advised America as the safer course. While they were still settling in at Malmaison, the good Marchand, practical and solicitous for his master as ever, stayed on for a few hours at the Elysée to gather more of the Emperor's personal treasures and pack them into a carriage and follow with them to Malmaison.[13] He had already salvaged some of the cash, jewels and other valuables from Napoleon's carriage before the Prussians had pillaged it after Waterloo.

In a bizarre sort of way, life at Malmaison for a few days almost assumed the pattern of a house party from old times rather than an emergency venue for a critical council of war. Hortense played hostess, and a houseful of family, old friends, colleagues and personal retainers moved in to join them. Among them were the Generals Bertrand, Gourgaud and Montholon, all of whom were to accompany Napoleon, more or less willingly, to St Helena; the Duke of Rovigo (the former General Savary, one of Napoleon's most able and trusted subordinates, who had at one time also served as Minister of Police); and Count Emmanuel de Las Cases, a chamberlain of the court, who was not yet quite among the inner elects, but angling to join them. Apart from Hortense, feminine company was provided by two of the generals' wives, Mesdames Bertrand and Montholon, both now countesses, an array of duchesses and other countesses of the new aristocracy, who owed their recent elevations to Napoleon, and even his favourite mistress, the beautiful Polish Countess Maria Walewska, the mother of his son and the only one of his paramours who had visited him on Elba.[14]

Although for some of the time he appeared outwardly relaxed, Napoleon was in shock and in no hurry to move on or indeed take any fresh decisions. He wanted the provisional government to make the first move and he remained suspicious and uneasy. In many ways he was like a fugitive with no fixed abode. He was unwilling to leave unless he was assured he could control his ultimate destination, but there was no news of the passports he had requested from the British Government and he waited impatiently for confirmation that the two French frigates were in position and ready to sail from the port of Rochefort on the Atlantic coast. Time was now beginning to run out but the provisional government were also stalling as they did not want to incur the opprobrium of the French public by being seen to hand Napoleon over to the British. Fouché, however, who had continued to maintain discreet contact with the British, despite a state of war still formally existing between Britain and France, was quite ready to use him as a bargaining counter with them. On 26 June General Becker arrived at Malmaison from Paris, ostensibly sent by the provisional government to guarantee his safety but in reality dispatched by Fouché to keep a close eye on Napoleon and to get him away and out of the country as soon as possible. Napoleon's suspicions were further aroused and so, turning his attention to practical matters for a moment, he arranged to set up an emergency credit account of more than three million francs with the banker, Lafitte, in Paris.

There followed a continuing period of indecision, or at best reluctance to take the initiative, on all sides. The frigates *Saale* and *Méduse* had been ordered to be armed and ready at Rochefort, but the British Government, through the Duke of Wellington in Paris, made it clear to the provisional government that no safe conducts would be provided. Their main objective now was to seize Napoleon in person, and this was the instruction given to Admiral Hotham, who was in command of the naval detachment sailing to Rochefort to blockade the port. On the night of 28/29 June Napoleon had received a peremptory letter from Fouché ordering him to leave at once for Rochefort and set sail. The Prussians were drawing near to Paris and Marshal Blücher had sent a flying column to seize the bridge at Chatou over the Seine, not far from Malmaison. Wellington had so far dissuaded Blücher from pursuing his wish to execute Napoleon, but there was no knowing what would happen if the Prussian flying columns arrived at Malmaison first. After one final repeated offer to the Government through Becker to take command of the French troops around Paris, which was summarily declined, Napoleon bowed to the inevitable. At 5.30pm on 29 June, after tearful farewells – with Hortense, who handed him a valuable diamond necklace, and with his other relatives and friends left behind, including Maria Walewska – he left Malmaison for Rochefort. Before leaving he also paid a silent and tearful visit on his own to the room in which his beloved Josephine had died.

The departure was chaotic. Although there had been plenty of time to plan it, little preparation had in fact been done. The various carriages were assembled in the courtyard at Malmaison but in the panic no-one had ordered the horses. There was a mountain of luggage to load, including no less than 1,099 pieces of silver plate, 127 pieces of Sèvres porcelain, and a host of table accessories and linen to go with it. Together with all the other personal items and necessities that Napoleon wished to take with him, the whole lot was packed into fifty chests, each specially designed to accommodate and safeguard its contents. The loaded convoy eventually consisted in all of some sixty people. Napoleon was determined that, whatever happened to him, he would still retain all the outward trappings and insignia of the imperial court. There were more practical considerations also: the silver could come in useful if he ran out of money.

Despite his determination to maintain his imperial dignity Napoleon was so concerned for his personal safety on the journey that on leaving he abandoned his favourite green uniform of the Chasseurs de la Garde and travelled in 'habit bourgeois', wearing a large round hat with a broad brim for disguise.[15] This was not the first time he had resorted to this tactic: after his first abdication in April 1814 he had donned civilian clothes and later the uniform of an Austrian army general in order to avoid recognition by hostile crowds on the route. On this second occasion he was accompanied in a four-horse *calèche* by Generals Bertrand and Becker and the Duke of Rovigo, similarly dressed in civilian clothes. Sitting up on the front seat of the coach was number two valet, Louis-Etienne St Denis, known as 'Mameluke Ali', who had prudently supplied the coach with ample provisions for the journey, together with six pairs of pistols, two for himself and one each for the inside passengers. First valet Louis-Joseph Marchand followed in another coach, which was stuffed with as many of Napoleon's most personal possessions from Malmaison and the Elysée that he could cram into it. General Gourgaud also followed Napoleon in a separate carriage, but the Montholon family and Las Cases and his son were sent off by a different route. Fanny Bertrand and her three children – showing the independence of spirit that was later to mark her stay on St Helena and so irritate Napoleon – together with Napoleon's brother Joseph and General Lallemand set off separately on the following day, she having first returned to Paris with Hortense. Nevertheless, the destination for all of them was the naval arsenal of Rochefort, where the two frigates were waiting.

Napoleon's convoy travelled via Rambouillet, Chartres, Châteaudun, Tours and Poitiers before reaching the small town of Niort at around 10pm, pausing there for forty-eight hours. After a brief rest at the somewhat uncomfortable hotel La Boule d'Or, and as news spread round the town of his arrival – despite the civilian disguise it could hardly be kept a secret when such a procession of great people in grand coaches arrived out of the blue in this relatively minor provincial centre – Napoleon was invited by the Prefect to move to his more comfortable residence.[16] Here he appeared to relax again for a while as he was acclaimed by a gathering crowd of local residents, wined, dined and serenaded by the local band, and exhorted by the still-loyal soldiers of the resident garrison to rejoin the army. However, this could not last for long. The news was bad: General Becker, who had accompanied the party, reported in a letter to the provisional government that Napoleon had been informed at Niort by the Prefect that the English had strengthened their blockade of Rochefort, making escape without their permission virtually impossible. On receiving this news, Napoleon, who had already sent General Gourgaud ahead to appraise the situation at Rochefort, asked the Prefect to find out whether a deal could be struck with the commander of the English squadron, failing which he would, as a mere general, once more offer his services to the forces still defending Paris and the homeland.

It was, however, far too late for any further such self-delusion: Paris was on the verge of capitulation, and at 4am on 3 July Napoleon set off for Rochefort. A troop of hussars provided an escort out of the town with drawn swords as they rolled on through the valley of the River Charente. They passed through the great gateway in the city walls of Rochefort and headed straight for the house of the Maritime Sub-Prefect, Captain Casimir de Bonnefaux, arriving there mid-afternoon. Bonnefaux was no friend of Napoleon, who had held back his promotion some years previously, but he put his apartments at the disposal of the ex-Emperor. The rest of the party, including Joseph, who had already made his plans to sail to America, arrived during the night and over the next two days.

The next few days were utterly critical for Napoleon. If he was to have any chance at all of avoiding exile and further indignity, or an even worse fate, he had to act quickly and decisively. Luck had generally been on his side throughout his meteoric career and now was the time to make the most of it again. But luck was starting to run out and the options now before him were narrowing rapidly. There are differing views on how far Napoleon's will and energy had in fact been sapped by this stage, but there can be little doubt that his capacity for decisive and resolute action had been seriously damaged by the defeat and resulting depression of Waterloo, and the harassment and humiliation of his treatment by the Chamber of Deputies and the new government. There are also differing accounts of the state of his physical health at this time. He was still only forty-six, the same age as Wellington, and over the years had been tough enough to endure unbelievable hardships on campaign, from the parched and burning sands of Egypt to the freezing steppes of Russia. He had also become habituated to little sleep, rising at early and irregular hours to review his troops.

Nonetheless it is difficult also to believe that his physical condition had not now deteriorated significantly – and no wonder, given the ceaseless physical and mental strain he had been under ever since the return from Elba. The loyal Marchand claims that he was not unwell at Waterloo – specifically, that he was not suffering from the piles or cystitis to which some historians have attributed his listlessness and lack of energy and initiative on the battlefield.[17] However, many witnesses have remarked on the unusual pallor of his complexion and his increasing corpulence: he had put on a great deal of weight round the middle. His companions were mystified by his inertia and lack of decisiveness and could not understand what had overtaken him. As General Montholon wrote later, 'The reasons for our staying at Rochefort until the evening of July 8, when we embarked for the frigate *Saale*, were a mystery that I have never succeeded in fathoming, for I shall always refuse to believe that we remained five days at Rochefort merely to await packing cases and wagons.'[18]

Napoleon initially installed himself at the Rochefort Prefecture. There was much discussion among his advisers as to what course he should now take, but he seemed content once more to bide his time until every possibility had been explored and definitive news about the passports had arrived. On 6 July he finally stirred himself and made his first positive decision since arriving, to transfer to the frigate *Saale*.[19] He now had broadly three options before him. The first option, whether or not the Chamber of Deputies supported him, was to return to the army and try to rally the troops and fight on. Although this was still urged on him by some of the younger loyal officers, it was a forlorn hope and no longer a serious possibility. Paris was now in enemy hands and the white Bourbon flag was being raised throughout France. It was in any case uncertain how far any significant number of troops would follow the Eagle again, despite the acclamations he had received on the triumphant march from Antibes to Paris after the return from Elba, and subsequent local demonstrations of loyalty and affection.

The second option was to try to break through the English naval block-ade. Unbeknown to Napoleon, this might just have been possible during the first few days after his arrival at Rochefort. The approaches to the roads of Rochefort contain two large islands, the Ile de Ré and the Ile d'Oléron, as well as a number of smaller ones, and these create three entrances or chan-nels to the Basque Roads, where the French frigates were stationed. The Basque Roads were the most important French naval base on the Atlantic coast after Brest, the main anchorage being sheltered from Atlantic storms and defended by the heavily fortified Ile d'Aix, with its ramparts, walls, gun emplacements and a small garrison town. There had in fact only been one English ship on guard during that time, the 74-gun ship-of-the-line *Bellerophon*, under the command of the thirty-seven-year-old Scotsman, Captain Frederick Maitland. Even this doughty old warship, which had fought at the battle of the Glorious First of June and later with Nelson at both the battle of the Nile and at Trafalgar, could not have controlled all the three entrances on its own at the same time, especially at night. Within a few days, however, the *Bellerophon*, or 'Billy Ruffian', as the sailors who had not had the benefit of a classical education called her, had been reinforced by two frigates, the *Myrmidon* and the *Slaney*, and on 12 July by two well-armed sloops, the *Daphne* and the *Cyrus*. Maitland had deployed them so as to block all three possible exits. Maitland had also already received clear instructions from his commanding officer, Admiral Hotham, to prevent Napoleon from escaping in either of the French frigates, and he knew that London had refused the application for passports and guarantees of safe passage. But there had been a short window of opportunity during the first days of his arrival at Rochefort that Napoleon had been too ignorant or indecisive to seize.

Despite the odds against him, Napoleon toyed with, or at least purported to, the idea of a breakout for a time. Philibert, the captain of the *Saale*, a loyal Bourbon at heart, was himself unwilling to try it. He was in communication with the provisional government in Paris and both he and his officers were unsympathetic to Napoleon and were in fact much relieved when he finally left the *Saale* and transferred to the Ile d'Aix on 12 July. Las Cases refers ruefully to the 'faiblesse de caractère de la part du commandant' (the weakness of character of the captain).[20] But there was no shortage of offers from other quarters to tread the road of glory and run Napoleon through the blockade. Captain Ponée of the other French frigate, *La Méduse*, offered to lead a diversionary attack on the *Bellerophon* and thus allow Napoleon to make for the open sea in a fast French sloop.[21] However, Philibert would not go along with this plan. A young French lieutenant, Victor Besson, offered to take command of a Danish ship, *La Madeleine*, which also happened to be in port at the time, and take Napoleon on board secretly and make a break for it.[22] But it would have obliged Napoleon to travel in disguise, hidden down in the bowels of the ship, and resulted in utter humiliation in the likely event of interception. It is not difficult to imagine what the cartoonists in the English press would have made of this.

A similar offer came from the young, enthusiastic and still-loyal naval cadets on the Ile d'Aix, whom Napoleon met when he left the *Saale* on 9 July to spend the day on the island inspecting its fortifications and testing the loyalty of the garrison there. They proposed making a dash for it in a *chasse-marée*, a type of small armed coastal vessel noted for her speed.[23] They obviously inherited the fiercely anti-British spirit of the inhabitants of the island, where a French fleet had been utterly humiliated and largely destroyed by English fireships under Captain Thomas Cochrane at the battle of Aix Roads in April 1809. Napoleon's brother Joseph, the former King of Naples and then Spain, bravely and unselfishly even offered to abandon his own plans to go to America and impersonate Napoleon and surrender to the English in his place, thus allowing Napoleon to slip away unrecognized in another vessel. Perhaps Napoleon should have taken this chance – Joseph later made his way successfully to America and ended up living in great style as the rich owner of vast plantations and returning to Europe, including London, without fear of imprisonment or prosecution.

Napoleon was now in an almost impossible predicament. Whichever way he turned posed formidable problems. When he had returned to the *Saale* from his first visit to the Ile d'Aix on 9 July, he had been informed by the Prefect that the provisional government had decided that anyone who helped him to disembark on French territory would be declared a traitor. They clearly wanted to drive him into English hands. The views of Napoleon's inner circle were still divided.[24] The majority, including General Bertrand, the Duke of Rovigo and Las Cases, appeared to favour the option of Napoleon throwing himself voluntarily on the mercy of the English. Bertrand was enthusiastically urged on in this by his wife, Fanny, who, given her Anglo-Irish background, and tired of everlastingly following in the Napoleonic baggage train, certainly preferred a comfortable retirement in England to an uncertain future in America or who knows where. As we have seen, she had been the main advocate of trusting the British in the earlier discussions at Malmaison. Apart from General Lallemand there was little support for trying to break the British blockade. It was evident to them that Maitland would resist it, and the frigates were no match for a British ship-of-the-line. In response to an approach by Las Cases and the Duke of Rovigo, whom Napoleon had sent on 10 July to sound him out yet again, Maitland had confirmed to them that his instructions were to prevent any ship of war putting out from the port of Rochefort.[25] Although Montholon and Gourgaud still had doubts about trusting in the hospitality of their sworn enemy, perfidious Albion, the ayes in favour of surrendering to Maitland on the *Bellerophon* seemed to have it.

Even then Napoleon remained incapable of reaching a final decision. On 12 July, however, he left the *Saale*, where the atmosphere was increasingly unsympathetic, and transferred to the Ile d'Aix. This small island, which it is easy to walk round in a couple of hours, is now a quiet holiday resort better known outside France for its delicious oysters, pleasant beaches and tree-hidden holiday villas than for any connection with Napoleon. It was, however, familiar territory to the Emperor. He had always regarded it as pivotal to the defence of the great naval arsenal at Rochefort, which was second only in importance to Brest. He had visited it in great style and imperial pomp in August 1808 and personally approved the plans for fortifying it and building the handsome commandant's house (now converted into an excellent museum), in which he was to spend his last three nights on French soil. On 14 July he sent Las Cases and Lallemand once more on a mission to sound out Maitland.[26] After an unconvincing ruse, in which they claimed that Napoleon was so anxious to avoid further bloodshed that he would be ready to travel to America in any way the British Government permitted, whether in a French or English vessel, Maitland made it finally clear that he could not guarantee that passports for America would be granted but that he had been authorized by his Government to receive Napoleon and his suite and treat them with the greatest consideration and convey them to England.

There have been allegations that Captain Maitland played a double game and gave assurances to Napoleon of an honourable reception in England on which he subsequently reneged. The balance of evidence, however, is that Maitland acted with great skill, honesty, prudence and discretion. He was in an extraordinarily difficult position. Although said to be a 'natural diplomat' with a courteous and charming manner, he was a hardened sea-fighting captain, not a professional envoy. He was tightly bound by his orders, and he simply could not enter into any commitment beyond that of conveying Napoleon and his party to England. In any case, also looking over his shoulder now was his commanding officer, Admiral Hotham, who had arrived outside Rochefort on his flagship, the *Superb*, on 15 July.

In his more considered moments later on St Helena Napoleon himself exonerated Maitland from blame[27] and in his voluminous *Mémorial*, published in 1823 to immortalize Napoleon and glorify his career and martyrdom (and *en passant* to earn himself a pretty penny), Las Cases cleared him completely. According to Las Cases, who must have discussed it with Napoleon, Maitland made it clear that he could not guarantee safe conducts to America, and he concludes by saying of Maitland 'Je lui rends la justice de croire qu'il était sincère et de bonne foi, ainsi que les autres officiers, dans la peinture qu'ils nous avaient faite des sentiments de l'Angleterre' (I do him the justice of believing that he and his officers acted sincerely and in good faith in the picture they gave us of feelings in England).[28] Coming from this source the acquittal of Maitland is convincing.

When all this was reported to Napoleon at a council held in his room in the commandant's house he finally reached what in effect was the most momentous and irrevocable decision of his life – to hand himself over voluntarily to the British, thus ending for ever any aspiration to rule France as emperor again and, though he did not yet know it, condemning himself to the rocky isolation of imprisonment on St Helena. He must have realized, however, that at this stage, after delaying for so long, he really had no other choice. If he tried to escape by land there was a high probability that he would be quickly captured by the newly restored Bourbons or, perhaps even worse, by the Prussians or Austrians, with the prospect of early execution. If he tried the direct sea route, the chances were that he would be blown out of the water by the waiting British warships, along with the men, women and children who had loyally followed him so far. And to try to steal away in disguise like a common fugitive in the grubby hold of some smaller vessel was entirely inconsistent with the acute sense of personal honour and dignity to which he attached great importance. He therefore rejected the various escape plans and, according to Marchand, he summed his final decision up in the following words: 'il n'est pas sans quelques dangers de se mettre entre les mains de ses ennemis, mais mieux vaut risquer de se confier à leur honneur que d'être entre leurs mains prisonnier de droit' (it is not without a certain danger to put oneself in the hands of one's enemies, but it is better to risk trusting oneself to their sense of honour than to be in their hands as a prisoner of right).[29]

There is a touching anecdote about this fatal decision to surrender to the British which is attributed to Gourgaud. A tiny wren is said to have flown into Napoleon's bedroom in the commandant's house on the Ile d'Aix. Gourgaud caught it in his hand but Napoleon said 'Ah, rendez-lui la liberté, il y a assez de malheureux!' (Ah, give it its freedom, there is enough unhappiness already!)[30] As Gourgaud released it and the little bird flew away Napoleon asked whether this should be taken as an omen. Gourgaud replied 'Sire, il vole vers la croisière anglaise' (Sire, it is flying towards the English squadron).

This concept of surrendering voluntarily and trusting to the British sense of honour and fair play, and therefore not waiting to be taken and made a 'prisoner of right', but in effect becoming an asylum-seeking guest, was absolutely fundamental to Napoleon's utter rejection of, and resistance to, his subsequent deportation to St Helena and his treatment there. In an astonishing and bizarre way he attempted to enshrine this concept in the following letter, which, drawing on his familiarity with classical history, he dictated to the Prince Regent, who was acting head of state during the illness of his father, King George III, for delivery after his decision to surrender had been taken:

> Your Royal Highness,
>   A victim to the factions which distract my country, and to the enmity of the greatest powers of Europe, I have terminated my political career, and I come, like Themistocles, to throw myself upon the hospitality of the British people. I put myself under the protection of their laws, which I claim from your Royal Highness, as the most powerful, the most constant, and the most generous of my enemies.
>
> Rochefort, 13 July
Napoleon[31]

On the evening of 14 July Las Cases and General Gourgaud were sent over for the last time to the *Bellerophon* with a letter to Captain Maitland from Napoleon, announcing that he would proceed on board the ship the next morning. It also enclosed a list of the fifty members of his entourage who would accompany him. Maitland was asked to arrange for Gourgaud to be sent ahead to England to deliver the letter to the Prince Regent personally. Maitland agreed to these requests and arranged for the sloop *Slaney* to sail ahead to England with Gourgaud on board, along with his own dispatches to the Admiralty. He then discussed with Las Cases the arrangements for accommodating Napoleon and his party on the ship, and stayed up to the early hours supervising them.

The die was now truly cast, but it beggars belief that Napoleon, who had boasted before the Trafalgar disaster: 'With God's help I will put an end to the future and very existence of England,' and whose paramount objective for many years had been to destroy British commercial power and economic influence, could have been so apparently naïve as to expect his now victorious enemy to receive him as an honoured guest and allow him to live comfortably as a country gentleman somewhere in the Home Counties. As the Duke of Wellington's friend, Mrs Arbuthnot, subsequently commented when reading some papers about what Napoleon had told Las Cases he would have done if the Prince Regent had responded favourably to his Themistocles letter: 'He must have thought John Bull a greater fool than he really is.'[32] In any case he must have known that circumstances would never have allowed him to settle down for long as an apolitical animal in England. His remaining supporters – both in England, where surprisingly there was a significant number, and in France and America – would not have let him rest. He would inevitably have become a rallying point again, and would have found it impossible to resist.

He may have been influenced by the experience of his younger brother, Lucien, who had been captured by a British warship in 1810 and allowed to settle in a country house near Worcester, with minimum supervision. However, the traumatic events of the previous weeks had clouded his judgement, if not temporarily destroyed it completely, and throughout the rest of his life on St Helena he continued to protest with frustrated outrage at what he regarded as the British Government's shameful and treacherous abuse of the laws of hospitality.

Napoleon spent the night of 14/15 July at the commandant's house on the Ile d'Aix. He was woken soon after midnight as he had to be down on the quayside by 2am. Once more, assisted by Marchand, he donned the white waistcoat and breeches, military boots and green uniform coat with scarlet cuffs and lapels of a colonel of the Chasseurs de la Garde. On this was pinned the grand cross of the Légion d'Honneur, and over it, to protect himself against the chilly early morning breeze, he buttoned up his famous olive-coloured greatcoat and his unmistakable black tricorn hat, with its tricolour cockade. Despite his depression and despair, if he was to surrender to the British, he would do so as a soldier, not as an anonymous civilian seeking to avoid attention.

He was slowly rowed out from the landing stage at Aix to the French vessel, *Epervier*, a 'brick de l'état' (naval brig) with eighteen guns and a crew of ninety-five.[33] As he stepped aboard there were cries of 'Vive l'Empereur'. He was accompanied on the *Epervier* by General and Madame Bertrand, General and Madame Montholon, General Lallemand and a few domestic servants. General Becker had also asked Napoleon if he wished him to accompany him to the *Bellerophon*. Napoleon's revealing reply was: 'Non, general Becker, il ne faut pas qu'on puisse dire que la France m'a livré aux Anglais' (No, General Becker, no-one must be allowed to say that France handed me over to the English).[34] Napoleon was determined to make it clear right from the start that his act of surrender was an entirely voluntary and personal one.

According to Marchand's account, there was a profound look of sadness on the faces of the crew as they sailed the *Epervier* slowly out into the middle of the Roads, to meet the barges sent by Maitland to convey him and his party to the *Bellerophon*.[35] Whether by chance or design the crews of the barges were largely composed of French sailors who had been taken prisoner. The crew of the *Epervier* simply could not believe that their former Emperor could trust himself to the generosity of a nation whose perfidy was so well known. Their huzzahs were mingled with tears as they saw Napoleon leave them for the last time. Their despair was such that some are said to have torn their hair out and trampled their hats beneath their feet. One of them exclaimed, 'Oh Napoleon. What fate is in store for you? You are counting on the generosity of the English. I pray to God that your faith will not be let down.'[36]

But it was too late. Napoleon reached the *Bellerophon* and, after requesting Mesdames Bertrand and Montholon to precede him, climbed up the ladder onto the deck. He was received by Count de Las Cases, who had gone in advance and who presented Captain Maitland to him.

According to the strict protocol procedures of the Royal Navy, it was, to the great relief of Maitland, too early in the morning for a full ceremonial welcome of any kind. He was thus spared the tricky decision as to whether to accord Napoleon full head-of-state honours. But the marines on board were under arms, the officers lined up on the quarter deck, and the yardarms fully manned. Napoleon simply said: 'Je viens à votre bord me mettre sous la protection des lois d'Angleterre' (I come aboard to put myself under the protection of the laws of England).[37] Maitland limited his response to 'un salut profond' (a deep bow), and led him down quickly to the saloon, where the ship's officers were presented to him. The rest of his suite were left on deck until they could be conveyed to their improvised quarters.

TWO

THE JOURNEY
FROM ROCHEFORT
TO PLYMOUTH

THE *BELLEROPHON* HAD HAD a glorious history since its launch at
Frindsbury near the Chatham dockyard in 1786. At that time Nelson was
a twenty-eight-year-old sea captain, and a recently commissioned young
artillery lieutenant, still known by his Corsican family name, Napoleone
Buonaparte, had just returned from military college in France to his
childhood home at Ajaccio in Corsica. He did not change his name to the
more familiar Bonaparte until some ten years later. The ship had fought in
most of the great naval engagements of the Napoleonic wars; after Trafalgar,
where its captain was killed by a musket ball in the same way that Nelson
himself was fatally wounded on the *Victory*, it had been engaged on the
Jamaica station guarding the West Indian colonies and escorting convoys
across the Atlantic. Immediately before the events that were to write its

name even more famously into the history books, it had formed part of the squadrons keeping watch on the Spanish fleet at Cadiz. As Cordingly in his brilliant history of the *Bellerophon*, titled *Billy Ruffian*, puts it, it was 'a crucial link in the wooden walls of England, that extended line of British ships which finally put an end to Napoleon's ambitious plans to invade England and march on London.'[1]

Captain Maitland went to enormous trouble to accommodate as comfortably as possible the most distinguished company of unexpected guests that had ever been thrust at short notice on a British warship – one former emperor, three generals, two French counts and countesses, two cooks, twenty-six servants and a mountain of baggage, including the imperial dinner service and silver plate. After Napoleon had been taken on a tour of the ship – during which he questioned Maitland incessantly on every aspect of it, not least on what was the secret of the Royal Navy's ability, time and time again, to defeat so easily their French counterparts – at 9am a typical English-style breakfast was served. Soon afterwards the commander of the *Bellerophon*'s squadron, Admiral Hotham, arrived in his flagship, the *Superb*, and anchored alongside the *Bellerophon*. The afternoon was spent loading the French party's baggage onto the *Bellerophon* and at 5pm a formal dinner was served in the great stern cabin – arranged by Maitland, but on his instructions prepared by Napoleon's own kitchen team. Napoleon seems to have lorded it over the occasion, seating himself at the centre of the table, with the Admiral on his right, Countess Bertrand on his left, and Captain Maitland opposite him. Since Napoleon could speak and understand little English, Fanny Bertrand proved to be a very useful interpreter.

The next day was spent in completing preparations to set sail for England. While these were under way Admiral Hotham invited Napoleon to cross over to visit the *Superb*. As he reached the flagship he was piped aboard and received ceremonially with honours that were appropriate for a head of state. St Denis, Napoleon's second valet, commonly known as Mameluke Ali – a curiously patronizing and egocentric indulgence by Napoleon, dating from his Egyptian days – described the reception as 'toute souveraine' (quite princely).[2] It was the last time that the English would accord him such imperial treatment. He was given a tour of the ship and a flash of the old soldier was sparked as he inspected the marine guard of honour drawn up to salute him on the deck. After giving them several sharp arms drill commands, he advanced into the middle of them, reproved one of the marines in the rear rank for not holding his musket firmly enough at the present, seized it from him and demonstrated how to do it correctly.[3] It was not only the marines who were amazed; Napoleon's own companions were horrified at seeing him at such close quarters, for the first time, at the business end of a bristling line of English bayonets.

Napoleon was ferried back to the *Bellerophon* around midday and they set course for England in the early afternoon. He was greatly impressed with the speed and efficiency with which everything was done, particularly with the silence with which orders were given and instantly carried out, and stayed on deck to observe it throughout. In the evening another convivial dinner was held in the great cabin. General Bertrand, usurping the role of host, as befits a former grand marshal of the imperial court, invited the First Lieutenant and the Captain of Marines to join them. Conversation was free and cordial and a surprisingly relaxed Napoleon appeared, for the moment, quite transformed from the tired, listless and indecisive person who had been paralysed by indecision for so long. Perhaps the sheer relief at having at last taken a positive decision, whatever its consequences, and a still delusional optimism about the reception that the British had in store had at least temporarily cleared some of the darker concerns from his mind.

He was, of course, an object of intense curiosity and observation for the crew, rather like a rare and exotic animal, captured and put on display in a zoo for the first time. All accounts suggest that both officers and matelots were greatly impressed with the most famous person any of them was ever remotely likely to see again. Many recorded their impressions. Lieutenant Smart found him 'affable and pleasing in his manners, he speaks to everyone he comes athwart and is always in a good humour and bears his misfortunes with a great deal of fortitude.'[4] For him, Napoleon's outstanding feature was his keen and penetrating eye with which 'like a hawke's, he never sees anything once but he recollects it again'. One of the most vivid portraits is that left by Lieutenant Bowerbank, who wrote:

Napoleon Bonaparte is about five feet seven inches high, rather corpulent, remarkably well made. His hair is very black, cut close, whiskers shaved off; large eyebrows, grey eyes, the most piercing I ever saw; rather full face, dark but peculiar complexion, his nose and mouth proportionate, broad shoulders and apparently strongly built. Upon the whole he is a good looking man, and when young must have been handsome.[5]

Napoleon may not exactly have appreciated the last double-edged remark, but it was overall a flattering portrait and demonstrates the legendary ability of the old master to mesmerize people and subject them to his charm and influence. It worked also on Captain Maitland, as is evidenced by the following extract from the preface to Maitland's journal of these historic days:

> It may appear surprising, that a possibility could exist of a British officer, being prejudiced in favour of one who had caused so many calamities to his country: but to such an extent did he possess the power of pleasing, there are few people who could have sat at the same table with him for nearly a month, as I did, without feeling a sensation of pity, allied perhaps to regret, that a man possessed of so many fascinating qualities, and who had held so high a station in life, should be reduced to the situation in which I saw him.[6]

The voyage proceeded smoothly and without untoward incident. For a time Napoleon maintained his outwardly relaxed and insouciant manner. In a perverse way he may have felt flattered by being given such regal treatment on an English man-of-war. He had little time for the English army. He later admitted that the English infantry had performed well at Waterloo and claimed that Wellington had owed his victory to their firmness and bravery rather than to his own conduct as a general.[7] However, he always maintained that Britain should stick to its ships (a whale) and that there was no point in Britain trying to maintain a standing army (an elephant) to fight on the continent. Its strength lay in its sea power and mercantile supremacy, and he had huge respect and admiration for the Royal Navy, which, by controlling the English Channel, had thwarted his plans to invade Britain. They had not relaxed their stranglehold for even twenty-four hours – the minimum time Napoleon needed to get his Army of England, over 100,000 strong, across the Dover Straits from their assembly point at Boulogne. He therefore appeared to enjoy the company of Maitland and his officers, and the attention of Admiral Hotham – rather in the way that later on he preferred Admiral Sir George Cockburn and his successor on St Helena, Admiral Sir Pulteney

Malcolm, to the soldier Governor, locally promoted Lieutenant-General Sir Hudson Lowe.

As the short voyage progressed, however, Napoleon's initially almost exuberant spirit began to dampen and he withdrew more to his cabin, only appearing on deck in the afternoons and, as was his long-standing custom, spending at most twenty minutes at the dinner table (he detested what he regarded as the uncivilized English tradition of staying at the table for coffee and port or liqueurs and left as soon as the dessert had been served). He must have begun to reflect again more soberly on what kind of reception awaited him in England. Would the Prince Regent grant his request for civilized and honourable political asylum? Would he be allowed to live the life of a retired country gentleman in comparative comfort and freedom? The gravity of the step he had taken came forcefully and perhaps emotionally to him as, at dawn on 23 July, the ship passed the lighthouse on the Isle of Ushant, the westernmost point of France. Did it occur to him that this might be the last time he would ever see his, albeit adopted, native land? It is recorded that, to the surprise of the crew, he rose at 4am to go on deck to gaze at the island and the disappearing mainland beyond, and remained there in a kind of reverie for the rest of the morning.

On 24 July the *Bellerophon* arrived off Torbay on the Devon coast. The events of the next days began to unfold like a classical Greek tragedy, determined by the fates and leading to an inexorable conclusion that Napoleon was powerless to prevent. The analogy of the suffering Prometheus, which Napoleon himself, who was familiar with the great Greek playwrights, liked to draw – chained to a rock in the Caucasus, his liver devoured each evening by a giant eagle – was becoming appropriate in more senses than one. As the days passed, the omens for Napoleon became grimmer.

The first disappointment was the news that General Gourgaud had not been allowed to land and travel to London to deliver personally Napoleon's appeal to the Prince Regent. The sloop *Slaney* was effectively placed in quarantine and Captain Maitland, who had reported immediately on arrival to the Admiral in command at Plymouth, Lord Keith, had also received very firm instructions that no-one, except authorized officers and other personnel, was to be allowed to leave or board the *Bellerophon* without his written permission. This applied even to his own wife. There was certainly no question of Napoleon or any member of his party being permitted to go ashore.

*   *   *

Lord Keith, who was now approaching seventy, had spent most of his naval
career fighting the French. He had been an admiral for some twenty years
and between 1803 and 1814 he had held the key posts of Commander in
Chief of the North Sea Fleet and then of the Channel Fleet. He had no love
for Napoleon but during the next few days he was to play an important role
as the British Government's intermediary with him. He must have been
intrigued, if not apprehensive, at last to meet his legendary enemy face to
face, but perhaps not entirely displeased to be the bearer of the grim news
of his final place of exile. His orders to Maitland were detailed and precise,
designed to eliminate any possibility of escape at this stage.

Despite the embargo and the comparatively primitive state of communications at the time, news of Napoleon's arrival spread astonishingly widely
and quickly. According to one contemporary account some inquisitive and
enterprising local bakers, who had seen the two great warships arrive off
Torbay, rowed out to it to see if they could make a quick profit by selling
some of their newly baked loaves of bread. Incoming vessels were notoriously desperate for fresh supplies. They were warned to move off, but in
so doing they saw a sailor beckoning to them who let a small object fall
into the sea from a lower port. After turning away temporarily they managed to retrieve the object without being intercepted. It turned out to be a
small bottle containing a message which read: 'We have got Napoleon on
board.'[8]

Whether it was as a result of this or other events that the news spread, in
no time the *Bellerophon* was besieged with dozens of small craft – thousands
of them, according to *The Times* – filled with excited sightseers, all anxious
to get a glimpse of the fabulous 'Boney', the 'ogre' who had been threatening
to invade their country for the past decade. He was now there, a prisoner,
mortal and harmless. The *Bellerophon's* crew tried to keep them away, even
sending armed launches among them to head them off and causing at
least one with women and children onboard to capsize. It was a bit like a
maritime version of the jostling crowds portrayed in Frith's famous picture
of Derby Day, only on water in a harbour instead of upon Epsom Downs.
After staying in his cabin for a short time, Napoleon went up on the bridge
to acknowledge the cheering spectators, even raising his famous cockaded
tricorn hat to them in salute in response to their hurrahs – rather like an
actor taking a curtain call. Many of those present subsequently recorded

their impressions. John Smart was surprised at how small he seemed and thought he was rather fat.[9] A *Times* correspondent reported that he appeared 'rather stout, very full in the face, but very stern and thoughtful in his manner'.[10] But the atmosphere was festive, and everyone present would long remember the day when they had seen the dreaded Napoleon brought as a captive to English shores.

After this reception, which Napoleon appeared outwardly to revel in (he had always maintained that if only he had been able to go to England he would soon have conquered the hearts of the English), the atmosphere on the ship began to change and the realities of his circumstances became more apparent. In the early hours of 26 July the *Bellerophon* was ordered to move to Plymouth. This was partly to escape the Torbay crowds and partly because the presence of Admiral Keith's flagship and other warships in the sheltered Plymouth naval base would minimize any further possibilities of Napoleon escaping. The first objective was not, however, met in the slightest. As the word continued to spread, a multitude of sightseeing day-trippers came out in boats to catch a glimpse of Napoleon on the *Bellerophon*, and they were met with the same, somewhat brutal tactics.

On the vessel itself Marchand records that the general climate of feeling among Napoleon's party also became decidedly more ominous and sombre. The dreaded words 'St Helena' even began to be mentioned. One of the two sentries stationed outside the dining room, an Irishman, when he thought no-one was looking, whispered to Marchand that he was a Catholic and, in a very low voice, said: 'No good for Empereur Sainte Hélène.'[11] It was not in fact the first time that St Helena had been mentioned in the context of Napoleon's future. At the Congress of Vienna in 1814, there was talk, even reported in some newspapers, of transferring Napoleon there from Elba – which may have precipitated Napoleon's early flight from Elba, the timing of which he later claimed to regret. Hortense Beauharnais also records that the dreaded words were uttered during Napoleon's few days at Malmaison before the flight to Rochefort.[12] But it was the first time it had been mentioned in relation to Napoleon's current fate. Suspicions were further aroused when on the following day Bertrand was told by Maitland that all the French officers who were not part of Napoleon's personal suite must be transferred to the frigate *Eurotas*, and that Lord Keith would be coming aboard to speak privately to Napoleon. In the event, Lord Keith's first call turned out to be purely a courtesy call, at which nothing of great substance was said. Keith was presumably testing the temperature for sterner conversations to come.

While these developments were taking place at Plymouth, critical deliberations were under way in Whitehall to decide on Napoleon's fate. The Paris Convention, signed on 2 August 1815 by Britain, Austria, Prussia and Russia, but which had presumably been negotiated in draft form some time beforehand, explicitly identified Napoleon as a prisoner and recorded the joint agreement of the allied powers that Napoleon should never again have an opportunity to disturb the peace of Europe. They entrusted specifically to Britain the responsibility for deciding the place and the measures necessary to secure this objective. The role of the co-signatories would be confined to sending commissioners to the place where Napoleon was held, without any responsibility for his safe-keeping, but to assure themselves and their governments of his continued presence. The restored King of France, Louis XVIII, was similarly invited to send his own commissioner. Although Marshal Blücher would certainly have applied summary justice, there was no formal discussion of the possibility of trying and executing Napoleon. No doubt the British Government felt that this would make him an instant martyr and that it was better to exile him far away, where with luck he would soon be forgotten – how wrong in the event they were!

The British Government alone, therefore, had to decide what to do with the former Emperor. The principal ministers involved were the Prime Minister, Lord Liverpool; the Foreign Secretary, Lord Castlereagh; the Secretary for War and the Colonies, Lord Bathurst; the First Lord of the Admiralty, Lord Melville; and the senior civil servant at the Admiralty, a Mr John Barrow. Contrary to Napoleon's later claims, the Duke of Wellington, who was still in Paris, appears to have played no part at the time in the decision. No doubt Napoleon assumed that because Wellington was familiar with St Helena, having spent a few days there on his return from India in 1805, he had inspired the idea of confining him there. In a later conversation with Dr O'Meara, who said he did not believe that Wellington was responsible for the decision, Napoleon said that if he had been it would reflect little honour on him in the eyes of posterity.[13] Nevertheless we can safely acquit the Duke of the charge.

Lord Liverpool had no sympathy for Napoleon. He wanted him out of harm's way as soon as possible. He wrote frankly to Lord Castlereagh:

'We wish that the King of France would hang or shoot Buonaparte [sic], as the best termination of the business.'[14] Time was also pressing. Among the opposition ranks at Westminster were several powerful supporters for clement treatment of Napoleon, including the prominent Whig, Lord Holland, and even a royal prince, the Duke of Sussex. Several possible places of confinement were mentioned in the press, both abroad and in Britain, including the Tower of London or Dumbarton Castle in Scotland. For Lord Liverpool none of these would do. Anywhere in Europe would become an immediate rallying point for Napoleon's remaining supporters, and in the United States he would be completely outside the control of the allies, and a potential focus for disturbance. Equally, if he remained in Britain he would, as the Prime Minister again wrote to Lord Castlereagh, 'become an object of compassion in the course of a few months.'[15] The welcome that Napoleon had received at Torbay and Plymouth, although largely inspired by sheer 'celebrity' curiosity, had amply demonstrated this. Evidence shows also that even the battle-toughened crews of the *Bellerophon* and subsequently of the *Northumberland* succumbed to the Napoleonic charm and charisma. 'He is a fine fellow, who does not deserve his fate,' recorded one *Northumberland* matelot.[16]

Lord Liverpool's attitude is hardly surprising in view of the devastation that Napoleon's megalomaniac adventures had caused for Britain and the rest of Europe. In his biography of Napoleon, Lord Rosebery said that it had been estimated that it had cost Britain more than 800 million pounds sterling to effect Napoleon's removal to Elba, and millions more as a result of his return.[17] In human terms it has been estimated that he was probably directly or indirectly responsible for some two million deaths, many of them of his own compatriots. It was not therefore unreasonable for the British Government to wish to place him somewhere totally isolated and inaccessible where, as the Paris Convention stipulated, he could not disturb Europe's peace again. St Helena was quite well known in White-hall from the reports of various traders, East India Company officials and military commanders who had visited the island over the years. Accordingly, on the very specific advice of Mr Barrow of the Admiralty, it was chosen as the place for Napoleon's detention and Lord Keith was deputed to break the news to him. St Helena had every conceivable advantage for its intended purpose. Apart from its isolation, it was small and compact, almost entirely surrounded by steep, towering cliffs, devoid of any easy landing place, already heavily fortified and easy to defend, and possessed of a small population, which meant that no stranger could penetrate the island without quickly being noticed.

On 31 July, Lord Keith, accompanied by the Under Secretary of State of War, Major-General Sir Henry Bunbury, came aboard the *Bellerophon* and presented to Napoleon a letter announcing the British Government's decision. Bunbury translated it for Napoleon. The crucial passage read:

> It would be inconsistent with our duty to this country, and to his Majesty's allies, if we were to leave General Bonaparte the means or opportunity of again disturbing the peace of Europe, and renewing the calamities of war; it is therefore unavoidable that he should be restrained in his personal liberty to whatever extent may be necessary to secure our first and paramount objective.
>
> The island of St Helena has been selected for his future residence. The climate is healthy, and its local situation will admit of his being treated with more indulgence than would be compatible with adequate security elsewhere.[18]

It is not clear whether the last sentence was drafted tongue in cheek, or simply, in the absence of the Duke of Wellington, out of sheer ignorance. The severity of the damp and windy climate for much of the year on the high plateau where his residence was situated was to become one of Napoleon's principal grievances on St Helena.

The rest of the letter also stipulated that Napoleon would be allowed to take with him three officers, together with a doctor and twelve personal domestics or servants. Rear-Admiral Sir George Cockburn, who had been promoted Commander in Chief of the Cape Station, would be conducting Napoleon to St Helena and would be ready to leave in a few days. Napoleon should therefore quickly select the members of his party who were to accompany him.

Although it was not the first time that St Helena had been mentioned as a possible place of exile the decision came as a bombshell. It left the rest of his followers in shock when they heard it, but Napoleon, according to Marchand, received it 'avec un calme profond, et sans laisser paraître la moindre émotion' (with a profound calm and without revealing the least emotion).[19] Perhaps in his heart of hearts he realized that his hopes for a quiet non-political life in the country – let alone the preposterous

1. Napoleon boarding the *Bellerophon*, 15 July 1815

2. First view of St Helena, December 2007

3. Jamestown harbour as Napoleon would have known it in 1815

4. Jamestown harbour, 2007

5. Napoleon gazing out to sea, with Sir Hudson Lowe and Major Gorrequer looking on

6. Napoleon at Longwood dictating to Count de Las Cases

7. The pavilion at the Briars, where Napoleon stayed from October to December 1815

8. The Briars pavilion in 2007 – now a small museum

9. *(top)* Sandy Bay, with the rusting cannon barrels lying across the beach, December 2007

10. *(centre)* Longwood House, front view, December 2007

11. *(bottom)* Plantation House, the Governor's official residence, December 2007

12. *(above)* Napoleon working in the Longwood garden

13. *(left)* Napoleon at Longwood being watched by British sentries

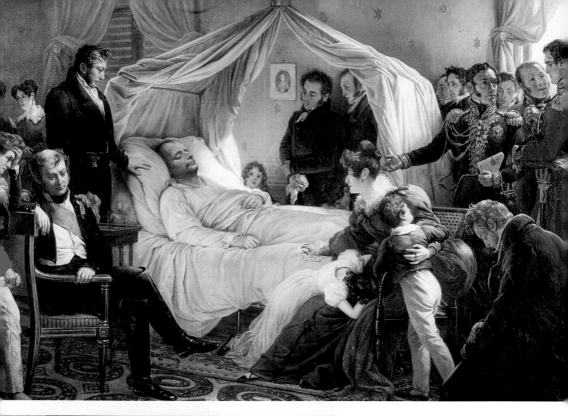

14. (*above*) Napoleon on his deathbed, surrounded by his faithful companions, 5 May 1821

15. (*left*) Fanny Bertrand and her children at Napoleon's deathbed (detail)

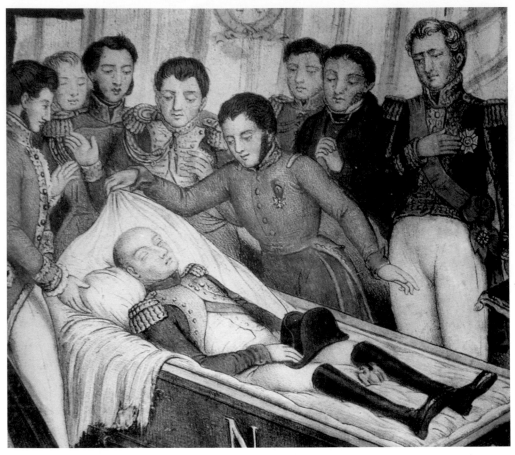

16. Exhumation of Napoleon's remains, October 1840

17. Napoleon's tomb, Geranium Valley, December 2007

suggestion attributed to him, surely apocryphally, of the bestowal by the Prince Regent of the Order of the Garter – were illusory. Nevertheless, when Lord Keith and General Bunbury had finished talking, he registered a strong formal protest against what he regarded as a disgraceful violation of the laws of England, of common human rights and of the sacred right of hospitality – all principles, of course, which, by his own admission, he had no doubt meticulously observed throughout his own career. He appealed to the sense of 'l'honneur Britannique', and later that day handed a letter to Captain Maitland for Lord Keith more formally expressing his outrage at his treatment. He asserted that he was not a prisoner of war, since he had put himself voluntarily in the hands of the English, under whose laws he sought protection. Despite his profound concern and distress, however, when he subsequently went out onto the deck with General Bertrand, he showed himself to the still-expectant crowds of sightseers impassively, 'avec le même visage que les jours précédents' (with the same expression as on the previous days).[20] Further gloom for the French, however, was cast on the occasion by the fortuitous passing-by of several British transport ships carrying French wounded prisoners captured at the battle of Waterloo.

Despite Napoleon's own immediate appearance of calmness and stoicism the news of St Helena was a terrible blow for Bertrand and the other members, or potential members, of his party. It was a severe test of their continuing loyalty. They had been prepared to sacrifice their futures to accompany their Emperor in a reasonable life in exile in England or America, but they had not bargained on being transported to a small inaccessible island, thousands of miles from their native country and indeed from almost anywhere. It is difficult to overstate the horror and despair that most of them must have felt. Madame Bertrand took the decision particularly badly. She was a feisty woman who, as we have already seen, had always had a strong will of her own. When Napoleon had left Elba, where she and her husband had accompanied him, she was told to stay put until arrangements were made to take her to Rome and then on to France. She disregarded this and made her own way back to France where she was initially arrested by royalist forces before being got out of jail by Napoleon and allowed to proceed to join him and her husband at Malmaison. Now she was absolutely horrified at the thought of being banished to St Helena. She had three young children and fresh in her mind was the fact that she had lost one child already while in exile with Napoleon on Elba. She rushed down to Napoleon's cabin, burst in unannounced, and begged him not to force her husband to go to St Helena with him. When he refused, and attempted to calm her, she hurried back to her own cabin and tried to throw herself out of the window into the sea. Only the intervention of General Montholon, who heard all the commotion and shouting, saved her. He followed her into the cabin, grabbed her legs and pulled her back in, although it is claimed that at the same time the Duke of Rovigo, who also heard the row that was going on, shouted unsympathetically 'Let her go'! She eventually calmed down, but for the next few days she continued to pester an increasingly irritated Maitland with protests about the British Government's conduct.[21]

The transfer to the ship that was chosen to take them to St Helena was delayed for a few days while the necessary arrangements were being made. The British Government was anxious to get them away as soon as possible, not least because there were reports of a legal challenge based on the serving of a writ of habeas corpus being prepared by Napoleonic sympathizers. The chosen ship, the 78-gun ship-of-the-line Northumberland, was not yet, however, equipped or ready. Its selection for the purpose was somewhat ironic, since it was not built to a British design but copied from one of the French warships captured at the battle of the Glorious First of June. It required extensive refitting and provisioning and many of the crew were in a mutinous mood, having just returned from a long spell of duty at sea and now at short notice deprived of their eagerly awaited shore leave. It would also take some time to scrutinize the huge amount of baggage that Napoleon's party wished to take on board. Dr William Warden, a naval surgeon aboard the Northumberland, later described it in somewhat uncomplimentary terms as 'no better than the properties of an itinerant theatre.'[22]

While all this frantic activity was taking place Napoleon, at least outwardly, still kept up an impassive demeanour. He was determined, says Marchand, to show to Europe 'ce que peut une grande âme aux prises avec l'adversité' (what a great spirit can do when faced with adversity).[23] In consultation with General Bertrand he reviewed and settled the list of those whom he wished to accompany him. The British had excluded General Lallemand and the Duke of Rovigo, who were on the proscribed list in Bourbon France, and were to be sent back initially as prisoners to Malta. The only outstanding issue was whether Count de Las Cases, a former naval officer, would be allowed to accompany him, given the restriction of three officers in the party. In the end Lord Keith agreed to a compromise that he could travel as Napoleon's secretary. The rest of the party, apart from General Bertrand and his wife and children, comprised Generals Gourgaud and Montholon (the latter also with his wife and one child), and from Napoleon's personal household: the two senior valets, Marchand and Ali; Noverazz; Cipriani, a fellow Corsican; the two brothers Archembault; Lepage, Rousseau and Gentilini – all of whom had, except Lepage, also been with Napoleon on Elba. The senior officers and their wives were also allowed to take with them their own domestic servants.

Events then began to move in earnest. On 4 August the *Bellerophon* moved from Plymouth to Start Point, once more seeking to shake off the never-ending flotillas of small craft crammed with men, women and children still trying to get a glimpse of the celebrated Napoleon. A bizarre incident occurred when the departure from Plymouth harbour only just took place in time to pull away from a rowing boat following hard after them – it contained a lawyer brandishing what Maitland later learned was a subpoena for Napoleon's release.[24] This was further evidence of the sympathy for Napoleon that surprisingly still existed in some political circles.

Napoleon now at last began to appear more depressed but he still had the spirit and energy to dictate to Las Cases yet another long letter of protest for Captain Maitland to deliver to Lord Keith. Two days later they were joined by the *Northumberland*, which was accompanied by two troop ships, the *Bucephalus* and the *Ceylon*. The united squadron sailed on together to Torbay and anchored to the west of Berry Head. At the same time Admiral Sir George Cockburn received his detailed instructions from London as to how he should treat 'General Bonaparte' and his party when they joined the *Northumberland*, including the requirement for a formal customs inspection to ensure control over both the money and other valuables taken on board.

Probably for the first time in his life Napoleon was made to suffer the indignity of an examination by a junior officer from that historic department of state, His Majesty's Customs and Excise.[25] He was accompanied by Marchand, who had carefully supervised his packing, making sure that the bulk of his available cash was distributed – strictly, of course, to be handed back later – for concealment in body belts by other members of his party, and that only a modest amount, some 4,000 napoleons, was openly declared. The rest of Napoleon's baggage consisted of various cases of valuable household effects – silver plate, Sèvres porcelain and other china, table linen, personal ornaments, portraits, etc. – and the inevitable collection of books, which Napoleon had always insisted should even accompany him on his campaigns.

Admiral Cockburn at least had the decency to absent himself from the customs inspection but in the afternoon he accompanied Lord Keith, under instruction, to request Napoleon and his officers to hand over their personal weapons. However, on seeing Napoleon's sharp reaction to this request – Ali said that: 'Le regard de l'Empereur était terrible' (the Emperor's look was terrible)[26] – Lord Keith spared them this final indignity and allowed them to keep their swords, taking away only their firearms. Napoleon's only remaining task, since his own French doctor had withdrawn from the party, was to nominate a doctor. He invited Dr Barry O'Meara, an Irish naval surgeon who had also attended him on the *Bellerophon*, and who spoke fluent French and Italian, to accompany him in that capacity to St Helena.[27] Lord Keith agreed to this, and a very close relationship developed between them, which had profound consequences for the future relationship between Napoleon and the Governor, Sir Hudson Lowe, on St Helena, and for Lowe's own subsequent reputation.

On 7 August, after a cordial farewell to Captain Maitland, for whom he seems to have developed a genuine respect and admiration, which was reciprocal, Napoleon appeared on the deck of the *Bellerophon* for the last time, ready to transfer to the *Northumberland*. After doing so he said to Lord Lyttleton, who had accompanied the party on deck, 'You have soiled your flag and your national honour by imprisoning me as you are doing.'[28] His appearance now shocked the crew who were lined up to see him depart. The strain was beginning to tell and he was described as looking corpulent, unshaven, his face pale and drawn, and his clothes ill-fitting. As he crossed the quarter deck and climbed down to the waiting barge, followed by his companions, the marines presented arms – no checking of their arms drill by Napoleon this time – accompanied by three drum rolls, the salute that was decreed for an officer of general rank. When he reached the *Northumberland* he received a similar formal reception from the sailors and marines lined up on the deck. The rules of the game were now clear. It was General Bonaparte who was now on board – His Excellency, but no longer His Majesty.

The *Northumberland* set sail on the following morning, 8 August 1815, after thirteen days of waiting off Plymouth and the Devon coast and forty days since Napoleon had left Paris. On that same day, in contrast to the tension and bustle on the *Northumberland*, in the peace and quiet of the small Hampshire village of Chawton, Jane Austen, who had two brothers in the Royal Navy, began work on *Persuasion*, the most naval of all her novels. On the following day, aboard the now steadily progressing *Northumberland*, the French party caught a brief glimpse through the mist of the coast of France, positively the last sight that Napoleon would ever have of his beloved country. He removed his hat and cried: 'Adieu, terre de braves! Adieu France! Adieu!'[29]

THREE

THE VOYAGE TO
ST HELENA

THE *NORTHUMBERLAND* WAS NOT the most suitable ship in the Royal Navy to take the former Emperor and his high-level delegation on the arduous two-month, 5,000-mile journey to St Helena. Its accommodation was limited and cramped, and in addition to Napoleon and his party (including the women and children), it was required to act as a troop ship and carry 200 of the nearly 2,000 extra soldiers sent out by the British Government to guard Napoleon and ensure that he could not escape. In all there were about 1,100 people on board, 'packed', as Lord Rosebery put it, 'like herrings in a barrel'.[1]

The ship had to be hurriedly cleaned up, refitted and provisioned, for which there was simply not enough time. One serious casualty of the haste was the failure to renew the freshwater supplies. This meant that for at least the first part of the voyage the passengers and crew had to put up with stale and discoloured drinking water left over from the *Northumberland*'s recent return trip from India – a source of constant and justifiable complaint, particularly by the ladies in Napoleon's suite. In fact, they were reduced to drinking weak beer in place of water. The departure of the ship had also been accompanied by a number of events usually regarded as ill omens by superstitious sailors. The captain had been forced to bring on board a large party of soldiers to quell an incipient mutiny among members of the crew who were furious at losing their long-anticipated shore leave. At one point, they were refusing to raise the anchor to get the ship away. Moreover, just as the ship sailed, a cutter, dispatched to clear away yet more of the sightseeing boats that still surrounded them, caused one of them to capsize, drowning two female passengers. About the only merit of the *Northumberland* was that, despite these problems, it was reasonably quickly available.

The captain of the *Northumberland* was Charles Bayne Hodgson Ross, thirty-seven years old, another experienced sea warrior, who had spent much of his career as a post captain in the American war rather than in the Napoleonic wars in Europe. Although he was the senior officer in direct control of the ship he was subordinate to the flag officer on board, Rear-Admiral Sir George Cockburn, to whom he was related as a brother-in-law. Cockburn was in overall command of the rest of the accompanying flotilla that set sail, including two frigates and several troop carriers, and was also designated to take over as interim Commander in Chief on St Helena until a new military governor could be appointed and sent out. Thereafter, as Commander in Chief of the Cape Station, he was to remain in charge of the naval squadron detailed to maintain a twenty-four-hour watch on the island. It would, therefore, be his responsibility when they reached St Helena to see that Napoleon was properly housed and guarded – for which he had received detailed written instructions from Whitehall – and in the meantime to ensure appropriate treatment of Napoleon and his party on the voyage.

Admiral Cockburn, as to be expected from someone who had spent so many years of his career fighting against him, was not a natural Napoleon admirer. His task was in one sense made easier by the British Government's decision to, as it were, demote Napoleon to the rank of a 'half pay general not in employ'.[2] This meant that he did not have to bother with the elaborate protocol and courtesies normally due to a head of state. This made life much simpler and, as a no-nonsense sailor, he declared that he was quite ready to put down any remaining imperial pretensions on Napoleon's part if need be. In his diary he recorded: 'It is clear that he is still inclined to act the Sovereign occasionally, but I cannot allow it.'[3] Nevertheless, like Captain Ross, he was a man of great courtesy and common sense and he took the trouble to ensure that Napoleon was housed as comfortably as the ship would reasonably allow. According to Las Cases his attitude gradually mellowed during the voyage – even to the extent of proposing a toast to Napoleon's health on his birthday on 15 August. The old Napoleonic charm had evidently begun to work once again, even with the battle-hardened Admiral.

Marchand, Ali and Las Cases have left us detailed descriptions of the accommodation arrangements for Napoleon on board.[4] There were two small cabins leading from the relatively large officers' dining room and saloon at the stern of the ship, one to the left and the other to the right. Each of these had two doors connecting with the dining room and saloon. Cockburn allocated the room on the right to himself and the one on the left to Napoleon. It was made clear to Napoleon at the outset, however, that the adjacent larger rooms were for common use, in which the ship's officers would freely come and go, and not for his private use alone, although Cockburn in practice seldom appeared in them himself except in order to gain access to his own cabin or to come to dinner. Napoleon's cabin was sparsely furnished but included his famous iron bed – the 19th-century equivalent of a narrow folding camp bed – which had always accompanied him on his campaigns. Ever watchful, like twin Cerberuses at the gate of Hades, Marchand slept on a mattress just inside Napoleon's cabin and Ali on the floor outside it in the saloon. The generals and their wives, and the remainder of Napoleon's party, were housed wherever tolerable privacy and space could be found in a warship not built for that purpose. For the wives and their children the dark claustrophobic atmosphere and the lack of space and hygiene, above all of clean water, must have been almost insupportable. But for Bertrand and Gourgaud, who had survived many tough campaigns with Napoleon, including the murderous retreat from Moscow, it was probably not too bad, except for the prolonged tedium. Las Cases too, as a former naval officer, must have known how to adapt to conditions on board.

The prospect for the captive Napoleon – sailing helplessly into the unknown, to a remote and isolated prison island that could well be his home to the end of his days – was an awful one. The voyage got hotter and clammier as they approached the tropics. On 22 August they arrived off Madeira, where at least it was possible to obtain and bring fresh supplies of fruit, vegetables and even live cattle aboard. However, the ship remained well off shore and the captives were not allowed to disembark; this would have been extremely hazardous anyway because of a violent sirocco wind that left the *Northumberland* covered with fine sand and most of the passengers ill and seasick. On Sunday 27 August they passed right through the Canaries, not even catching a glimpse of the 12,000-foot volcanic peak of El Teide because of the bad weather.

From there onwards the ship trudged slowly on towards its destination, mostly with a favourable wind behind it. There were only occasional diversions from the tedious daily routine, such as the traditional ceremony of 'crossing the line' on 23 September.[5] This is an age-old maritime custom that requires all passengers on board, no matter what their rank or status, who have not previously crossed the equator at sea, to take part and submit to the indignities of being shaved and ducked in a pool of water on the deck by a character dressed up as the sea god Neptune. The role of Neptune on this occasion was played by the oldest sailor on the ship, who demanded that Napoleon be handed over to him. Admiral Cockburn tactfully saved the day for Napoleon, however, by exclaiming that he had crossed the line before and could therefore be excused this doubtful ceremony. The somewhat relieved Napoleon rewarded Neptune with an excessive tip – 500 napoleons – which went down extremely well both with him and with the rest of the crew. Napoleon was later much impressed by the way in which discipline on the ship was quickly and smoothly restored at the end of a day of festivities during which chaos had reigned and rank and protocol had been completely reversed.

Another diversion occurred when a man was lost overboard on 29 September, and by the hauling in, another time, of a six-foot shark weighing an estimated 120 pounds.[6] In his eagerness to see it on the deck at close quarters, Napoleon was nearly struck by its thrashing tail. Marchand, who recorded the incident, noted coolly that when it was subsequently opened they found the remnants of human clothes inside it. Otherwise, as Las Cases commented ruefully, 'Rien n'interrompait l'uniformité de nos moments; chaque jour passait lentement en detail' (Nothing interrupted the uniformity of our journey; each day passed slowly in every respect).[7]

The accounts of the voyage credibly reflect the growing atmosphere of boredom, discomfort and despair.

This sense of boredom and frustration was at the very heart of one of the main problems that was to confront Napoleon on St Helena. For so many years he had been used to a life of continual action and, as he grew in power and status, to unquestioned command of both his own destiny and that of millions of others. Now he was reduced to inactivity and dependency on his captors, and there was not much he could do about it. He was by nature an absolute workaholic who used to say of himself: 'le travail est mon élément' (work is my very nature). He was now stripped of his power and responsibilities and had to try to find some alternative means of using up his energy, occupying time and diverting his mind from the darker forebodings of what was in store for him on St Helena.

His first recourse was to start dictating his memoirs, which were to be the public testimony or authorized version of his glorious career for future generations. It was crucial to complete this since they would in effect be a huge 'spin' and set out what he wanted posterity to believe about him. Las Cases comments in his magnum opus, *Mémorial de Sainte Hélène*, 'Le travail seul pouvait nous faire supporter la longeur et l'ennui de nos journées' (Work alone could enable us to endure the length and tedium of our days).[8] Although General Gourgaud was required to take down some of the dictation, Las Cases bore the brunt of it. This was not unexpected as he was the most literary member of Napoleon's inner circle of four and the one whom Napoleon found it most comfortable to communicate with. He was the author of a celebrated *Atlas Historique, Généalogique et Géographique*, which Napoleon was familiar with and much admired, and he was described by Lord Rosebery as 'the most Boswellian of Napoleon's biographers.'[9] He therefore gradually began to be given the lion's share of the dictation, which sowed the first seeds of the intense jealousy on Gourgaud's part that later poisoned the relationship between them on St Helena. According to Marchand, Napoleon also aggravated the situation by awarding Las Cases the Légion d'Honneur in the course of the voyage. It is not quite clear what authority, as an ex-emperor, he now had to do this, but it was all part of the maintenance of the imperial status.

Taking dictation from Napoleon was a hazardous and exhausting business. He had long since given up writing in manuscript himself. This was partly because his handwriting was awful and almost illegible, and partly because, somewhat like Churchill, his own hand could not possibly keep up with the rapidly cascading stream of thoughts coming from his mind. This meant that his desperate secretaries found it extremely difficult to get all his words down and Las Cases in fact devised a form of hieroglyphic shorthand that just about enabled him, with the subsequent help of his co-opted son, to cope. Napoleon often boasted, according to Ali, that he was capable of killing six secretaries and he often employed four or five at a time.[10] Dictation took place at all hours, often after dinner and sometimes in the small hours when Napoleon woke up during the night and could not get back to sleep. There was no dodging the outcome either. He normally demanded to see the results early the next morning, after which he made corrections to the text before proceeding to the next piece of dictation.

At one stage Las Cases, perhaps to give himself a breather from the constant dictation, persuaded Napoleon, who was frustrated at not being able to read the English newspapers, to start having lessons in English. Las Cases was a fluent English speaker, having spent several years in England. Napoleon soon, however, became bored and the experiment only lasted for two or three days. Perversely Napoleon blamed Las Cases for discontinuing the lessons, to which Las Cases was bold enough to reply that he was still ready with the medicine if only Napoleon had the courage to swallow it.

It might be expected that eating and dining, the traditional time consumers and waist expanders of modern cruise ships, would help to occupy time and provide a welcome diversion from the daily monotony of the voyage. Again, however, this was not for Napoleon, who had always regarded eating as a purely functional necessity and otherwise a waste of time. Admiral Cockburn, despite his professed determination to keep Napoleon in his place, ceded the honours to him at the dining table by inviting him to occupy the centre place, with himself on his left and Madame Bertrand on his right.[11] Moreover, Napoleon was allowed to be served, as if he were back at the Elysée, by his own personal staff: by Ali from the right and by Noverazz from the left. The usual custom in Royal Navy ward rooms was to take up to an hour and a half or even more at the dinner table, remaining for conversation after the dessert for more drinks and coffee. But Napoleon would have none of this – he would not vary his long-standing habit. He normally spent no more than twenty minutes at the table, except very exceptionally out of courtesy to Cockburn. Straight after the dessert he was up and out and back to his cabin, sometimes after a short stroll on deck – usually then followed by another session of dictation for his hard-put-upon secretaries. On one occasion Admiral Cockburn indicated by his expression or body language his disapproval of this habit. Madame Bertrand, not always the first to defend Napoleon, turned on him and rebuked him sharply, saying: 'N'oubliez pas, monsieur amiral, que vous avez affaire avec celui qui a été maître du monde, et que les rois briguaient l'honneur d'être admis à sa table' (Do not forget, Admiral, that you are dealing with someone who was master of the world, and that kings solicited the honour of being admitted to his table).[12] Cockburn's response is not recorded, but he did not discontinue his own custom of staying on for the port, brandy and liqueurs with his fellow officers long after Napoleon had left the table. The only concession that Napoleon seems to have made at the dinner table, if Dr Warden, one of the ship's surgeons, is to be believed, is that he asked for the ship's band to play both 'God Save the King' and 'Rule Britannia' on the first dinner occasion.[13] Perhaps, underneath the growing depression and boredom, there was still a sense of humour or at least irony lurking in him somewhere.

With none of the other distractions now found as a matter of course on any modern cruise ship, and perhaps even on the contemporary equivalent of Royal Navy ships-of-the-line, Napoleon had to find other ways, in addition to dictating, of occupying time and alleviating the tedium. An important one was reading and being read to. He had always been a voracious reader, with a remarkably wide range of interests for someone whose early education had been almost exclusively military. He was well versed in the classics, ancient and modern, both prose and verse. Though unable to understand English, he was familiar with Shakespeare and Milton and, curiously, his favourite writer was the fictitious epic poet Ossian – perhaps another example of being deceived by the British (though he was not alone in this – David Hume, Adam Smith, Schiller and Goethe were taken in too). It had always been his practice to take a substantial mobile library with him on his campaigns. Before leaving Paris in June he had instructed his librarian at the Elysée, Monsieur Barbier, to assemble a library, which Marchand had then arranged in six mahogany cases. He had initially asked for an incredible 10,000 volumes, but had to be content with a mere 588. As Napoleon began to spend more and more time in his cabins in the mornings, Las Cases was often required, instead of taking dictation, to read to him, as necessary translating from any English texts as he went along. In this way he read aloud everything contained in the *Encyclopaedia Britannica* and several other books about St Helena.[14] Maintaining the habits of a supreme general he always reconnoitred the terrain thoroughly before the next battle.

Apart from reading and dictating, Napoleon allowed himself the more frivolous pursuits of playing cards (mainly vingt-et-un and piquet), and sometimes chess, usually after dinner.[15] The problem for his companions was that he expected to win and they were afraid to commit *lèse majesté* by not allowing him to do so. This caused the occasional embarrassment when Napoleon saw through their deception and began to ask why someone to whom he had lost was then easily beaten by someone else whom he himself had beaten.

Physical exercise was difficult in view both of the motion of the ship and of the lack of space on deck or elsewhere, but Napoleon often roamed round the ship to quiz members of the crew about their jobs. This reflected his interest in and respect for the Royal Navy and also his general insatiable curiosity and desire to get other people on his side. He was a formidable inquisitor, almost in Socratic fashion. As on the *Bellerophon* the old charm seemed to work once again. There are many testimonies to the admiration and even affection that the crew developed for him as the journey progressed. One of his habits was to lean against a particular great gun, which the young sailors who often accompanied him, forgetful of their Government's instructions on how to address him, then named the 'cannon of the Emperor'. It may be significant too that in the muster books of the *Northumberland* preserved in the National Archives, wherever the words 'General Bonaparte' appear the word 'General' has been scratched out by some unknown hand and 'Emp' written over it.[16]

On one occasion, after being impressed by a conversation with him, Napoleon invited the master of the ship, a very senior non-commissioned warrant officer, to dine with him at the Admiral's table. Although it was not Napoleon's place to determine who should dine with the Admiral and the commissioned officers, on this occasion Admiral Cockburn, despite his declared resolution to keep Napoleon in his place, agreed. He told Napoleon that anyone he invited to dinner was welcome at his table. This and other incidents were evidence of the mutual respect that developed over the voyage between Napoleon and Cockburn, as well as with Captain Ross.

After some delay, due to the course chosen by Cockburn, who had decided to run down along the coast of Africa rather than Brazil – thus losing nearly a fortnight – the end of the long, hot and tedious journey was in sight. The *Northumberland* began to approach its destination, St Helena. In the late afternoon of 14 October the cry of 'Land' sounded across the ship. The island was said at last to be in view, a tiny dark dot on the far distant horizon. According to Las Cases, the former naval expert, who was apparently most impressed with the scientific marvels of modern navigational techniques, this occurred only fifteen minutes after the time predicted.[17] Napoleon and his companions rushed to the bows of the ship to try to see it. Napoleon said he thought he could, but it was still some distance away, and Las Cases maintained he could see nothing.[18] Marchand, however, claimed to be able to catch a glimpse of Diana's Peak, at nearly 2,700 feet the highest point on the island.[19] It was now beginning to get dark and at 9pm the *Northumberland* stayed its course for the night and a corvette was dispatched from the squadron to sail ahead to the island and warn of their arrival. They had, however, been preceded by the frigate *Havannah* and the bark *Furet* from the squadron, which had taken the Brazil route and arrived seventeen days earlier, so that news of their imminent arrival had already spread to the astonished islanders.

The next morning the *Northumberland* moved in closer and took up a position in James Bay, half a mile or so out from the town's only landing stage – exactly the same procedure as is still followed to this day by the only regular ship to visit the island, the RMS *St Helena*, the last Royal Mail Ship now in service. Even now all passengers are still required to climb down to a pontoon, don life jackets and be ferried in small launches to the landing stage on the island. Napoleon was up and dressed early and joined his colleagues on the bridge to get his first close view of the island.

It is difficult to imagine a more forbidding view, and Napoleon's heart must have sunk even further. From the sea, as you approach it, the distant dark dot on the horizon gradually expands to become a solid mass of towering, precipitous, jagged volcanic rocks, in some cases rising up more than 500 feet sheer from the sea, and often capped, like a mini Table Mountain, with mist and cloud. There are no beaches or other obvious landing places except for the jetty at the capital, Jamestown, which itself is squeezed into a narrow valley running for a few hundred yards inland from the sea and overtopped on both sides by steep bare cliffs. From the angle where the ship had anchored Napoleon could not, because of the cliffs, and even with the aid of his field glasses, see much of Jamestown itself, except for the top of the tower of the Anglican church of St James, said to be the oldest in the southern hemisphere. For Marchand the sight of the island was 'repoussant' (repulsive). Las Cases was struck by the 'énormes rochers arides et pelés qui s'élevaient jusqu'aux nues' (enormous bald and arid rocks which rose right up to the clouds).[20]

It is not difficult to imagine the feelings Napoleon must have had as he saw for the first time this remote, rocky and impregnable outpost, which was to become his prison for the rest of his life – 'le moderne Prométhée sur son roc' (the modern Prometheus on his rock), as Las Cases, catching the classical literary habit, put it.[21] His companions were utterly horrified. Madame Bertrand, who was seldom slow to speak up, later described it vulgarly but vividly as 'une île que le diable a chié en volant d'un monde à l'autre' (an island that the devil shat when flying from one world to another).[22] The naval surgeon, Dr Barry O'Meara, said: 'Nothing can be more desolate or repulsive than the appearance of the exterior of the island.'[23] Napoleon no doubt shared all these sentiments at heart, but he refused to show his feelings and remained impassive; after a few moments he returned to his cabin to resume work. He summoned Las Cases to go with him, 'faisant aucune observation et ne laissant rien deviner de ce qui passait dans son âme' (making no comment and giving no indication of what was passing in his heart).[24]

FOUR

ARRIVAL AT ST HELENA

ISOLATED IN THE MIDDLE of the South Atlantic Ocean, 1,200 miles from the coast of Angola, the nearest mainland to the east, and nearly 2,000 miles from Brazil to the west, St Helena is still just about as remote a place as you can find. The nearest land is Ascension Island, located just over 700 miles to the north-west (still referred to on the island as 'nearby Ascension'). It is not difficult to understand why, if Napoleon had to be allowed to remain alive, the British Government chose it as the place to bury, literally and metaphorically, the prisoner whom they and their allies wished to prevent ever disturbing the peace of Europe again. They chose it as a prison again in 1900–1 at the time of the Boer War when over 5,000 Boer prisoners of war were interned in camps on the island, several hundred of whom now rest in neat white lines of unnamed graves on a hillside at Knollcombes. Even today, although there are plans to build an airfield and encourage tourism – there have been for the last sixty years and still no final decision has been taken – the island is in some ways even less accessible than it was then. It remains reachable only by sea, and there is only one ship, the RMS *St Helena*, that regularly visits it and provides a lifeline to the island. This compares with the hundreds of vessels that called there for refitting or fresh supplies in the 18th and 19th centuries on their way from the United Kingdom to and from India, many of them belonging to the East India Company, which then owned the island.

St Helena measures only around ten and a half miles by six and a half, covering a territory of some forty-seven square miles.' Since it is of volcanic origin the terrain is steep and rocky, with scattered valleys, plateaus and plains in the interior. Beyond the bare fortress-like cliffs, the outer fringes of St Helena are extremely arid and contrast sharply with a surprisingly lush and green interior. There are grasslands and pastures in the valleys lower down and bush and semi-tropical vegetation, including prehistoric-looking indigenous tree ferns, on the higher central ground. This is why the island has been described as an 'emerald set in a ring of bronze'. Sadly, however, many of the endemic flora have now been overwhelmed by alien species such as the rampant New Zealand flax, which was cultivated to form the basis of the island's industry and economic prosperity during the first half of the 20th century, but which now, in unyielding and difficult-to-extirpate uniformity, covers whole swathes of hill and mountainside with its tough, tall, green, spear-like leaves. Keen conservationists on the island, mainly volunteers, are trying hard to remove it and replant in its place some of the original endemic trees and shrubs – gumwood, ebony and cabbage trees (both 'he' and 'she'!) as well as tree ferns – but it is a formidable task and will take many years to achieve. There are also few native fauna. Imported goats, cats, rats, rabbits and mynah birds have dominated and driven out many of the small number of original species, and in so doing created their own problems. The only endemic bird – the symbol of the island – the wirebird (*charadrius sanctae-helenae*) struggles to breed and survive. The highest point on the island is Diana's Peak, from where the whole circumference of St Helena can be seen in panorama, with the endless shimmering Atlantic Ocean surrounding it beyond.

The most striking features of the island to any approaching visitor are the sheer, dark, bare, often jagged cliffs, which in places rise dramatically straight from the sea and encircle it like prison walls. Charles Darwin, who spent a few days there in 1836 during the homeward journey of the *Beagle*, and walked all over the island, noted in his diary: 'It is a curious little world within itself. The habitable part is surrounded by a broad band of black desolate rocks, as if the wide barrier of the ocean were not sufficient to guard the precious spot.'[2] Napoleon often later made this same point, asking why, given the natural impregnability of the island, it was necessary to impose such tight additional internal restrictions in order to keep him there. Unlike Napoleon, however, Darwin reportedly enjoyed his rambles on the island more than anything he had done for a long time.

Access to and from the sea is only possible (except to an experienced rock climber) at three points – the landing place at Jamestown itself, Rupert's Bay nearby, where there is now a small fish-canning factory, and Sandy Bay, on the southern coast of the island. The last, however, is a cruel misnomer. It can only be reached by a long, narrow and hair-raisingly steep and winding road, with hairpin bends of a gradient of one in three; the so-called sand consists of a narrow stretch of unpromising dark gravel, bounded now at the upper tide line by the rusting barrels of long since discarded cannons, once mounted there in a fortified emplacement to deter and destroy any potential invaders. Even at Jamestown there is still no proper harbour. Arriving passengers still have to be ferried to the landing stage as Napoleon and his companions had to be nearly 200 years ago.

In spite of the fact that the island is situated well within the tropics, the climate – which Lord Liverpool, in choosing it for Napoleon, was assured was healthy and reputed to be a 'tropical paradise'[3] – is kept fairly mild and equable by the prevailing south-east trade winds. In general, summers, which stretch from November to March, are warm and sunny, and winters cool and mild with only moderate rain. There are, however, substantial climate and temperature variations within the island. It can sometimes be as much as ten degrees centigrade warmer down in humid sunny Jamestown, on the northern coast of the island, than up in the interior, which is more prone to wind, mist and rain. Longwood Plain, where Napoleon's permanent place of residence was to be situated, falls into the latter category.

There are no indigenous inhabitants on the island. It was uninhabited when it was discovered by the Portuguese navigator, Juan de Nova Castella, on 21 May 1502 – the anniversary of St Helena, the mother of the Roman Emperor Constantine, after whom the island is called. The Portuguese kept its existence a secret for over eighty years until an English explorer, Thomas Cavendish, landed there in June 1588 on the last stage of a round-the-world voyage. By the early 17th century the Portuguese had virtually given it up and in 1633 the rival Dutch, already present in the Cape, landed there and proclaimed it as their possession. Their tenure was, however, short. In May 1659 Captain John Dutton took over the island in the name of the English East India Company. In 1660 this de facto annexation was ratified by a royal charter of King Charles II, which confirmed the Company's right to possess, fortify and settle the island on behalf of the Crown.

The further development of the island was, however, halting and troubled. Settlers hardly flocked in to set up there and take advantage of the Crown's new possession; periodically there were severe shortages of food and other essential supplies. This led to civil unrest and even a mutiny of discontented islanders in August 1672 – only with difficulty was this suppressed by the small military garrison before the Dutch arrived again and announced that they were once more masters of the island. This occupation was even shorter than their previous one. They were soon driven out by a new squadron from England under Captain Richard Munden, and since then St Helena has remained in the hands of the United Kingdom, the rights of the East India Company being again confirmed in a fresh charter by Charles II on 16 December 1673. It is still a British dependent territory today (the British Government having taken it over from the East India Company on 28 August 1833), with a Governor, a Chief Secretary, an Attorney General and a classical colonial administration in miniature reporting to the Foreign and Commonwealth Office in London.

When Napoleon and his party arrived in October 1815 the island was still under the control and administration of the East India Company. It had generally prospered, its chief source of revenue coming from the duties paid and other expenditure by ships calling in there for victualling and repairs on the long voyage between India, the Cape and the United Kingdom. Over 1,000 vessels a year used it as a staging point in its heyday, before the opening of the Suez Canal virtually obliterated this trade later in the century. The Governor, who was at that time the popular Colonel Mark Wilks, was appointed by and responsible to the Company, as were the members of his Council and the remaining officials of the civil admin-istration, ranging from the Judge Advocate down to the humblest clerks. Estimates vary as to the population at the time, but it was probably in the region of 4,500 to 5,000 – a little larger than that today – including a sub-stantial number of slaves, mainly from Madagascar, a smaller number of

Chinese indentured workers and some freed slaves. It is noteworthy that at that time slavery was still legal on St Helena and the children of female slaves automatically became slaves themselves. The primarily Indonesian ancestry of the former slaves is evident in many of the Saints today, as the islanders call themselves.

The arrival of the *Northumberland* and its accompanying flotilla on 15 October 1815 caused as great a shock to the islanders as the earthquake that was to occur three years later while Napoleon was there. Until the *Havannah* and the *Furet* had arrived just over a fortnight earlier they had not even heard about Napoleon's escape from Elba and Wellington's decisive victory at Waterloo, let alone the choice of their island to house his defeated victim, the most famous man on earth. And this was not all. In addition to Napoleon and his immediate entourage they were to be faced with the indefinite presence of the astonishing number of more than 2,000 extra soldiers and sailors, brought specially to the island to ensure that their principal guest stayed on to enjoy their hospitality. This had the immediate effect of increasing the island's population by nearly fifty percent.

In economic terms this represented a sharp increase in output and a great boost to the economy. But it also created a serious scarcity of supplies, including fresh water (of which the island had a natural abundance, but – like the United Kingdom still today – an inadequate distribution system), rapid price inflation and a range of unwelcome restrictions, including a nightly curfew, which began to affect everyone living on the island, though they were intended for the purpose of the safe-keeping of Napoleon. In the days to come on St Helena there was frequent resentment among the residents that both the army and the French household at Longwood were given preferential access to scarce commodities on the island. Indeed, to some of the poorer and hard-pressed islanders, the eventual standard of living at Longwood, where wine and meat were plentiful, seemed to be on a Lucullan scale. It may just be the folk memory of this, or some other hereditary trait, that explains why the present-day Saints seem curiously uninterested in Napoleon, although his captivity there is probably the only reason why most people in the world have ever heard of the island.

After the *Northumberland* had moored out in the Jamestown Roads on 15 October, Admiral Cockburn and Brigadier-General George Bingham, the military commander designate of the greatly reinforced army garrison on the island, went ashore to start looking for suitable interim accommodation for Napoleon and his party, pending the identification and preparation of a more appropriate and secure long-term residence.[4] It seems incredible now that, because of the difficulty and slowness of communications at the time, such critical arrangements had to be made so extempore and at such short notice. They returned a few hours later together with the Company's Governor, Colonel Mark Wilks, who remained formally in this post until Sir Hudson Lowe arrived in April 1816. However, he was immediately superseded on the spot as Commander in Chief of all the military forces on the island by Admiral Cockburn. For the duration of Napoleon's captivity the control of the island was then formally taken over by the British Government, to which the Governor reported on all matters appertaining to Napoleon's safekeeping, although he continued to be accountable to the Company for its civil administration.

When Admiral Cockburn, Brigadier-General Bingham and Colonel Wilks returned to the *Northumberland* they were cross-examined eagerly and impatiently by the frustrated and expectant French party. They were tired of being cooped up for so long on the cramped and unhygienic ship and longed to get ashore – albeit on such an 'île maudite' (accursed island),[5] as Fanny Bertrand, once again not mincing her words, put it. They had, however, to be patient a little longer. The next day, 16 October, passed in similar frustration on board until Cockburn and Bingham returned in the evening from another reconnaissance ashore. They announced that they had found a suitable lodging place in Jamestown for the short term until the longer-term residence that Colonel Wilks had recommended – on the plateau of Longwood, about four and a half miles from Jamestown – could be suitably modified and improved to accommodate Napoleon and his suite.

The house in question at Longwood had been built as a rather rambling single-storey farmhouse, and had been used as such, but it had more recently been improved and used by the Lieutenant-Governor as a temporary summer residence. It still, however, needed a good deal of both refurbishment and extension if it was to be remotely suitable for its new purpose, particularly given the size and composition of Napoleon's party. Admiral Cockburn's instructions from ministers in London were to keep the party safely under guard on the ship until a secure permanent residence was available, but, just as he had allowed Napoleon and the generals to keep their swords, he turned out to be 'plus humain que les ministres' (more humane than the ministers), as Marchand put it, and decided to let them disembark on the following day.[6]

On 17 October the disembarkation, news of which had spread through the island like a bush fire, finally took place. The islanders, who had initially been warned of the approach of the *Northumberland* by an alarm gun fired from the fort high up on Ladder Hill, which overlooks Jamestown, flocked to the harbour to see the show. They had, however, to wait until the evening as it took some time to unload all the troops, baggage and stores; Napoleon also wished to bid a proper, and even amicable, farewell to Captain Ross, his officers and crew. Once again the Royal Navy was exempted from the contempt that Napoleon sometimes showed towards the British army.

It was thus growing dark when Napoleon at last climbed up out of the *Northumberland's* barge on to the landing stage. According to one eyewitness, the fifteen-year-old Betsy Balcombe, about whom there will be more to say later, he walked slowly up between the lines of astonished and gawping spectators, with Admiral Cockburn and General Bertrand on either side of him.[7] In the gloom all she could see of him was the occasional glimmer of a diamond star that he wore on his breast. Betsy, in her later memoirs *To Befriend an Emperor*, says that the pressure of the crowd became so great that the sentries were ordered to stand with fixed bayonets at the entrance from the lines to the town, to prevent the multitude from pouring in. Although the crowd was enormous – almost the whole population of St Helena seemed to have turned out and it was, according to Betsy, difficult to believe it contained so many inhabitants – it remained for the most part respectfully silent. Napoleon again remained silent and impassive, determined not to reveal his inner feelings to the crowd, but this did not prevent him from expressing irritation later that he had been made the subject of such a public peep show.

The house that Admiral Cockburn had identified as a temporary lodging place was Porteous House, named after its owner, Henry Porteous, who was superintendent of the East India Company's gardens. It was entirely inadequate. Jamestown then, as now, consists essentially of one fairly broad main street leading inland from the so-called Castle (the Governor's office and official administrative headquarters) until after a few hundred yards it divides into two lesser streets. The right fork eventually leads up a steep, narrow, winding hill to Ladder Hill Fort, where an artillery detachment was stationed, and beyond that, through what is now the straggling community of Half Tree Hollow scattered over the hillside, to the Governor's fine 18th-century residence, Plantation House, about three and a half miles away. The left fork leads up a twisting road past the sharp bend at Hutt's Gate and the precipitous Devil's Punch Bowl to Longwood Plain, some 1,800 feet above sea level. Jamestown, with many attractive Georgian buildings still remaining, is now rather like a very small English village of fifty or sixty years ago, apart from the number of cars, which is astonishing for such a small population and the hazardous nature of many of the roads. Napoleon later in his stay disparagingly referred to it as just a few wretched hovels. Porteous House, now long since demolished and replaced by a modern office block, was situated on the left of the main street just a few yards up beyond the Castle.

Porteous House is where the Duke of Wellington, then Major-General Sir Arthur Wellesley, fresh from his triumphs as a 'sepoy general', is believed to have stayed initially when he called at St Helena on his return voyage from India in 1805. But it had no other merits, if indeed the fact that Wellington boarded and lodged there for a short time can be regarded as a merit from Napoleon's point of view. Accessed by a short staircase, it faced directly onto the road, which meant that it was public and noisy, especially as the caterwauling feral cats – which are still a pest on the island – roamed the street at night howling and searching for something to eat. It did not even have a garden or small courtyard at the back where Napoleon and his party could escape the eyes of curious onlookers and relax in private; worse still, the rooms were small, pokey and flea ridden, little better than the cramped cabins on the *Northumberland* that they had been so eager to leave. Marchand, who as usual went ahead to prepare the way for Napoleon, leaves us in no doubt in his memoirs that he thought it entirely unsuitable for his master, who slept badly that first night.[8] Before going to bed he told Marchand that he wished to go and see Longwood and its state of readiness for himself the next morning.

At 8am the next morning Napoleon duly set off on horseback with Admiral Cockburn, General Bertrand and his second valet, Ali, to inspect Longwood House. Although just less than five miles from Jamestown, it is a slow and, in the conditions of that time, an arduous and even hazardous journey. The route is steep and winding, and there are frequent unfenced descents on each side. In particular, on the right of the road as they climbed they had to skirt the Devil's Punch Bowl, a seemingly bottomless abyss of ravine after ravine, which eventually descended some distance away into the sea. On arrival at their destination Napoleon could quickly see from its dilapidated state that Longwood was not remotely ready for occupation by himself and his extended family. Marchand, with some understatement, described him as having been 'médiocrement charmé de l'habitation qui était sans ombre, sans eau et exposé au vent du sud-est qui y régnait constamment' (moderately charmed with the dwelling, which lacked shade and water and was exposed to the south-west wind which blew there constantly).[9] They therefore decided, after a short stop for lunch in the garden with Mr and Mrs Skelton, the Lieutenant-Governor and his wife, to return to Jamestown. Ali describes the lunch as 'servi à l'anglaise' (served in English fashion), and notes that Mrs Skelton was an attractive thirty-six-year-old blonde who, having been educated in France, spoke French fluently. Her charms evidently did not escape Napoleon, who 'prit grand plaisir à causer avec elle' (took great pleasure in chatting with her).[10]

On the ride up to Longwood Napoleon had spotted a small house with a beautiful garden in a little valley about a mile out of Jamestown and he asked Cockburn if he could go and view it on the way back.[11] The house, which was called the Briars, turned out to belong to Mr William Balcombe, who had come to St Helena in 1807. He was superintendent of public sales for the East India Company and was soon to be appointed official purveyor, or supplier, to Longwood. He lived there with his attractive wife, Jane, who increasingly came to remind Napoleon of his own first wife, Josephine, and they had two lively teenage daughters, Jane and Betsy. Betsy, the younger one, then fifteen years old, recorded her memories of the time that Napoleon went on to spend at the Briars in her book, *To Befriend an Emperor*, which was published in 1844 under her married name, Mrs Abell, when she was living in London after the death of her own husband. Although it provides a delightfully vivid and entertaining account of that period, some allowance should perhaps be made for the imaginative recollections, some time after the event, of a young and impressionable teenager who found herself spending nearly two months cheek by jowl with the most celebrated man in the western world.

The Briars, which has now disappeared, was a relatively modest house, built largely in a single-storey, Indian fashion. Its glory, however, was its setting, a verdant oasis in a landscape dominated by dark, barren, towering rocks. Betsy described it as 'a perfect little paradise – an Eden blooming in the midst of desolation'. It was surrounded by gardens blossoming with colourful trees and shrubs, and 'a beautiful avenue of banyan trees led up to it, and either side was flanked by evergreen and gigantic lacos, interspersed with pomegranate and myrtle, and a profusion of large white roses, much resembling our sweetbriar, from which, indeed, the place derived its name.' There was a pond in the garden and to the west of the house a cascading waterfall, which 'in that hot climate … was a delightful next-door neigh-bour'. By a further coincidence Wellington had also stayed at the Briars for a few nights during his visit in 1805 and in a letter from Paris dated 3 April 1816 to Admiral Malcolm he mischievously said: 'You may tell Bony that I find his apartments at the Elysée-Bourbon very convenient and that I hope he likes mine at the Balcombes.'[12]

In the garden of the Briars, not much more than fifty yards from the house, was a fairly large one-room pavilion, with an attic room above, which Mr Balcombe had had built as a ball-room or a rather up-market summer house. It was protected by a low fence and had its own small lawn and garden in front. Although it is now surrounded by other houses, which destroy the original isolated atmosphere, the pavilion still exists and has been well restored. It can be visited today, with much of the original fur-niture and other contents still on display inside it. Like Longwood House it is now owned by the French Government, who are responsible for its upkeep. It was bought in 1959 and presented to the French Ministry of Foreign Affairs by Dame Mabel Brookes of Melbourne – a descendant of Sir William Doveton, a member of the island Council during Napoleon's time there, who visited St Helena and wished to save it. She was subse-quently made a Chevalier of the Légion d'Honneur, one of Napoleon's most lasting creations, in recognition of this generous gesture. After inspecting the pavilion Napoleon asked if he could stay there rather than return to Jamestown until the renovation of Longwood House was finished. He was ready to live almost anywhere rather than to go back to the unsatisfactory Porteous House. Balcombe was willing – he even offered to accommodate Napoleon in the main house – and Admiral Cockburn gave his agreement. Arrangements were accordingly made for Napoleon to move in immedi-ately. The Balcombes did what they could to make it more comfortable by moving over at once a number of items of furniture and other articles from the main house.

Napoleon later described the next few weeks as the happiest time he spent on St Helena. It was, however, in a sense a period of 'phoney war', an interval or distraction until he had to face the hard realities of captivity at Longwood. But it was certainly not all roses (or even myrtles) for him from the standpoint of living conditions. For a start, as a residence for a former emperor, who had known the great marble halls and galleries of the likes of the Elysée Palace, Versailles, Fontainbleau and Schönbrün, it was not very grand, to say the least. Las Cases recorded ruefully that he had never known 'un logement plus exigu, ni autant de privation' (such a cramped dwelling, nor so much hardship).[13] This was because there was only the one square, though well-lit, room at ground level, which Napoleon occupied, with a door flanked by two windows at the front leading onto the lawn and garden. Las Cases and his son, whom Napoleon also asked to be with him, had to sleep up above in a stuffy loft reached by a narrow staircase – father on a camp bed and son on a mattress on the floor. There were no other facilities inside the pavilion.

After a short time Brigadier-General Bingham, showing consideration for them, arranged for a large tent like a marquee to be erected in front of the pavilion. This served both as a dining room and place of work for Napoleon – and later as a sleeping place, on another camp bed, for General Gourgaud when he joined them on 30 November. Gourgaud was not a man for discomfort, but he was getting increasingly twitchy about the growing precedence that Las Cases seemed to be establishing in Napoleon's attention and affections. This development was also noticed by Marchand, who wrote about the growing intimacy between Las Cases and Napoleon, indicating that the former's position became 'avec raison enviée de tous' (not surprisingly envied by everyone).[14] It was a further warning signal of the internal household squabbles that were to plague Napoleon's life at Longwood in the future. Marchand and Ali maintained their usual faithful vigil by sleeping, like shepherds watching their flocks by night, on the floor in front of the door leading to Napoleon's room.

There were other disadvantages too. Napoleon, so wedded to the comfort of long and regular hot baths, and deprived of them during the voyage on the *Northumberland*, was still unable to have one until he left the Briars. He also liked his meals to be served piping hot, even though he spent such little time over them. This was initially impossible as all the cooked meals had to be prepared in Jamestown and then carried laboriously up the hill by servants and slaves, so that they were cold when they arrived. This was only remedied at a later stage when Napoleon's maître d'hôtel, Cipriani, a fellow Corsican and very close to him, set up a sort of mobile camp kitchen at the Briars and cooked on the spot. All this was not only inconvenient for Napoleon himself but also a great bore for his companions, who were frequently invited – or rather commanded – to come up from Jamestown to join him for a generally cold dinner. They then had to trek back down the hazardous route in the dusk of the early evening – they could not afford to linger because they were at risk of being arrested under the strict curfew which required everyone to be off the road by 9pm.

The imposition of this curfew and other related security restrictions also began to weigh on Napoleon and his companions, and threatened to sour the hitherto generally amicable relationship of mutual respect that he had developed with Admiral Cockburn. In addition to the curfew, his companions were required to be escorted by a soldier when they came to visit him at the Briars and they were forbidden to carry arms. Two sentries were also posted in the garden at the Briars to keep watch on him and only moved a little further outside after a complaint by William Balcombe himself, who was alarmed at having the military encamped on his own property. Napoleon was likewise forbidden to go for a walk or ride outside the garden boundaries unless accompanied by an English officer. He objected strongly to this, and this very same issue in due course became one of the bitterest bones of contention in his subsequent battles of will with Sir Hudson Lowe over the restrictions imposed at Longwood. Nevertheless, despite this (and unlike the situation at Longwood later on when he spent days and even weeks virtually confined to his own damp and stuffy rooms), according to Betsy Balcombe he took a good deal of exercise, exploring walks in the valley and adjacent mountainside. On one occasion, when taking a walk with General Gourgaud, he was said to have been threatened by a disturbed and angry cow, which advanced on him *à pas de charge*. Gourgaud, however, valiantly stood his ground and, drawing his sword, threw himself between his sovereign and the cow, exclaiming: 'This is the second time I have saved the Emperor's life.'[5] All in jest, no doubt, but in time Napoleon found Gourgaud's boasts about saving his life increasingly tiresome.

A minor crisis developed when Napoleon reacted angrily at being shown a copy of Admiral Cockburn's detailed instructions to the police on the measures imposed to control all ships approaching or leaving the island, and on would-be visitors from those ships to the Briars or Longwood. A distinct element of disenchantment with the upright and imposing Admiral Cockburn began to set in, although in later times Napoleon tended to look back on Cockburn's temporary spell in command as a golden age compared with Hudson Lowe's.

The flip side of Napoleon's stay at the Briars is described in vibrant and amusing detail in Betsy Balcombe's memoirs. There seems little doubt that Napoleon took a great fancy to the attractive and boisterous fifteen-year-old tomboy, who was said to look two or three years older than her age. Added to her natural attractions she could speak and understand French reasonably fluently – at one time she even started to build on Las Cases' earlier work and teach him English – so that they could converse fairly freely. At their first meeting Napoleon, discovering she could speak French, quizzed her closely on her studies, and particularly on geography. He asked her to name the capitals of the different countries of Europe and when, in reply to the question, 'What is the capital of Russia?', she replied: 'Petersburg now, Moscow formerly', he demanded sternly: 'Who burnt it?' Betsy was initially terrified and unable to reply, whereupon Napoleon, laughing violently, said: 'You know very well that it was I who burnt it.' Taking courage, and seeing him laugh, she then ventured to say, 'I believe, sir, the Russians burnt it to get rid of the French.'[16]

After this the ice was broken and Betsy began to feel at ease in his society. She was allowed to take liberties with him, which would have amazed and shocked his most senior colleagues and even the closest members of his family who, except for his mother, were required always to pay to him the formal respect and deference due to their sovereign and Emperor. According to her account they often played games together, including whist, chess and even on one occasion blind-man's buff, together with her sister, General Bertrand's young son, Napoleon, and some other members of the French party. Napoleon insisted that they should draw lots for who should be blindfolded first and, whether genuinely by chance or by Napoleon's deliberate contrivance, Betsy was the first victim. Napoleon then entered fully into the spirit of the game, creeping up on Betsy and tweaking her nose and ear, and eluding all her attempts to catch him. He was summoned away, however, before he could take a turn at being blindfolded.

She sometimes invited her own young friends to come and play with them too, and relates how on one occasion Napoleon brushed up his hair, howled, shook his head and made horrible faces at a little girl, the daughter of a friend, in order to justify the frightening stories she had been told about him. The little girl was terrified and screamed so violently that her mother was afraid she would go into hysterics and took her out of the room. He then tried the same on Betsy, again distorting his features and giving what he called a 'Cossack howl', but Betsy only laughed at him. The household also possessed a billiard table and Napoleon started to teach her how to play. She preferred, however, to try to send the balls shooting across the table to trap his fingers. On another occasion, upset by something he had done or said earlier in the day, and determined to punish him, she snatched his ceremonial sword quickly from its richly embossed scabbard, flourished it over his head, made passes at him, pinned him into a corner, and threatened him with the point of the sword at his throat, telling him that he had better say his prayers as she was going to kill him. Las Cases and Gourgaud were utterly horrified to see this. Las Cases was so indignant at the unprecedented insult offered to his Emperor by a mere slip of an English girl that she said he looked as if he could annihilate her on the spot.

Betsy's own conversion to Napoleon's charm was a sudden and dramatic one. She was not, however, the first or last person to submit to the extra-ordinary charisma that Napoleon seemed to be able to impose on even his most hardened critics and enemies. Like all good English children she had been brought up to hate and dread him. The picture she had had presented to her was of a 'huge ogre or giant, with one large flaming red eye in the mid-dle of his forehead, and long teeth protruding from his mouth, with which he tore to pieces and devoured naughty little girls, especially those who did not know their lessons.'[17] This childhood image, however, was quickly transformed when she saw him in the flesh. Moving to the other extreme, she was soon describing him as 'the most majestic person I have ever seen', and admiring every aspect of his features and physiognomy. She said that his smile and the expression of his eyes constituted his chief charm, and that these could not be transmitted to canvas. Once he began to speak, 'his fascinating smile and kind manner removed every vestige of the fear with which I had hitherto regarded him.'[18] This was far from the all-power-ful authoritarian victor of Ulm and Austerlitz and so many other bloody battlefields, and she clearly had an adolescent crush on him, in addition to being overawed by the prominence of his former position and renown.

There is little doubt also that Napoleon became very fond of Betsy and indeed of the rest of her family, with whom he found at least temporary relaxation and distraction in this kind of make-believe land that he was able to share with them for a time. It is impossible to dismiss entirely a sexual element in his relationship with the precocious and attractive young teenager (a love affair that was later made a central feature of the entertaining but over-imaginative French film *Monsieur N*) but it seems more likely that he was desperate for any sympathetic human contact away from the soldiers, sailors and other companions with whom he had been cooped up on the *Northumberland* for two months. He had in fact had little first-hand experience of children and perhaps he saw Betsy as the daughter or granddaughter he had never had. He referred to her as his little *bambina* and he was by no means immune to the charms of her attractive mother. When he finally left the Briars he gave them all parting presents, including a lock of his hair to Betsy, which she had especially requested. They were also often invited to visit and even lunch or dine with him at Longwood later on, until the Balcombe family were removed from the island by the Governor in March 1818 – like most residents whom he believed were getting too close to, and being used by, Napoleon.

All good things come to an end and the realities now had to be faced. The works to extend and make Longwood House habitable had proceeded apace. Admiral Cockburn had spared no pains to get it finished as quickly as possible and 200–300 sailors had been employed on the work, together with fatigue parties from the 53rd regiment. Almost everything had to be carried by hand and the poor sweating soldiers and sailors must have cursed Napoleon and his companions as they toiled the nearly five miles up the long, hard and steep road from Jamestown, dragging and carrying the timber and other materials necessary for the renovation.

On 8 December Admiral Cockburn appeared at the Briars and announced that Longwood was now ready for occupation and that they should move to it.[19] Napoleon, although in many ways sorry to leave the Briars, but nevertheless ready now to establish himself in his more permanent home, suggested moving on the following day. There was, however, a further day's postponement because General Bertrand had been to inspect it and reported that there was still a very strong smell of fresh paint, which

Napoleon could never stand.[20] They finally left the Briars on 10 December and after fond farewells to all and sundry set off for Longwood. Napoleon once more donned his favourite green uniform of the Chasseurs de la Garde and mounted a new horse sent to him, by Cockburn's arrangement, from the Cape. The journey took them initially back in the direction of Jamestown and then round and up the steep, winding road to Longwood – past Hutt's Gate, where General and Madame Bertrand were to live in a small cottage for a time, before moving in October 1816 into a new house specially built for them just across the road from Longwood.

Word of their move had quickly got around. Many islanders turned out on the road to watch them go. As they approached the entrance to Longwood House a guard of honour presented arms. Napoleon entered the house. The first thing he did, getting his personal priorities right once again, was to order a hot bath, which the Admiral had thoughtfully had installed. A new chapter in the St Helena story was to begin.

FIVE

LONGWOOD HOUSE

ALTHOUGH IT IS ONLY about four and a half miles from Jamestown to Longwood, as the crow flies – or, more accurately on St Helena, the mynah bird, peaceful dove or fairy tern – and a mile less by a cross-country route from the Governor's residence, it was quite a journey to undertake, especially in bad weather. In the best of times the road was steep, twisting and narrow, with dangerous drops along much of the way on either side. In wet, misty or windy conditions it must have been a formidable challenge. Journeys were on foot, horseback, or – for the lucky few – in a horse-drawn carriage. There are many accounts of mishaps when carriages got stuck in the mud or struck rocks that had fallen onto the road, and were damaged or overturned. Betsy Balcombe recounts how on one occasion she was being taken with Mesdames Bertrand and Montholon to a ball given by one of the regiments of the garrison, and their carriage broke down, leaving them to complete the journey up to the ankles in mud and drenched to the skin.[1] The tall and elegant Fanny Bertrand had to borrow a change of clothes and went on to the ball in a dress that was far too short for her.

The journey between the Governor's residence, Plantation House, and Longwood was not an easy one either. Sir Hudson Lowe, who arrived and took over as governor in April 1816, must often have sat brooding at Plantation House, or in the Castle in Jamestown, wondering nervously whether Napoleon was still safely installed at Longwood. This was why, as an essential part of the security restrictions, he posted an orderly officer of captain's rank to reside permanently at Longwood with instructions to report to him twice a day that he had actually seen Napoleon there. This requirement caused huge friction in the days to come and occasioned some almost farcical games of hide-and-seek as Napoleon shut himself away, loaded his pistols and threatened to shoot anyone who tried to cross his threshold and force themselves into his presence. The poor orderly officers were between the devil and the deep blue sea, having to choose between incurring the wrath of the Governor, or risking being shot by Napoleon. On occasions their only recourse was to lurk outside in the garden, and hope to catch a glimpse of Napoleon through his windows, if the shutters were not closed.

Longwood House had originally been built as a farmhouse, and used for some time as such, but more recently had been adapted as a summer residence for the Lieutenant-Governor. It is situated on Longwood Plain and looks directly across to Deadwood Plain, separated from it by a deep ravine. In the distance can be seen the conical peak of Flagstaff Hill on the left, which had originally been the site of a signalling station, and on the right the Barn, a huge bare hostile lump of very ancient volcanic rock thrown up out of the sea when, or even before, St Helena was formed. Napoleon is said always to have been depressed when he looked out to the Barn. He was probably even more depressed, however, by the inescapable sight of the scarlet tunics and neat rows of white tents of the British regiments that were encamped on Deadwood Plain, less than a mile from Longwood. He could not avoid seeing them and being reminded of his captive status whenever he looked out.

Longwood House is now surrounded by attractive lawns, shade-providing trees and well-tended shrubs and flower beds, restored and maintained by the French Government, which has owned both the house, its gardens and also the area around Napoleon's tomb in Geranium Valley since they were sold to France by the British Government in 1858. The French tricolor now flies proudly and challengingly over Longwood, an unexpected sight on an island where the Union Jack and pictures of the British royal family normally dominate. It is looked after by Michel Danceoise-Martineau, a Napoleonic scholar and painter who combines the task of *conservateur* of the Longwood museum with the post of honorary consul of France. In 1815, however, when Napoleon arrived, there was little vegetation around the house except for a few scattered gum trees, which can grow quite tall but notoriously offer little shade. It is true that the house was exposed to the prevailing south-east trade winds and often shrouded in mist or drizzle, and occasionally in the summer months baked under a hot sun. However, despite Napoleon's constant complaints, the weather was not always unfavourable, otherwise there would not be so many records of al fresco meals, and strolls and dictating sessions out in the garden. Napoleon's main grievance was the lack of shade. This is partly why later on he discovered an unaccustomed passion for gardening and had everyone, including himself, working hard at it from the early mornings – to create some natural screens and barriers. The other reason for this new horticultural enthusiasm was his determination to establish some privacy and conceal himself from the eyes of the nearby English sentries.

The extensions and renovation that Cockburn had commissioned had made some improvement to Longwood but hardly turned it into a deluxe residence appropriate for the former Emperor of Europe. Napoleon on many occasions – while refusing to discuss the proposed new and better New Longwood House, which the British Government decided to build alongside the old one – demanded to be moved to Plantation House, the Governor's elegant thirty-five-roomed official residence, which was set in a delightful park, much like an English country house. But, like his delusions about living a gentleman's life in retirement in England, it was another rather ridiculous pipe dream. Apart from the fact that the Governor not unreasonably wished to live in the house expressly designated for the Governor, the East India Company, who owned it, had forbidden it to be used by Napoleon. At one point in November 1818 Napoleon also proposed to the Governor that he should be allowed to move to Farm Lodge, an attractive late-17th-century planter's house, now a comfortable guest house, set in beautifully shaded lawns and gardens in Rosemary Plain not far from Plantation House.[2] Again, the Governor was deaf to Napoleon's proposal.

Longwood was and remains a rambling aggregation of mostly single-storey rooms, thrown together with no obvious pattern or logic. It had a central yard in the middle and various servants' quarters and domestic offices off it to the rear. The main addition by Cockburn was a spacious room projecting at the front, from which a short, covered verandah and a flight of steps led down into the garden. The full frontal view of this is the most familiar picture postcard shot of Longwood. The new room was about twenty-six feet long by seventeen feet wide, with narrow windows flanking the front entrance and larger windows on either side of the room's length. It was, however, only built of wood, with no proper foundations and the ceilings covered with brown paper and smeared with pitch and tar. This meant that in warm weather the tar melted in the sun and it became hot and stifling, and in bad weather it let in the rain. Even now, though the house has been restored and is well-maintained, there are signs of damp and the paper is peeling here and there from the walls.

The single fireplace in this room turned out to be a mixed blessing. It created as much smoke as heat and added to the general unpleasantness and unhealthiness of the atmosphere of the room. Another serious problem throughout the house was an infestation of rats. Every attempt to get rid of them failed, even when the whole household turned out on a rat-killing orgy with drawn swords and knives to hunt and cut them down. Dr O'Meara records how on one occasion in January 1817 Napoleon moved his hat, which was placed on a sideboard, and a large rat jumped out of it and ran away between his feet.[3] The fragile floors and partitions were not tough enough to resist the rats' sharp, gnawing teeth. There were rat holes everywhere and O'Meara claims that they ran over him in bed at night. Given the proximity of everyone in the house, and the presence of children, it was not feasible to put down rat poison except under the very strictest control.

The initial use of the spacious new entrance room was as a reception chamber where visitors could be formally received by the Grand Marshal of the Court, General Bertrand, before being ushered into the imperial presence in the adjacent salon. In view of its dimensions it also offered Napoleon an opportunity to take some exercise when he was unable, or did not choose, to go outside into the garden. From July 1816, however, when the necessary table had been built and installed, it served also as a billiard room. Neither Napoleon's enthusiasm for, nor skill at, playing billiards was very great and he soon employed the table to spread out his maps and other papers when he was dictating or reminiscing, almost as if setting up an operations room for briefing his generals prior to a battle.

The billiard room led at its far end to the salon. This is where Napoleon received his visitors, who were expected to remain standing unless the Emperor indicated that they had his permission to sit. It was to here also that Napoleon was moved from his bedroom during his final illness and where he eventually died. In January 1816 a piano was also installed in this room to allow Madame Montholon, who was an accomplished pianist, to practise and entertain the company after dinner.

Napoleon's own accommodation was spartan. It consisted of two small chambers of roughly equal size to which access inside the house was gained through the dining room that led off the salon. One of them was his work room, or *cabinet de travail*, and the other his bedroom. He had one of his famous iron campaign beds placed in each of them so that he could move from one room to the other when, as frequently, he could not sleep. As time went on he spent more and more time sitting, lying and brooding in the bedroom. Both rooms were often damp and stuffy and Dr O'Meara once described entering the bedroom as like going into a damp cave.[4]

For Napoleon perhaps the most important room, which was next to his bedroom, was the small bathroom, where he progressively spent more and more hours reading and being read to, dictating, eating and even holding conversations while relaxing in the deep, hot water. There were no taps in the Longwood bath. The hot water flowed in through a pipe connected to the outside where it was heated in a boiler stoked up by Chinese labourers. In view of the shortages of both water and wood for fuel on the island, the mind boggles at how Napoleon's constant demands for copious amounts of hot water were met. Hudson Lowe later became extremely irritated by the water, which he believed Napoleon wasted, when often the troops in the camp were seriously short of it. Three different bathtubs were in fact successively installed while he was there. The present one, still in its original position in the house, was manufactured in England and dates from 1816. It was removed from Longwood at one stage to France after Napoleon's death but later brought back again. It is copper-lined and encased in a handsome oak panel, and is remarkably deep by modern standards. Since Napoleon was barely five feet, seven inches tall, it probably had some kind of seat fixed in it so that he could keep his head above water. Marchand also made for him a wooden tray that fitted across the bath on which he could lay his books and papers. Next to the bathroom is another small room where Marchand normally slept in order to be available to Napoleon at all times.

Such were Napoleon's quarters. The rest of his entourage, except for the Bertrands, were crammed here and there into the house where space allowed. They consisted of the Montholons and their son, Tristan; Las Cases and his son, Emmanuel; Gourgaud, a bachelor and alone; the valets Marchand and Ali; Cipriani; the two Archambault brothers; Noverazz, the groom; and Santini and a number of other servants who had either travelled with them on the voyage on the *Northumberland* or were locally employed. In addition, accommodation within the house had to be provided for Napoleon's surgeon, Dr O'Meara, and the resident British orderly officer. It is difficult to be precise about the total number accommodated in the house but there must have been forty or more at any one time. As well as this, other people employed around the house, such as the Chinese workers and gardeners, lived in a variety of quarters nearby.

With that spirit of independence that she had already shown on more than one occasion Fanny Bertrand insisted that she, her husband and three children (a fourth, Arthur, was born on the island) should live separately. At first they occupied a small cottage at Hutt's Gate, which was on a sharp bend by the roadside about three and a half miles from Jamestown and a relatively short cross-country walk from Longwood. About a year after their arrival, however, they moved to a comfortable house built specially for them just across the road from Longwood. She therefore spared herself the problems and temptations of living under the same roof and physically close to Napoleon. This separation, and her frequent absence at dinner (on the grounds that she was unwell or needed to stay at home to look after the children) became a great source of irritation to Napoleon and created friction between them. It did not prevent him, however, from going over quite often to visit the Bertrands, for example to get an unseen view from the upper windows of the race meetings organized by the army on Deadwood Plain (to which he was always invited, but declined to attend). Bertrand's cottage still stands opposite Longwood and is in a reasonable state of repair. There is a current project to restore it and convert it into an international Napoleonic study centre – on the assumption that an airfield, vital to attract the necessary visitors, is in due course built on the island.

* * *

Napoleon's main companions were Generals Bertrand and Montholon, both accompanied by their wives and children, and General Gourgaud and Count de Las Cases. They became known collectively as the four evangelists as each of them left memoirs of the time they spent with Napoleon. The differences in character and behaviour of these four, and the relationships between them, are important to an understanding of the St Helena story and how Napoleon endured his captivity. Valuable information and insight is also available from the memoirs of other inhabitants of the house: notably the two remarkably literate principal valets, Marchand and Ali; Napoleon's doctor, Dr Barry O'Meara, in his significant volume of recollections, *A Voice from St Helena*; and from the brief and spicy journals of Albine de Montholon.

General Bertrand must be discussed first. As well as being the most senior he was the most loyal, forbearing and constant of Napoleon's companions. In his 1912 *Napoléon et sa Famille*, the French historian Frédéric Masson wrote: 'Of all the people that surrounded the Emperor at St Helena, one stands out above the others. This is Grand Marshal Bertrand. He did not make a speculation of his devotion but filled all his duties with a fine serenity.' Every record of Bertrand's conduct, including his own modest and self-effacing memoirs, bears out this judgement.

Henri Gratien Bertrand was born in 1773 and was thus four years younger than Napoleon. After military college at Metz he served alongside Napoleon in the Army of Italy and thereafter accompanied him on most of his great campaigns, including the disastrous invasion of Russia in 1812. His speciality was engineering, and he was responsible for the miraculous construction of the bridges over the Berezina that saved the returning remnants of the Grande Armée from complete annihilation. Napoleon described him as the best engineer in Europe. He accompanied Napoleon to Elba, where he served as Minister of the Interior, and returned with him to Paris in March 1815. He was with Napoleon at Waterloo, withdrawing at the end of the battle in the same infantry square formed by the Old Guard, and elected to accompany him to St Helena, despite the strong and emotional protests of his wife.

He was probably not as bright as his companions. In her diaries Albine de Montholon says that Napoleon described him to her as 'mediocre' and was very critical of him,[5] and he quite undeservedly suffered abuse from

Napoleon on many occasions, particularly during the last months of the latter's fatal illness. This was partly, however, due to Napoleon's increasing anger and frustration with Bertrand's wife, Fanny. But Bertrand had a great deal to put up with. As the principal intermediary between Napoleon and the Governor, Sir Hudson Lowe, he was frequently the unfortunate messenger bearing bad news. Lady Malcolm, the wife of Cockburn's successor as naval commander, Admiral Sir Pulteney Malcolm, described him in her memoir, *A Diary of St Helena, 1816–17,* as a 'melancholy man and not giving the idea of a man of talents' but nevertheless a 'kind husband and father'.[6]

There is no doubt, however, that Bertrand was a tower of faithful strength to Napoleon throughout his stay on St Helena. He was his 'fidus Achates' par excellence. He remained touchingly loyal right to the end, and shared with Marchand and Ali many of the unpleasant physical duties of nursing the incontinent and dying Napoleon during his last agonizing days. He may have been pushed around at times by his feisty wife, whom he had married at Napoleon's command – Napoleon revelled in being a marriage broker both within his family and among his senior aides – but his devotion was unquestionable. Despite the peremptory manner in which he often dealt with Bertrand, one of Napoleon's greatest fears was that Bertrand and his wife might leave him. It is revealing of Bertrand's accommodating character that immediately after Napoleon's death he enjoyed, until his departure from the island, a cordial and civilized relationship with the Governor.

The other evangelist to stay the course to the end was Charles Jean Tristan de Montholon, who was only thirty-two when he went to St Helena. He had had a more erratic military career than Bertrand, with a touch of the Vicar of Bray about it. A colonel at the age of twenty-six, he left the army and in 1809, largely due to his friendship with her son, Eugène de Beauharnais, secured a place as chamberlain in the Empress Josephine's household. After then occupying the post of French Minister at Würzburg he blotted his copybook with Napoleon by marrying the twice-divorced Albine-Hélène de Montholon against the Emperor's wishes. He did not regain his spurs until 1814, when he commanded the National Guard in the Loire region when the allies invaded France, but then rapidly switched allegiance back to the (temporarily) restored Louis XVIII. Undeterred, he shifted camp once more back to Napoleon when the latter returned from Elba, and was promoted to general shortly before Waterloo. Thereafter he accompanied Napoleon to Rochefort and Plymouth and insisted on continuing with him to St Helena with his wife, now restored to Napoleon's favour, and young son, Tristan.

Montholon was the complete opposite of Bertrand, and therein perhaps lay his particular appeal to Napoleon. Elegant and above average height, with curly hair and an aristocratic background and manner, he was an agreeable charmer and entertaining companion, with an attractive wife, and his earlier peccadillos were easily forgiven by Napoleon. As Gilbert Martineau, the curator at Longwood from 1956 to 1987, put it in his book *La Vie Quotidienne à Sainte Hélène au Temps de Napoléon*, he was perhaps more suited for the boudoir and antechamber than for the bivouac.[7] Although lower down in the pecking order with Napoleon at the start of their exile, after the departure of Las Cases he gradually became his most privileged and constant confidant. At the end he became the principal executor of Napoleon's extraordinarily long and detailed will, even taking precedence over Bertrand – and he benefited substantially from it.

His adherence to Napoleon throughout five and a half dreary years of self-imposed captivity, during which he was frequently ill and for much of the time without his wife and children, was, however, substantially motivated by the prospect of fame and fortune. He was heavily in debt in 1815 and had been involved in a suspected misappropriation of funds during his time in command in the Loire. He nonetheless served his Emperor loyally on St Helena and shared fully in the duties of care at the end.

The third member of the quartet was General Gaspar Gourgaud, who was also only thirty-two when he went to St Helena. Like Napoleon, he had trained as an artillery officer and was present at the battles of Austerlitz and Wagram. In July 1811 he was appointed an aide de camp and, although wounded at Smolensk, survived the horrendous Russian campaign. When Napoleon was sent to Elba, Gourgaud temporarily attached himself to the restored Bourbon court. At the beginning of the Hundred Days, however, he rejoined Napoleon and, with Bertrand, was present at Waterloo, also taking refuge with them in the square of the Old Guard that covered their retreat on the evening of 18 June. He was promoted to general on 21 June and it was natural that he should press his claim to be a member of the party that eventually sailed to St Helena.

Unlike his three senior colleagues, Gourgaud remained single and his real love affair was in effect with his idol and hero, Napoleon himself. Napoleon appears to have been genuinely fond of him and in earlier times described him as 'mon premier officier d'ordonnance' (my number one military aide).[8] However, Gourgaud's obsessive and unconcealed quest always to be the first in Napoleon's attention and affections led to serious friction both with Napoleon and with his colleagues. He particularly resented the fact that Napoleon generally preferred to dictate to and converse with Las Cases. After Las Cases' departure from St Helena his jealousy of Montholon, who had begun to take over Las Cases' position, was so intense that in February 1818 he challenged Montholon to a duel, which was only prevented by the intervention of Napoleon himself.

When not engaged in these feuds, or secure for a time in Napoleon's affection, Gourgaud was plagued by boredom. The word 'ennui' occurs time and time again in his journal, which was published in 1898. He had too much time to spare, in which his jealousies and grievances could increase and fester. This was bound in the end to exhaust the patience of Napoleon, who had been prepared to put up with some of his moods and ill temper, and had for the most part sought to treat him gently. They began to quarrel openly and Gourgaud sometimes answered back in words that would have provoked instant dismissal in the old days. He reacted furiously, for example, when on one occasion Napoleon called him a child – Napoleon is recorded as exclaiming: 'Je ne suis pas sa femme, je ne peux tout de même coucher avec lui' (I am not his wife and I really can't go to bed with him).[9]

Matters came to a head early in 1818 when Gourgaud declared that he wanted to leave the island and sought medical certificates of illness to justify this. The succession of events following this is not entirely clear. He was almost certainly requested by Napoleon to convey certain secret messages to Europe, including an appeal to Tsar Alexander of Russia, with whom Napoleon still believed he had influence from the time when they signed the Treaty of Tilsit in June 1807. On the other hand, after Gourgaud left Longwood, he dined with the Governor at Plantation House and, as well as receiving a personal loan from him, appears to have spilled some of the beans on life at Longwood – including the ease with which Napoleon and his colleagues had been able to communicate with the outside world. He also spoke in bitter terms of the way in which he had been treated by Napoleon ('like a dog').[10] When this was reported by the Governor to Lord Bathurst in London it led to an immediate instruction to Lowe to tighten further the security restrictions on Longwood. Gourgaud also told similar

stories to Bathurst after he arrived in London. Whether this was a double
bluff by Gourgaud with Napoleon's connivance to distract attention from
his real purpose in returning to Europe, or simply the effect of pent-up
boredom and frustration, it is impossible to tell. The reality is that the
tense and claustrophobic atmosphere at Longwood, and the strain it had
placed on Napoleon, could simply not continue without an explosion of
some kind. Although it perhaps cleared the air at Longwood, Gourgaud's
departure was a sad one because he still worshipped the Emperor he
left behind, as was shown twenty-two years later when he returned with
Bertrand to bring his exhumed body back to France and occupied a place
of honour in the internment ceremony at Les Invalides in December 1820.

The fourth and last member of the evangelists was the odd man out,
Emmanuel-Auguste-Dieudonné-Marius-Joseph de Las Cases. At forty-
nine, he was older than both Napoleon and the other three and his military
career had been confined to service at relatively junior rank in the royalist
navy. Nonetheless he was already an established author, fluent in English,
and, significantly, the only one of the four who was shorter than Napoleon.

Like Montholon, Las Cases came from an old aristocratic family, being
the son of the Marquis de Las Cases. He fled to London during the
Revolution, returning to France in 1802 when he rallied to Napoleon's cause
and became a Chamberlain and Counsellor of State. After being created
successively a baron and a count, and conducting a mission in Holland, he
joined Napoleon on his return from Elba and clung tightly to his coat tails
after Waterloo, following him to Malmaison, Rochefort and Plymouth
and insisting on sharing his exile with him. When the choice was made
of companions to proceed with Napoleon to St Helena, he was at first
excluded by the British, who stipulated that only three senior officers could
accompany him. He was, however, eventually allowed to travel as Napoleon's
secretary; he promptly collected some money, summoned his fifteen-year-
old son, also Emmanuel, and climbed aboard. He was criticized widely for
abandoning his wife and other children, but his response was that it was
in their greater long-term interest that by hitching himself to Napoleon he
should win fame and fortune.

This he certainly did. Although he undoubtedly admired Napoleon,
whom he once described as his god, his principal motives were mercenary.
He guessed correctly that Napoleon would want to write or dictate his
memoirs and he was well qualified to help him do this. Gourgaud accused

him of only coming to St Helena to write a book, and Hudson Lowe told Dr O'Meara that Las Cases had not followed Napoleon out of affection 'but merely to have an opportunity of obtaining materials from him to publish his life'.[11] He quickly became the principal amanuensis, took dictation from Napoleon on both the *Bellerophon* and the *Northumberland*, and was summoned with his son to share Napoleon's temporary accommodation at the Briars during his first few weeks on St Helena. Thereafter he shared dictation duties with Gourgaud but it was clear that Napoleon found him the most congenial of his colleagues to converse with, particularly given his knowledge of England and the English language and his expertise in naval matters. All this provoked enormous jealousy on the part of Gourgaud in particular, and he was known by his colleagues as the Jesuit, partly for the extreme care he took in drafting and looking after his journals.

His output in the form of the massive *Mémorial*, which was published in 1823, far outshone in both length and celebrity the writings of his colleagues. He was a truly Boswellian rapporteur, using his journal not only to record every detail of Napoleon's daily life on the island, but, more importantly, to transcribe for posterity Napoleon's own account of his great and glorious career. As such it was a supreme work of propaganda, sometimes even sycophantic, which achieved instant success and for years to come was regarded as the definitive work on both the glory of Napoleon and the outrageous treatment he received from the perfidious English. From Napoleon's point of view, once he began to realize that St Helena could be the end, his overriding objective was to leave a lasting testament to the great achievements of his life's work – from the perspective from which he wanted them to be interpreted.

Las Cases achieved his objectives superbly. In November 1816 he was expelled from St Helena by the Governor on a charge of conducting clandestine correspondence for Napoleon. His great work, *Mémorial de Sainte Hélène*, according to Lord Rosebery, earned him some 80,000 pounds and he had only had to spend thirteen months on the island to earn that.[12] Napoleon too could be satisfied in the knowledge that his current fate was made known all over Europe and his own version of his career read in almost every town and country.

The four senior companions described in this chapter, of whom only Bertrand and Montholon stayed on to the end, were the main protagonists on Napoleon's side on St Helena. They had their own supporting cast in

Marchand, Ali, Noverazz, Cipriani and the other loyal servants who had elected to remain with Napoleon. Nevertheless it was they who bore the brunt of entertaining and assisting Napoleon, and the often disagreeable task of mediating between him and the Governor and his subordinates. Bertrand and Montholon also had their wives and children to look after, which brought a different set of personal strains and pressures.

Apart from Bertrand, who lived first at Hutt's Gate and then in the cottage across the road, all the others were shoehorned on top of each other into the one unsatisfactory house. This must have intensified the internal conflicts, particularly in bad weather when they were unable to go out and the damp and sometimes smoky atmosphere inside Longwood became particularly unhealthy and unpleasant. During the early months of this extraordinary cohabitation, however, they settled into a regular and disciplined family routine, even if Gourgaud had, for a time, to camp out like a servant in the rear courtyard.

Each of the evangelists was given a specific household role by Napoleon. Bertrand, the Grand Marshal, presided in a rather grand way over them all, but since he did not live in the house, Montholon acted as a kind of delegated household chamberlain in his place, with responsibility for controlling the servants and overall administration. Gourgaud was put in charge of the stables – not the most exalted role for a distinguished general of thirteen campaigns – and Las Cases was made nominally responsible for the household goods and chattels, including the daily provisions supplied by the British. In practice this was a sinecure as Marchand looked after these things, and Las Cases was in any case mostly occupied with taking dictation and conversing with Napoleon.

The daily routine in the early months followed a regular course, each day being divided into specific periods for specific purposes.[13] Napoleon usually rose between 6 and 7am. After a first cup of coffee and completing his toilet (he always shaved himself – a long-standing habit adopted for security reasons), and on most days an early morning consultation with his doctor, he would either, in good weather, go out for a walk or ride, or proceed to the billiard room or his own *cabinet de travail* to dictate.

After dictation or the morning excursion 'le déjeuner de Sa Majesté' was served with strict protocol at about 10am. The rest of the day would be spent resting, reading, dictating, receiving approved visitors and in the late afternoon taking another excursion, sometimes in a carriage with the two leading wives. Dinner was normally served at 7pm or soon afterwards, but not before Napoleon had taken his daily hot bath. This was not simply a quasi-medicinal occasion for Napoleon to soak and relax, but often a theatre for holding court (like Winston Churchill many years later) with Las Cases or another favoured companion.

Dinner was served, again with absolutely strict protocol, in the dining room and seldom lasted for more than twenty minutes – it is a wonder that the entourage did not suffer from chronic indigestion. Coffee was taken in the salon, served on the magnificent Sèvres service that Napoleon had brought with him. After coffee the party either stayed in the salon or moved to the billiard room and the rest of the evening's agenda was determined by Napoleon. The assembled company were entirely at his mercy, according to whether he wished to read aloud or to be read to (often one of the great French or classical tragedies, such as *Andromache* or *Phèdre*, with which Napoleon was familiar and could quote from), play cards, regale them with his memoirs, or ask Albine de Montholon to play and sing at the piano. Whatever the choice, no-one was allowed to leave until Napoleon himself retired and gave his permission to the others to do so. It is not difficult to imagine how tedious and fatiguing some of these evenings must have been, and Napoleon was not best pleased when he observed one of his companions nodding off. One incident is recorded when he had a sharp exchange with Madame de Montholon, who had clearly fallen asleep.

A feature of all these occasions, including the receiving of visitors, was their absolute formality. Napoleon insisted on behaving exactly as he would have done in his pomp at the Elysée or the Tuileries. Callers were first received in the garden in front of the house by a liveried servant and then handed over to Grand Marshal Bertrand in full military uniform, who ushered them from the billiard room into the presence of the Emperor in the salon. As Napoleon normally remained standing (ever since Admiral Cockburn had once offended him by having the temerity to sit down without being invited to!) this must have been very intimidating. Full dress uniform for the officers was also mandatory for dinner, whatever the weather or temperature. Napoleon's defiantly desperate attempts to maintain his imperial dignity and status may perhaps be understandable, but as time went on they verged on the absurd or pathetic, and became more difficult for both himself and his companions to sustain.

So passed the first few weeks and months at Longwood House. There were no major crises and relations with the acting Governor, Admiral Cockburn, remained reasonably amicable, despite progressive disenchantment as the restrictions he applied began to take effect. The fragile peace was, however, to be shattered by the arrival in April 1816 of the new Governor, Lieutenant-General Sir Hudson Lowe. Now the central act of the drama began in earnest.

SIX

THE ARRIVAL OF
SIR HUDSON LOWE

EVERY DRAMA NEEDS A villain. In the St Helena story the arch villain is traditionally cast as Sir Hudson Lowe, who arrived to take up the post of Governor and Commander in Chief on 14 April 1816. There are, however, two sides to most stories and it is only fair to examine more carefully Lowe's conduct and the circumstances into which he was pitched before uncritically accepting the traditional view of him as a cruel and sadistic *bourreau* (torturer), or as Napoleon described him, 'a hyena caught in a trap'.[1]

When Lowe arrived at St Helena he was, at forty-seven, virtually the same age as Napoleon (and incidentally as the Duke of Wellington). They both had a Corsican background, though this turned out to offend Napoleon rather than to commend Lowe to him as he thought that the selection of someone with a Corsican Ranger connection – they were rebels who fought for the British against France – was deliberately provocative. Both had also been soldiers since early childhood and had spent their whole careers in the army. But there the resemblance ends.

Lowe was born in 1769 in Ireland, the son of an army doctor who, after serving in Germany in the Seven Years' War, had been Chief Medical Officer to the military garrison in Gibraltar.[2] The young Lowe was sent away to school in Salisbury at the age of twelve and in September 1787 he was commissioned as an ensign into his father's regiment, the 50th of foot, in Gibraltar. He rose to the rank of captain in 1795 and obtained a furlough of eighteenth months, during which he travelled extensively in Italy, where he became fluent in both Italian and French. This linguistic ability was significant for his later relationship with Napoleon, who could only speak those two languages and in the view of many people never even spoke French properly.

Thereafter Lowe's army career was not spectacular but followed a steady course. He was dispatched to Toulon in 1793, only to arrive shortly after the British forces had withdrawn. He thus just missed coming under fire from the guns of the brilliant young French artillery officer, the then Napoleone Buonaparte, whose dash, courage and initiative had been largely responsible for the French success in recapturing the port. He then followed the 50th regiment to Agaccio, Napoleon's birthplace in Corsica, which the British had by then occupied, and although it would be nice to believe that he occupied the Bonaparte family home, he was probably quartered with other officers in the citadel. After the recapture of Corsica by the French he spent a short time on Elba – another connection with Napoleon – before returning via Gibraltar to Lisbon, where he learned both Spanish and Portuguese.

After two years in Lisbon he was posted with his regiment to Menorca, by now an important base for the British fleet, and was there appointed to the command that linked his future more closely to that of Napoleon. Probably chosen for his fluency in Italian, he was promoted to major in command of some 200 rebel Corsican volunteers, known as the Corsican Rangers, who were opposed to French domination of their island and had fled to the British side. He took the unit back to Gibraltar and in March 1801 they formed part of the force commanded by Sir John Moore in the landing at Aboukir in the Egyptian campaign. They took part in the battle of Canope and Lowe's conduct was highly commended by General Moore, no mean judge of soldiers, who said in a letter to him: 'When you are in an advance position, I am always sure of having a good night's sleep.'[3]

The Corsican Rangers were disbanded when the short-lasting Peace of Amiens was signed in 1802 and Lowe, thanks to the recommendation of General Moore, was posted to the 7th Royal Fusilier regiment and appointed aide de camp to the commanding general. He was then, again at Moore's personal request, sent on a secret mission to Portugal, on return from which he submitted an important report recommending the signing of a pact of alliance with Portugal and the establishment of a British base on the Peninsula. The fulfilment of this a few years later laid the foundations of the 'Spanish ulcer' – the term coined by Napoleon for the protracted Peninsular War that drew hundreds of thousands of French troops into Spain and Portugal – which contributed so much to Napoleon's eventual downfall. There is no evidence that Napoleon appreciated Lowe's part in this.

In December 1803, after war between England and France had resumed, Lowe was promoted to lieutenant-colonel and made responsible for raising the Corsican Rangers to the strength of a full regiment. In 1805 he took them to Naples to support the Bourbons who were being attacked by a French fleet. A British squadron under Sir Sydney Smith, one of the few British commanders apart from Nelson for whom Napoleon had any time at all, succeeded in capturing the island of Capri and Lowe with his Corsican Rangers was ordered in the summer of 1806 to occupy and hold it.

There are differing versions of the story of the capture of Capri in October 1808 by a French squadron under Marshal Murat. The island is difficult to assault, being protected, like St Helena, by high cliffs, and Lowe had two years in which to ensure that its fortifications were as strong as possible. It fell, however, to a daring assault by Murat's troops, who climbed the steep cliffs near La Punta Carena, where Lowe had concentrated most of his Corsicans, and established a vital beachhead on the island. Following a successful French assault later that day, and the inability of the British fleet to bring in reinforcements, Lowe was compelled to surrender ten days later, after first rejecting the harsh capitulation terms offered to him.

On St Helena Napoleon taunted Lowe insultingly with this failure.[4] He claimed that with some 1,360 troops under his command, mainly composed of the Corsican Rangers and the Royal Malta regiment, but with only a handful of British troops, it should have been easy for Lowe to hold out. He, Napoleon, would have held the island easily. There is, however, testimony to the contrary. Lowe's casualties were heavy and Major-General Forbes, Lowe's immediate commander, wrote of his conduct in high terms and said that he had done all that a man could have done.[5]

After negotiating an honourable withdrawal, in which none of his men was made prisoner, Lowe went on to take part, with his Corsicans, both in the capture of Ischia in the Mediterranean in June 1809 and in a number of other actions in the Ionian islands, distinguishing himself particularly in the successful attack on the island of Sainte-Maure on 16 April 1810. In January 1813 he was promoted to full colonel and sent on a special mission to inspect the German Legion, a mercenary force in the British army, largely composed of deserters from Napoleon's own Grande Armée. This was a significant move that brought him into contact with personalities at the very highest level, including Tsar Alexander, the young Emperor of Russia. He was subsequently present with the Russian army at the battle of Bautzen in May 1813, where he saw Napoleon in action on the opposite side for the first time.

At the end of 1813 the relationship he had developed with the Russians and Prussians was so appreciated in London that he was appointed British liaison officer to their combined armies. This enabled him to develop a close rapport with Marshal Blücher and his influential Chief of Staff, General Gneisenau, and he was present with them at the important battles of Leipzig and Moeckern. Blücher seemed to think highly of him and in a letter addressed to him wrote: 'We have learned to appreciate and respect you; the memory of you will be dear to us all our life.'[6] In the early weeks of 1814 he crossed the Rhine with Blücher's army and was present at a succession of battles against the desperately defending French forces before triumphantly entering Paris with him in March 1814. A mark of Lowe's standing with Blücher was that he was given the signal honour of taking the news of Napoleon's first abdication to the Prince Regent in London.[7] He was there appointed a Knight Commander of the Bath and soon afterwards promoted to major-general and appointed quartermaster-general to the allied troops in the Netherlands.

During this last appointment, when the news broke of Napoleon's return to France after escaping from Elba in March 1815, as the senior British officer on the spot he used his influence with the Prussian high command to persuade them to cross the River Meuse and act in close concert with the allied forces placed under the command of Wellington. He is also credited with having suggested the defensive position at Mont St Jean, although this is usually attributed to Wellington himself. These were absolutely crucial services to the allied cause, without which the battle of Waterloo would not have been won. Napoleon never showed any appreciation of this in his subsequent contemptuous disparagement of any pretensions Lowe had to being a decent soldier.

Lowe did not, however, go on to take part in the subsequent Waterloo campaign. Wellington preferred to have as his quartermaster-general the known qualities of Sir William Howe de Lancey, who had served with him in the Peninsula. He accordingly arranged for Lowe to be recalled and appointed commander of a force of some 1,500 British and 3,000 Italian troops at Genoa, which had been placed there to attack the south of France. It was at this point that the fates of Lowe and Napoleon were brought critically together, when Lowe was summoned from Marseilles on 1 August 1815 to become Governor of St Helena.

Although Lowe had never commanded large bodies of troops in battle, the above shows that his military career had been perfectly respectable, indeed well above average. He had won the respect and commendation of senior British and foreign commanders, including Sir John Moore, and had had the crucial insight to urge the strategy that secured a British foothold in the Peninsula and was vital to the success at Waterloo. He was, like anyone else, a military pygmy compared with Napoleon, but Napoleon's contempt for him as a soldier was ungracious and undeserved.

In appearance he was a little over medium height, and therefore slightly taller than Napoleon. His features were dark, with reddish-brown scrubby hair and thick prominent eyebrows, and his face a little narrow and bony, with a longish, thin nose. The most severe criticism that Lord Rosebery could find to make of him was the rather Trollopean one that he did not look like a 'gentleman'.[8] He had a trim, upright figure that contrasted with the growing portliness of Napoleon. Las Cases, who was adept at pen portraits, described him vividly in the following terms: 'On l'a trouvé un homme d'environ quarante cinq ans, d'un taille commune, mince, maigre, sec, rouge de visage et de chevelure, marqueté de taches de rousseur, des yeux obliques fixant à la dérobée et rarement en face, recouverts de sourcils d'un blond ardent, épais et fort proéminents' (We found him to be a man of about forty-five years of age, of average height, slim and slight, gaunt, red-haired and ruddy in appearance, with freckled skin. His eyes always glanced sideways and seldom looked you in the face and they were surmounted by very prominent bushy, reddish eyebrows). Napoleon at that stage was content with the one-word description of Lowe as 'hideux'.[9]

Why was he chosen for the governorship of St Helena? He had a number of obvious qualifications. He could speak fluent French and Italian; he had previous Corsican connections; he had experience of being in command of a small island; and he was well known to Britain's main allies, the Russians, Prussians and Austrians. Their agreement to his appointment was not formally required, but they would no doubt have assented if asked. He was also readily available, having been relieved of his command in the Netherlands and not yet fully established at Genoa. And above all he was a soldier, used to taking and carrying out orders without question.

There was much discussion of his appointment in London. The Foreign Secretary, Lord Castlereagh, who was still at the conference in Paris, was opposed to it, but more because he had his own candidate, Lord Treavour, than for any specific objection to Lowe.[10] He nevertheless questioned Lowe thoroughly in Paris about the measures he would take to ensure that Napoleon would not escape. Castlereagh was a hawk so far as Napoleon was concerned and urged him to impose an 'iron discipline'. Lowe also called on the Duke of Wellington in Paris and on his old friend, Marshal Blücher, who told him, somewhat intimidatingly, that the fate of Europe would depend on his vigilance.

There were still divided views in Westminster and in the country generally as to how the defeated Napoleon should be treated.[11] Somewhat surprisingly, the Whigs in Parliament were in favour of treating him clemently, and popular opinion was split between reluctant admiration for the arch demon 'Bony' and anger at the waste, loss of life and destruction, not to mention the huge cost to the British taxpayer, he had caused over the last fifteen years. Legal advice was sought within the Government, and the Lord Chancellor, Lord Eldon, expressed the opinion that the Paris Treaty gave the British Government no right to dispose of the life of a defeated enemy who had voluntarily handed himself over. However, both the Prime Minister, Lord Liverpool, and the Secretary of State, Lord Bathurst, took the more pragmatic approach, consistent in their view with the terms of the Paris Treaty, that it was imperative to prevent Napoleon doing any further harm in Europe and that nothing else mattered. They thus wanted someone who would carry out their orders without question like a good soldier. Who then was more suitable for this huge responsibility than Sir Hudson Lowe? However, it is doubtful whether Lowe, while flattered to be offered this unique chance of celebrity and glory, fully appreciated the acutely sensitive and political nature of the hot potato that he was being asked to handle. In a sense he was in a no-win situation. If he let Napoleon escape, his career was finished. If he succeeded in confining him, there could be no guarantee that a grateful British Government and people would thank him at the end of the day.

During his stay in London Lowe had long interviews with Lord Liverpool and Lord Bathurst, who assured him that he was the right man for the job and promised that if he accepted it his position would be reviewed after three years.[12] Bathurst, to whom as Secretary of State for War and the Colonies Lowe would directly report, then gave him a series of briefings in which he impressed on him the absolute necessity to carry out his instructions, which would be set out in writing in minute detail. On 23 August the Board of the East India Company, who remained formally in charge of the civil administration of the island, notified him of his appointment as Governor of St Helena, and on the same day he was promoted to the local rank of lieutenant-general, with the generous salary for the time of £12,000 (which compared with the £300 a year that a captain then earned).

Lowe had the good sense to seek reassurance as to the legal authority for his appointment and its terms of reference. In a letter of 13 April 1816, Bathurst wrote:

> You will receive the King's Warrant under my Grant and Seal authorizing you to detain keep and treat Napoleon Bonaparte as a Prisoner of War; and you will receive at the same time the Act of Parliament lately passed giving powers to the above effect. You will be pleased to regulate your conduct according to the spirit of the above Instruments.[13]

Lord Bathurst also set out for Lowe before his departure the broad principles which should govern the exercise of his powers. He assured him that within those general principles many matters would necessarily be left for local decision at Lowe's discretion, in which he had full confidence. He also stated as a basic tenet that every indulgence should be accorded to Napoleon (henceforward to be entitled General Bonaparte, not Emperor) that was compatible with his total security.[14] This mantra, which was said to have emanated from the Prince Regent himself, was to be repeated many times, but perhaps more for form's sake and public consumption than reflecting any benign feelings on Bathurst's part. Underneath all the verbiage Lowe was left in no doubt at all that security was paramount and that every other consideration should be subordinated to not letting Napoleon escape, as he had done from Elba. However the jurists might choose to interpret the law, Napoleon was to be treated as a prisoner of war and his companions, including the servants who had travelled with him, were to be required to sign a statement that they were on St Helena with him of their own free will and, on pain of deportation or other punishment, would submit to the same restrictions as those imposed on Napoleon.

Hudson Lowe's task was an awesomely heavy one, with the risks greater than the potential rewards. He set about the preparation for it, however, energetically and first started to select the military staff to accompany him to St Helena. As chief of staff he chose the Deputy Adjutant General, Lieutenant-Colonel Sir Thomas Reade, aged only thirty-one, who had served in various mainly diplomatic functions in the Mediterranean and had been knighted for them. On St Helena he soon became a hawk as far as Napoleon was concerned and thought that Lowe was too soft with him. Lady Lowe is even reported to have said that he was the real Governor and that her husband was his assistant. Subordinate to Reade was Lieutenant-Colonel Edward Wynyard, the Military Secretary. He was thirty-six and had become known to Lowe through his presence at the attacks on the islands of Ischia and Procida. Lowe also took with him another officer who had served with him in the Corsican Rangers and at the surrender of Capri: the army surgeon, Dr Alexander Baxter, whom he appointed Deputy-Inspector of Hospitals on St Helena. Baxter stayed on until 1819 and played an important part in the difficult politics of medical attendance on Napoleon.

To complete his immediate personal staff Lowe chose Major Gideon Gorrequer, aged thirty-five, as his aide de camp. Gorrequer had been a soldier since the age of sixteen and, like Wynyard, had served with Lowe in the Ionian islands. Although he was the junior member of the team, he became by far the most interesting and influential, and punched well above his military rank and weight. Like Lowe he spoke French and Italian fluently and he remained on the island with Lowe until Napoleon's death. He lived with the Lowes at Plantation House and was always at Lowe's side to take dictation, record meetings and conversations, and prepare reports to the Secretary of State in London. It was not until the discovery, deciphering and publication of his secret and private diaries by James Kemble in 1969 that the full extent of his relationship with Lowe and Lady Lowe became apparent. The diaries, which he wrote every night in a solitary cramped room at Plantation House (he continually complained that Lady Lowe, whom he detested, would not allow him a decent room or furniture), absolutely fester with pent-up anger, jealousy and frustration, combined with indignation for the lack of appreciation that he received from Lowe for all his hard work.

On the military side Lowe was also supported by Brigadier-General Sir George Bingham, the senior officer commanding the soldiers on St Helena, and by the successive admirals in charge of the naval squadron that kept a perpetual watch around the St Helena coast. When Lowe arrived, Admiral Sir George Cockburn, who had conducted Napoleon to St Helena on the *Northumberland*, was already in temporary command as acting Governor and had installed Napoleon at Longwood and set in place the restrictions on Napoleon ordered by the Government. He left in June 1816, soon after Lowe arrived, and was succeeded by Rear-Admiral Sir Pulteney Malcolm who, with his wife, Clementina, a niece of Lord Keith, quickly established a cordial relationship with Napoleon, who received them frequently. Many of their conversations are recorded in Lady Malcolm's diary (*The Journal of Lady Malcolm*) and although Admiral Malcolm remained formally supportive of Lowe, the closeness of his relationship with Napoleon made Lowe extremely suspicious of him and their relationship deteriorated. Lady Malcolm, like her husband, obviously also thought that Lowe at times acted unreasonably towards Napoleon and Napoleon took every opportunity to exploit this and encourage the division between them. Lowe was therefore relieved when Malcolm left in June 1817.

Malcolm was replaced by a more supportive naval commander, Rear-Admiral Robert Plampin, who was much less critical of Lowe. Napoleon took an instant dislike to him, describing him somewhat curiously on first acquaintance as 'looking like one of those drunken little Dutch skippers I have seen in Holland, sitting at a table with a pipe in his mouth, a cheese and a bottle of Geneva before him.'[15] Plampin achieved celebrity on the island when it was discovered that the lady he had brought with him was not his wife. This caused protocol problems for Lady Lowe at Plantation

House and stimulated a tirade of scandalized invective from the puritani-
cal and bigoted Rev. Mr Richard Boys in the pulpit of the country church
situated near Plantation House.[16] Plampin left in July 1820, to be succeeded
by Rear-Admiral Robert Lambert who was never received by the then very
sick Napoleon at Longwood and did not play a significant part in the St
Helena story.

Before his departure for St Helena, despite a pressing round of engagements
in London, Lowe found time to get married. His bride was the thirty-five-
year-old Susan de Lancey, the sister of the William de Lancey who had
displaced Lowe as Wellington's quartermaster-general for the Waterloo
campaign. She had been previously married to a Colonel Johnson, who had
died in 1812, and had two daughters by him who accompanied her to St
Helena. She was an elegant and attractive woman who was not afraid to
show a daring décolletage, and she was happy to play hostess and first lady
at Plantation House, where Lowe entertained generously.

Lowe and his family and staff sailed to St Helena on the frigate *Phaeton*
and arrived on 14 April 1816. There were great expectations on the island.
Napoleon was said to be becoming a little tired of Admiral Cockburn and
prepared to give a fellow soldier a chance, even though he had a suspicion
that the choice of someone who had commanded the Corsican Rangers was
deliberately provocative. The stage was thus set for the new Governor and
Napoleon to come face to face, and serious confrontation was inevitable.

SEVEN

CAPTIVITY AND CONFRONTATION

NAPOLEON HAD NOW BEEN on St Helena for about five months. The physical and psychological pressures on him were enormous. He was a closely guarded prisoner, confined by restrictions on all sides, and under the absolute control of a jailor whom he came to loathe and despise. He faced a number of acute problems. First, it was absolutely paramount for him to maintain his self-respect and dignity, above all his imperial status. He sought to do this by imposing on his retinue as much as possible of the protocol and outward trappings, in miniature, of the imperial court. Second, unless he was to give in at an early stage to absolute hopelessness and despair, he had to believe, or convince himself, that there were still political forces in Britain or Europe that would reverse policy and allow him to return – if not to France or elsewhere in Europe, at least to America or somewhere more civilized and congenial than St Helena. Third, he had to cope with the sheer physical conditions of the island – the unhealthy confinement, cheek by jowl with too many bickering and competing colleagues, in an inadequate, often damp and windswept house, with unsatisfactory medical care. Finally, when he was not sparring with the Governor, contesting and plotting to evade his restrictions, or trying to settle the interminable squabbles that developed within his own household, he had to find other ways of alleviating the long hours of growing boredom. Until now his life had been dominated by the incessant demands of an externally imposed structure – in more recent years the massive military and political demands of the Empire, with thousands of subordinates at his every beck and call and fresh problems every day. He now had to create a new structure, aided only by three generals, a counsellor of state, and a handful of loyal personal servants.

As we have seen, he passed the first two months in a kind of never-never dream land at the Briars, enjoying the hospitality of the Balcombes and the boisterous and irreverent companionship of the young and ebullient francophone Betsy. The first few weeks at Longwood were then fully occupied by settling in, allocating domestic duties and fixing the general structure and routine of the household. Although signs of later tensions started to appear, particularly in the jealousies increasingly aroused by the pre-eminent place that Las Cases was beginning to establish in his attention, there were no great crises in the early days. Longwood Plain was not the most comfortable of locations on the island, but they moved there at the most agreeable season of the year, St Helena's summer, and the residents of Longwood House were able to spend much of the time out of doors. Napoleon was, however, beginning to have second thoughts about Admiral Cockburn, as the severity of the restrictions that Cockburn had imposed gradually began to bite home, and he was now prepared to give a new governor, particularly a soldier, a chance. He told Brigadier-General Bingham: 'J'en suis fort aisé, je suis las de l'amiral. Il y a quelques sujets sur lesquels je causerais volontiers avec Sir Hudson Lowe. Il est militaire et il a servi. Il a été avec Blücher. En outré, il commendait un regiment Corse et il connaît plusieurs de mes amis' (I am pretty relaxed. I am tired of the admiral and there are several subjects which I would gladly discuss with Sir Hudson Lowe. He is a military man and has seen service, including with Blücher. Moreover, he commanded a Corsican regiment and knows a number of my friends).[1] On the face of it, this was a propitious start.

The main reason why Napoleon was becoming disenchanted with Admiral Cockburn was that the latter had made it quite clear that – despite the generally amicable relationship he had established with Napoleon on the *Northumberland* – on St Helena he would not be deterred from applying, to the letter, the strict security measures laid down in the detailed written instructions he had been given in London. He had so far combined firmness with a humane common sense. This had, for example, been shown in indulging Napoleon over the dinner seating and serving arrangements on the *Northumberland*, allowing Napoleon and his senior officers to keep their swords and permitting the whole party, contrary to instructions, to disembark on St Helena before the secure long-term accommodation was ready. So far as security on the island was concerned, however, with one small exception, he could not be smooth-talked into making concessions.

The restrictions imposed on Napoleon and his party were extremely rigorous. It was ordered that, on pain of severe punishment, there should be no written or verbal communication with the 'prisoners' without prior authorization. A curfew was imposed on any movement outside Jamestown after sunset and patrols were ordered to arrest anyone they found breaking the curfew who was not in possession of the appropriate password. These restrictions, together with the impact on prices and availability of goods and comestibles of the sudden and massive influx of troops on to the island, were hardly likely to endear the presence of the prisoners to the resident Saints.

The increased military presence on St Helena was astonishing for such a small island. Two full infantry regiments were brought out from England. The 53rd was stationed on Deadwood Plain, staring Napoleon and Longwood directly in the face (Napoleon had small holes bored in the shutters of the billiard room so that he could spy on them without being seen – the holes can be seen in the replica shutters at Longwood today). The 66th was largely billeted in barracks at Jamestown. Together with the existing East India Company's local troops, many of whom were ex Indian army, the total garrison now amounted to some 2,800 at its peak, of whom 1,000 or so were on guard duty each night. There were about 500 soldiers of officer or non-commissioned officer rank, which would normally have served an army of 10,000. Detachments of the troops, including artillery units, were established at fortified strategic points such as Sandy Bay, on the south coast, where the rusting barrels of cannons can still be seen lying across the top of the gravelly beach, and at supposedly vulnerable landing places such as Lemon Valley and Egg Island, which is now the home of thousands of nesting black and brown noddies rather than emplacements and field guns. Small detachments were also stationed at other locations from time to time, and the regiments, which never fired a shot in anger, and suffered badly from illness and disease, were regularly rotated and replaced during Napoleon's stay. The whole island was like an armoured porcupine, bristling with spiky muskets and guns.

Longwood House was itself also tightly guarded.[2] Two perimeter zones around it were defined. The inner one, enclosed by a dry stone wall, stretched for about four miles, and was in a sense the extended garden of Longwood. Within this area Napoleon and his party were free to walk, ride or otherwise exercise without restriction and without the presence of any soldiers. Immediately outside the wall, however, a sentry was placed at every fifty paces, and at sunset they moved in close to the house and spent the night standing against the walls and windows at fifteen-pace intervals, with muskets loaded and bayonets fixed, right under the noses of Napoleon and his sleeping companions. This more than any other measure belied any idea that Napoleon might have had that he was anything other than a very closely guarded prisoner.

The outer perimeter around Longwood stretched for about twelve miles. It covered virtually the whole of both Longwood and Deadwood Plains, and embraced the road to Jamestown as far as Hutt's Gate, where the Bertrands initially lived, the sentry post at Alarm House, and, with a space of about half a mile on each side, the road on from Hutt's Gate to Orange Grove and the bottom of Fisherman's Valley. Within this area Napoleon and his companions were also allowed to move where they wished, but they were liable to meet sentries. On the rest of the island Napoleon was also free to go anywhere he liked, except to fortified military posts, provided he gave prior notification to, and was accompanied by, the British orderly officer stationed at Longwood. Apart from the question of his title, this requirement was to become perhaps the bitterest cause of dispute between Napoleon and the Governor and was to have serious consequences for his health. The only derogation from his official instructions that Cockburn saw fit to allow was to order the sentries not to move in on the house until 9pm in order, during the warmer season, to allow the residents to enjoy the cooler air of the evening out of doors in the garden if they so wished.

As if these restrictions within the island were not enough, the Admiral, who was technically the Commander in Chief of the South Atlantic

Station, and would normally have been resident at the Cape, had under his command a small naval squadron consisting of his own flagship, the *Northumberland*, two frigates (initially the *Newcastle* and the *Orante*) and two armed brigs. Two of these vessels were perpetually on duty sailing round the island in opposite directions, with orders to prevent any unauthorized vessel entering St Helena waters. Every vessel, except British warships, was accompanied until it was either allowed to anchor or sent away. Signal posts on high ground on the island were positioned so that they could see ships at sea at twenty-four leagues' distance. In addition no embarkation or disembarkation at Jamestown was allowed between sunset and 10am, all fishing boats were numbered and anchored at sunset and the portcullis gate barring entry from the waterfront into the town was lowered each evening.

When Napoleon was shown a copy of these naval restrictions he was furious and this further contributed to his disenchantment with Cockburn. As a additional extreme safeguard, small naval forces were sent to occupy and annex the even less accessible volcanic islands of Tristan da Cunha and Ascension (both of which the present Governor of St Helena is still responsible for), in order to prevent any possibility of either of them being used as the base for a rescue attempt to release Napoleon.[3]

These then were the security dispositions already in place to greet Sir Hudson Lowe when he arrived to take up his command. Although there were to be some relatively minor modifications later, in both directions, and protracted and heated arguments about the nature of such modifications (Napoleon never ceased accusing Hudson Lowe of tightening the restrictions imposed by Cockburn), in essence they remained in force until Napoleon's death. Any casual observer might be forgiven for thinking, as Charles Darwin did, that, in view of the natural defences of the island, and its isolation, there was more than a small element of using a sledge hammer to crack a nut about them, but the British Government was paranoid about preventing Napoleon from escaping this time, and the possibility of escape and rescue plots became a recurrent theme.

Hudson Lowe lost no time after arriving in establishing himself at Plantation House, the Governor's official residence, which was a handsome country mansion, built as a summer residence by the East India Company Governor, John Roberts, between 1708 and 1711. It is set in a fine open park, with carefully tended lawns and shrub, flower and vegetable beds, surrounded by a small forest of fine oaks, birches and assorted conifers. With a more equable climate than Longwood and less exposed to the prevailing trade winds, it enjoyed many of the advantages that Napoleon craved at Longwood. The public rooms were spacious and high-ceilinged, making them ideal for entertaining, and Lowe made further substantial improvements while he was there, in particular by roofing-in an inner courtyard to create a handsome library.

The house remains today largely as it was in Lowe's time and, although it still serves as the Governor's official residence, it can be visited with permission. The grounds are normally open to the public and lumbering along in them can still be found the oldest inhabitant of St Helena, the giant tortoise, Jonathan, which was originally brought from the Seychelles as a mature adult in 1882. Jonathan is said to be about 180 years of age, and so just misses the distinction of being the oldest still-living creature to have existed contemporaneously with Napoleon.

Lowe used Plantation House as his military headquarters, and his offices in the Castle down in Jamestown for the civil administration of the island. He commuted between them, normally going down to Jamestown each morning to receive a report on any events of note that had occurred during the previous evening. He tended to use the afternoons for visiting the troops and for tours of inspection of the defensive positions of the island.

To Lowe, for all his experience, including consorting with great figures like Blücher and Tsar Alexander, the prospect of confronting Napoleon, whom he had never previously met in person, must have been an incredibly daunting one. He must try to impose his authority on his prisoner from the start and he knew that failure to prevent Napoleon escaping would bring his career to a rapid and catastrophic end – he would certainly earn a place in history, but it would be for the wrong reasons and an ignominious one. He therefore decided, perhaps not without some trepidation, to assert his position at the earliest possible opportunity and to make it clear that he was the boss and would suffer no nonsense with his prisoners.

Accordingly he set off to make his first call on Napoleon at Longwood on the early morning of the day after his arrival.[4] He rode straight to Longwood, accompanied by Admiral Cockburn, Brigadier-General Bingham and several other officers of his suite, and demanded to be shown into Napoleon's presence. To his absolute astonishment he was told by General Montholon, who came out of the house to meet him, that the

Emperor was indisposed and could not see visitors. In any case, Montholon added, the Governor really ought to know that 9am was not a time when emperors normally receive callers. However, if the Governor wished to make an appointment to meet him he should do so through Grand Marshal General Bertrand in the proper way.

Lowe was, not surprisingly, angry and utterly amazed. It had not occurred to him that His Excellency the Governor and Commander in Chief of the island was required to seek through an intermediary the favour of an interview with one of his own prisoners. His abortive visit had something of the farcical nature of William McGonagall's famous failed attempt to call at Balmoral Castle on Queen Victoria, who turned out not to be at home.

The fuming Governor blamed the orderly officer at Longwood, Captain Thomas Poppleton of the 53rd regiment, for not having prepared the path properly for his visit. Napoleon, however, according to Marchand, said that he suspected that Admiral Cockburn had deliberately failed to brief Lowe on the protocol that should have been observed. In any case, in Napoleon's view, as an officer and gentleman Lowe should have known that emperors simply do not receive callers unannounced at 9am, and he was sure that Lowe would never have dared to take such a presumptuous liberty with his own superiors, such as Lord Keith or Lord St Vincent.

Outraged and angry as he was, and humiliated before his subordinates so early in his governorship, Lowe had no option but to grit his teeth, swallow his pride and accept the situation. But this did not prevent him stalking with long strides around the outside of Longwood, and even up to Napoleon's windows, from where the concealed Napoleon, playing his first game of hide-and-seek with the Governor, spied him through the shutters of his bedroom without being seen. Lowe then rode off in high dudgeon to Hutt's Gate, where he complained to General Bertrand about the treatment he had received. After some discussion Bertrand agreed to try to make an appointment for him to call on Napoleon at 2pm on the following day. As Marchand later recorded with some understatement in his journal, 'Le début de Sir Hudson Lowe dans son nouveau gouvernement n'était pas heureux' (The start that Sir Hudson Lowe made in his new administration was not exactly a happy one).[5]

On the next day, 17 April, Bertrand went to Plantation House in the morning where Lowe, still presumably seething with anger at his humiliation on the previous day, immediately gave him notice that, on instructions from London, he would require all the occupants of Longwood to sign a declaration that they would comply with the same restrictions as those imposed on Napoleon. This would show Bertrand that there would be no nonsense with the new regime. Napoleon was furious when Bertrand, returning to Longwood, reported this to him and this did not augur well for the first meeting with Lowe later in the day.

At 2pm Lowe, again accompanied by Cockburn and their respective staffs, duly arrived at Longwood House for this first meeting. However, this was marred by one of the unfortunate misunderstandings that became a feature of the Lowe–Napoleon story.

On arrival Lowe was shown through into the billiard room – or parlour, as it was still known then – and General Bertrand, who was in the salon talking to Napoleon, was advised of his presence. Bertrand came out through the door between the salon and the parlour and instructed the servant on duty, Noverazz, to let the Governor enter to where Napoleon was standing waiting. Noverazz, however, apparently interpreting his instructions too narrowly and literally, let Lowe in but quickly closed the door behind him, thinking that only the Governor was to be allowed to enter. At that moment Admiral Cockburn, who expected to be required formally to introduce his successor to Napoleon, was in conversation at the far end of the parlour, near the door, and happened at that moment to have turned his back away from the salon. He was thus excluded from the meeting with Napoleon. According to Marchand he felt extremely insulted and strode out of the house in high dudgeon, jumped on his horse and rode away.[6] He was never to see Napoleon again in person before he left the island in June. The incident seems to have been a genuine mistake and although Napoleon found it very amusing when told afterwards about it, he later asked Dr O'Meara to express his regrets to the Admiral.

After such an ill-omened start, which would have been comic if it was not so tragic, this crucial first meeting lasted only some twenty minutes and was largely spent by the two protagonists in sizing each other up. They mostly conversed in Italian and Napoleon did much of the talking. He asked Lowe about his Corsican background and other aspects of his military service, and made polite enquiries about his recently acquired wife. Lowe was cautious and said very little and nothing was given away on either side. The result was rather like a no-score draw, with neither side gaining or conceding a significant point. After Lowe had received Napoleon's agreement to present his senior officers (minus Cockburn) to him, he withdrew. Napoleon was not very complimentary about Lowe afterwards; he said that he reminded him of a Botany Bay galley slave or a Sicilian brigand ('Shire'). Nevertheless he admitted at the same time that 'il paraît poli; on ne peut pas juger un homme que d'après sa conduite pendant un certain temps' (he seems courteous, and one cannot judge a man except by his behaviour over a certain period).[7] For the moment, therefore, honours were roughly even and Napoleon still seemed to be prepared to give Lowe the benefit of the doubt.

For his part, Lowe, perhaps to work out his frustration at this first inconclusive meeting and the nonsense that preceded it, set in hand a review of the dispositions of his troops and the state of the various fortified posts.[8] He commissioned his engineer officers to conduct a complete survey of all of them, so that they could be repaired or strengthened as judged necessary. Also, against Cockburn's advice, he took a number of steps to strengthen the guard on Longwood, including reinforcing the post at Alarm House, where his Military Secretary, Colonel Wynyard, now lived, and increasing from sixteen to eighteen the number of sentries on duty directly around Longwood each night. In addition, as became his regular habit after each meeting with Napoleon, he dictated and fired off a long detailed dispatch to the Secretary of State, Lord Bathurst. 'Firing off' may not be a suitable description of a missive that could take up to two months to reach London, and to which a reply would not be received for a similar time, plus however long it took to consider it and draft a reply in Whitehall. It is worth noting, however, in fairness to Lowe, that in this first dispatch, which was mainly about security concerns, Lowe expressed the view that Longwood House was not suitable for someone of Napoleon's stature, and was much inferior to his own residence, Plantation House.

The second meeting between them took place about a fortnight later.[9] Once more the atmosphere was soured in advance by Lowe's insistence on transmitting through Bertrand the text of the declaration that the Longwood residents were to be required to sign – certifying that they remained with Napoleon of their own free will and, on pain of punishment, would submit to the same restrictions that were imposed on Napoleon himself. Napoleon, when shown this, found it utterly unjust, arbitrary and insulting, particularly as it referred to him as General Bonaparte, and he dictated an amended version, which referred to the appalling treatment that he maintained was being served out to the threatened signatories 'volant continuer de rester au service de l'Empereur Napoléon' (who wished to remain in the service of the Emperor Napoleon).[10]

Several fractious exchanges followed, during which Lowe, who refused to accept any reference in the text to 'the Emperor', visited Longwood again in person to try to coerce the signatories. He finally secured their signatures against a text that, though not in the precise terms that Bathurst had laid down, was in his view sufficiently close to it and one that he could live with. Bertrand, after much soul searching, was the last to sign. Despite his sense of outrage Napoleon was in a serious dilemma. On the one hand he detested the whole concept and terms of the declaration; but on the other he was terrified to lose any of his companions and tacitly left it to them in the last resort to reach their own decisions. The fact that they signed in the end was probably secretly a great relief to him.

To compound Lowe's discomfort, the 30 April encounter, for which the prospect was already prejudiced, was almost unbelievably also preceded by yet another farcical non-event. Somewhat like the situation before the first meeting, Hudson Lowe went to Longwood on 26 April, but Napoleon, playing hide-and-seek again, refused to see him either that day or on the following one. The meeting eventually took place on the afternoon of 30 April, when Lowe was ushered into Napoleon's small bedroom and found him in his dressing gown, reclining on a sofa and complaining of indisposition. Lowe seized on this to offer him the services of Dr Alexander Baxter, the senior military surgeon whom he had brought out with him as Deputy-Inspector of Hospitals in St Helena. But Napoleon would hear nothing of this and changed the subject. His position was that if he was to have another doctor it would have to be on his own terms and not someone nominated by the Governor, who would doubtless be asked to spy on him. He then launched into a fierce tirade against the terms of the 2 August 1815 Paris Convention signed by the allied powers, along with a series of bitter complaints about the treatment accorded to himself and his companions, and in particular against the document that they had been forced to sign. Lowe had difficulty in getting a word in edgeways and, in any case, realizing that Napoleon was trying to provoke him into losing his temper, chose to say very little. They parted on very strained terms. As Marchand described it: 'Ils se séparerent plus brouillés que jamais' (They parted in a greater state of misunderstanding than ever).[11]

After the meeting Napoleon spoke to Las Cases of Lowe's 'ignoble et sinistre figure' (base and sinister countenance).[12] The extent of his growing mistrust of Lowe is shown by a subsequent remarkable comment to Dr O'Meara that he would never even drink a cup of coffee if Lowe had been left alone with it in the room for a moment.[13] Again, no significant points were scored on either side, but the prospect for any sort of sympathetic understanding or cooperation between the two men in the future was now practically zero. In his biography of Napoleon based on Napoleon's letters, Malraux quotes him as saying that he and Lowe were now becoming 'comme deux béliers qui allaient s'encorner' (like two rams who were about to lock horns).[14] Napoleon's initial willingness to give the soldier Lowe a fair hearing had quickly been exhausted.

Both men then retired to their corners to consult their seconds and reflect on their encounter. For Napoleon, Lowe now began to personify all the evils perpetrated on him by the British Government. Lowe must have felt utterly frustrated and perplexed, and his own reaction was again to take further measures that were under his control, that is to tighten further the security screw. He accordingly informed Bertrand that the orderly officer at Longwood would be under strict instructions to report to him twice a day that he had actually seen Napoleon. Bertrand protested that this was news both to him and to Napoleon, and had not been in the original official instructions implemented by Admiral Cockburn. Lowe's riposte to this was that, to the best of his understanding, it had in fact been communicated to them on the *Northumberland* by Cockburn, so that there was nothing new or inconsistent in it. Lowe also reiterated the prohibitions on any communication between the residents of Longwood and traders and suppliers in Jamestown (i.e. for the most part with the official purveyor to Longwood, William Balcombe, Betsy's father) without his authority – a prohibition that, in practice, the captives continued easily to evade. Then occurred yet another of the succession of *bêtises*, which further poisoned the relationship between Napoleon and Lowe.

On 6 May 1816 a British squadron was due to arrive at St Helena on its way back to Britain from India. Among the passengers was the Countess of Loudoun, the wife of the Governor-General of India, Lord Moira. Lowe, who, to give him his due, entertained generously, decided to give a grand dinner in her honour at Plantation House and to invite Napoleon to it.[15] He accordingly sent on 11 May a formal written invitation via General

Bertrand, which requested 'General Bonaparte' to attend the dinner. When he was shown the invitation Napoleon was said not to know whether to laugh or cry. He regarded the form of address in the invitation as a direct insult. He knew also that if he attended he would have to be escorted from Longwood by an English officer and he was not prepared to submit to this. He therefore instructed Bertrand simply to ignore it and not to reply. His view was that if Lady Loudoun herself wished to see him she was perfectly at liberty to come to Longwood and, after calling on Mesdames Bertrand and Montholon, seek an audience with him. The affair festered on and Lowe professed himself shocked by Napoleon's ill manners in not replying to the invitation. The dinner duly went ahead without Napoleon and was apparently a great success, attended by all the military and civilian grandees of the island. It was, however, yet another bad omen for the third meeting between Lowe and Napoleon, which was to take place on 16 May.

It is not clear whether there was any deliberate malice aforethought in the drafting of Lowe's invitation, which in any case only followed instructions as to the mode of address of Napoleon, or whether it was simply an example of his clumsiness and lack of common sense. The latter is more likely as Lowe said afterwards that if he had appreciated Napoleon's sensitivity to being escorted by a British officer he would gladly have gone to Longwood to conduct him to the dinner himself. That also, however, betrays Lowe's naïvety and insensitivity, as it was probably the last thing that Napoleon would have accepted or wanted.

The third round on 16 May did nothing to improve the relationship, which was already almost shipwrecked by then. It is described by Jean-Pierre Fournier La Touraille as the 'point de rupture' (breaking point)[16] and by Jean Tulard as a 'réception orageuse' (stormy reception).[17] The main purpose of the visit on Lowe's part was to obtain Napoleon's views on the construction of a new and more suitable house for him, to be called Longwood New House, which the British proposed to build right next to Longwood. The materials for building the house were due to arrive shortly and it was important to know soon what Napoleon thought before designs were completed and work begun. Napoleon, however, simply did not want to know and absolutely refused to discuss the matter. Instead he launched once more into a series of bitter complaints about his treatment, and in particular the gross insult of addressing him as General Bonaparte in the Loudoun invitation. 'Je ne suis pas le Général Bonaparte,' he claimed, 'je suis l'Empereur Napoléon' (I am not General Bonaparte, I am the Emperor Napoleon).[18]

Lowe could make no progress whatsoever and was hard pressed this time to keep his temper. In the end he told Napoleon that if he was not prepared to discuss the matter he had come to raise with him he would go away. After further insults from Napoleon, in which he accused Lowe of having been sent out with orders to assassinate him, Lowe left the room and went off to Hutt's Gate to let off steam to General Bertrand. He described Napoleon as living in a world of make-believe and, on returning to his office, he dictated yet another long and detailed dispatch to Lord Bathurst, concluding that it was impossible to deal rationally with Napoleon, whose sole object now was to gain more freedom and increase his contacts with people who would be favourable to his cause. For his part, Napoleon admitted at dinner that evening that he had gone over the top with Lowe, but he asked Dr O'Meara to tell Lowe never to come and see him again.[19]

Such was the dramatic deterioration in the relationship after barely a month had passed. Napoleon's unwillingness to discuss the proposals for the new house was, however, understandable. Since a new house would take a long time to build from scratch, to engage in such discussion would imply that he was resigned to staying on St Helena for the long term, whereas he still entertained hopes that he would be allowed to return to Europe. He knew that there were many sympathizers in Parliament at Westminster, notably Lord Holland, a leading member of the opposition Whig Party, whose wife frequently sent Napoleon gifts of books and other items while he was at Longwood. Napoleon also detested the windswept and often cloud-covered location of Longwood and would never have agreed to a new house subject to the same climatic conditions on virtually the same spot.

The month of June brought new developments. On 17 June the frigate *Newcastle* arrived at St Helena with Cockburn's replacement, Rear-Admiral Sir Pulteney Malcolm. He was accompanied by his well-connected wife, Clementina, who was the daughter of the Hon. William Fullarton Elphinstone, a director of the East India Company, and a niece of Lord Keith, who was the one who had broken the news of the decision to send him to St Helena to Napoleon at Plymouth. This combination of aristocracy and connection with perhaps the most distinguished serving admiral in the Royal Navy was bound to appeal to Napoleon. The ship also brought a letter to Lowe from the ever-vigilant and powerful Lord Bathurst about

the need to reduce expenses at Longwood and a secret missive from Under
Secretary Sir Henry Bunbury about an intercepted letter to Napoleon
relating to the possible financing of an escape plot.[20] This intelligence must
have made Lowe even more nervous about the security arrangements on
the island.

The *Newcastle* also brought a less welcome form of human cargo in the
shape of the three allied Commissioners sent out by the Russian, Austrian
and newly restored French Governments in the exercise of their rights
under the August 1815 Paris Convention (the Prussians had sensibly
decided not to send one).[21] The Convention authorized each government
to dispatch a Commissioner to St Helena in order, without having any
responsibility for the actual safe-keeping of Napoleon, to assure themselves
of his continuing presence. The three nominated were: Count Alexandre
Antonovitch Ramsay de Balmain, aged thirty-seven, for Russia; Baron
Barthelémey de Stürmer, aged only twenty-seven, for Austria; and the
oldest, and as events soon showed, the most ridiculous, the fifty-eight-
year-old *ancien régime* aristocrat from France, Count Claude-Marin-Henri
de Montchenu.

Although the Commissioners were a cross that Lowe had to bear, they
had little if any influence on his policy and conduct towards Napoleon.
Nontheless they were a nuisance and in the way, and Lowe constantly
had to be on his guard against the possibility that they would be used by
Napoleon as intermediaries or channels for communication with Europe.
For their part the French at Longwood intrigued to gain their sympathy
and use them as a means of lobbying with the outside world (a hopeless
task in any case with the Bourbon Montchenu); Lowe on his side hoped
equally that they might prove to be a useful source of intelligence on what
Napoleon and his household were up to. In fact they found themselves in
a farcical 'Catch 22' situation. Napoleon refused to receive them in their
official capacity as Commissioners. To do so would have implied that he
accepted the validity of the Paris Convention, which had appointed them,
and which he always contested. He once explained in conversation with
Lady Malcolm that if he saw them in their official role as Commissioners
it would amount to acknowledging that he was a prisoner to their masters,
which he was not.[22] On the other hand, Lowe adamantly refused to allow
them to see Napoleon in a private capacity – that would have conceded to
Napoleon his point.

They therefore wandered onto the scene like three comic stooges in a pantomime, often creeping round the perimeter of Longwood, hoping to catch a glimpse of Napoleon or to bump into one of his senior colleagues. They were also regular social callers on the Bertrands and Montholons, but they never once came face to face with Napoleon. Lowe nevertheless treated them formally with proper respect and handled their frequent complaints with reasonable courtesy and patience. He also took the trouble after their arrival to see them into temporary lodgings until they could establish themselves more permanently. In private, however, he abused and condemned them as fools and rascals. It is somewhat ironic, therefore, that in April 1820 he gave his elder stepdaughter away in marriage to the most sensible of the Commissioners, the Russian, Count Balmain, who soon spirited her away back to the court in St Petersburg. Perhaps Lady Lowe was bedazzled by the prospect of having access herself to the tsarist court in due course. Napoleon particularly despised the French Commissioner, whom he regarded as an imbecile and a poor old fool.

Having suffered three rebuffs, and been put on the defensive, as if he were the prisoner and not the reverse, Hudson Lowe now had to find a plausible reason for calling on Napoleon once again. Napoleon's attitude towards him had made it amply clear that it was not good enough, even though he was the Governor, simply to turn up at Longwood and expect to be received. Fortunately the arrival of the new naval commander, Rear-Admiral Malcolm, provided a suitable pretext. Lowe sought leave to present him formally to Napoleon and a meeting at Longwood was set up for 3pm on 21 June.[23]

On this occasion Napoleon appeared to be in better spirits and, true to his admiration for the Royal Navy, took an immediate liking to Admiral Malcolm, who had had a distinguished fighting career against the French. Sensing that here was a potential ally against Lowe, he concentrated most of his attention on him and spoke highly about him afterwards. He thought him frank and open, 'une physionomie franche et ouverte,'[24] and told Dr O'Meara that he had never met someone of whom he had immediately formed such a good opinion as that fine soldier-like old man. He also expressed regret that Admiral Malcolm was not now to be in command of the island rather than Lowe. Poor Lowe, to whom Napoleon hardly addressed a direct word at the meeting, must have felt completely snubbed; he sensed immediately that, although Malcolm turned out on the whole to be a loyal colleague, there was a serious potential problem here. Before they took their leave Napoleon readily agreed that Malcolm should pay a further call on him to present his wife. This foreshadowed a series of meetings that Lady Malcolm recorded in her journal.

In spite of Napoleon's request to Dr O'Meara to ask Lowe not to come and see him again, a fifth meeting between Napoleon and Lowe took place on 16 July.[25] This turned out to be as acrimonious and unproductive as the previous ones. Again, the build-up to it had not been conducive to a good atmosphere. Lowe had published on the island, on 28 June, the text of the Parliamentary legislative authority for his powers in relation to the custody of Napoleon; and there had been a spat about the handing over to Lowe by the French Commissioner, Montchenu, of letters given to him in Europe by the mother of Madame Bertrand and by Las Cases' wife. Lowe was accused of having held them back. Lowe had also been agitating again about breaches of his ban on unauthorized communications with and from Longwood, especially with the Commissioners.

At least the 16 July meeting was a long one: it lasted for nearly two hours. Once more, however, it was dominated by Napoleon's familiar list of grievances. He refused to respond to Lowe's renewed and well-meaning attempt to discuss the question of improvements to Longwood and strongly attacked him for the terms of a letter of reproof that Lowe had recently sent to General Bertrand forbidding him to allow visitors to Longwood to meet Napoleon without Lowe's permission. He said that it was an insult to Bertrand, a proper and distinguished soldier who ranked well above Lowe in every respect, and who would have been justified in cutting Lowe's throat. He then returned to the old theme that Lowe was exceeding his instructions in imposing on him a stricter regime than that which had been introduced and applied by Admiral Cockburn. Lowe appears to have tried hard once more not to be provoked into losing his temper and he finally left the discussion and returned to Plantation House, where he dictated his usual long post-match report to Lord Bathurst. In it he again endorsed the plan to build a new and better house for Napoleon near Longwood, although by now he must have been convinced that Napoleon would simply have nothing to do with it. He also sought Bathurst's agreement to be more flexible on the daytime limits imposed on Napoleon, provided extra precautions were taken to maintain security during the night.

These events took place in the context of a frustrating and acrimonious dispute about expenses at Longwood. In brief, the British Government had stipulated, in effect imposing a cash limit, that the household's annual expenditure met by the Treasury should not exceed £8,000.[26] This figure was based on the (false, as it turned out) assumption that the numbers at Longwood would quickly decrease as Napoleon's companions began to desert him. Anything beyond that would have to be met by Napoleon out of his own funds. Lowe (whose own salary, which presumably covered entertainment and related expenses at Plantation House, was £12,000 a year) was pressed by Bathurst and even by the Chancellor of the Exchequer himself to insist that this limit was observed. The position was, however, virtually impossible. Before he left, Admiral Cockburn's last forecast had estimated that spending in 1816 would amount to between £16,000 and £18,000, and by July this figure had increased to £20,000. Lowe tried unsuccessfully to air the subject with Bertrand, who sheltered behind an alleged assurance from Cockburn that in practice the British Government would ensure that Longwood was adequately resourced. He refused to discuss the matter further and passed it over to Montholon, who similarly declined to reply to Lowe's representations.

In desperation Lowe presented himself at Longwood on 16 August to try to raise the subject with Napoleon himself.[27] He was told once again, however, that Napoleon was in the bath and could not see him. The bath proved to be a very useful excuse to Napoleon on this and many further occasions. Frustrated, Lowe charged off to Hutt's Gate to see Bertrand, but found him equally uncommunicative. The most he would say was that he would speak to Napoleon about it. Lowe was thus back to square one, although he made one more attempt – he returned to Longwood, where he was again refused a meeting because Napoleon was still in the bath.

Lowe finally, however, achieved the meeting he wanted with Napoleon on 18 August.[28] He was accompanied by the full retinue of Admiral Malcolm, Sir Thomas Reade, and his Aide de Camp, Major Gorrequer. It was by far the most violent and hostile of all their confrontations and took place in the garden, where the atmosphere must have been unpleasantly tense. Once more Napoleon ostentatiously ignored Lowe and addressed most of his remarks to Malcolm. He reverted to the theme of Lowe's allegedly insulting behaviour towards Bertrand whom he had treated as if he was one of his corporals. Unlike Lowe, he said, Bertrand was a distinguished general who had commanded armies in the field. By contrast Lowe had never commanded anything in battle other than Corsican deserters and Piedmontese and Neopolitan renegades. He also again accused Lowe of having been ordered to assassinate him.

After a further long litany of insults and complaints – not least the by now familiar charge that Lowe had exceeded his instructions by worsening the regime he had inherited from Cockburn – Napoleon finally turned to Lowe and told him that although he was nominally by rank a lieutenant-general, his behaviour was no better than that of a sentry or a headquarters company clerk. He was certainly not a proper Englishman. This time Lowe's patience snapped. The insults were too much. He could not contain himself further. He riposted to Napoleon that he was only doing his duty accord-ing to his orders and had not sought his present job. Napoleon replied that a public hangman was also only doing his job, but that did not mean that when the noose was around the victim's neck he had to like him. Lowe's reply to this was to say that Napoleon made him smile. Napoleon said that this was simply the smile of the torturer at the scream of his victim.

On this bitter and unedifying note Lowe disengaged and left the meeting. It is difficult to credit that it was the last face-to-face meeting between the two of them on the island, only four months after Lowe had arrived to take up his post. Five more years passed without the two protagonists meeting directly again. The next time Lowe saw Napoleon at close quarters was when he was lying on his deathbed.

After this final unpleasant meeting, as on a previous occasion, Napoleon admitted that he had been out of humour and gone too far and that it would have been better not to have spoken to Lowe as he had done.[29] However, it was a mark of his growing sense of impotence and frustration that he had not been able to contain himself. He could not bear to be subject to Lowe's control and to be able to do so little about it, particularly as during their meetings Lowe had, until this last occasion, generally retained his composure in contrast to his own loss of temper. This time he decided firmly that he would never receive Lowe again.

Napoleon followed up the meeting with a very long and detailed letter, signed by Montholon, rehearsing all his grievances for transmission to the British Government.[30] Lowe received it on 24 August and sent it on in the usual way to Bathurst with a point-by-point commentary on all the matters raised.[31] In view of the offensive treatment he had received from Napoleon,

Lowe's letter was remarkably moderate and restrained. In it Lowe said that he was still 'reluctant to adopt any measures which might be considered as proceeding from motives of personal resentment for the treatment I have myself endured'. He also added, 'In proportion as he (Napoleon) has endeavoured to provoke me to some act of violence towards him, I have used a corresponding effort to preserve my temper and to render his design abortive'. His letter was, as usual, excessively verbose, but his words hardly displayed the sentiments of a vindictive man. It did not deter him, however, from once more strengthening the surveillance around Longwood as he was (rightly) convinced that they had established an extensive clandestine network of contacts both within the island and, with the help of sympathetic visiting ships and sailors, with the world outside. It was better once again to be safe than sorry.

Lowe received reassurance for his diligence and the manner in which he had handled the last meeting with Napoleon in a dispatch from Lord Bathurst, which said that the Prince Regent entirely approved of his conduct. It also referred again to reports of attempts to mount a rescue operation for Napoleon, and cautioned that the 'utmost vigilance and precaution were necessary'.[32] Lowe's pleasure at the royal commendation must, however, have been tempered by the reminder that 'Big Brother' Bathurst and the Government were always watching him closely and scrutinizing his every action.

The rancorous series of face-to-face meetings between Lowe and Napoleon was now over – six meetings in only four months, with nearly five more long years of captivity to come. It set the tone for the extreme tenseness between the jailor and his captive from then onwards. Its essence has been brilliantly portrayed in the short one-act play, *La Dernière Salve*, published by Jean-Claude Brisville in 1995, which compresses the duel between the two men into three tense meetings, in which Lowe – unusually in French accounts of the drama – is almost allowed to give as good as he gets.

Henceforward the battle would have to be renewed indirectly, through intermediaries, although Lowe on frequent occasions went to Longwood in the hope of obtaining a further meeting with Napoleon by arrangement or by chance. In one sense Lowe held all the cards. He remained, as Governor and Commander in Chief, in charge of the island and its considerable military forces and he had the authority to deal with Napoleon and his companions as he thought fit. As he said to Dr O'Meara after the 18 August meeting, 'It is in my power to render him (Napoleon) much more uncomfortable than he is. If he continues his abuse, I shall make him feel his situation. He is a prisoner of war and I have a right to treat him, according to his conduct.'[33] But in reality he was just as much a prisoner on St Helena as Napoleon, and Napoleon in practice continued to make most of the running. Despite the promise by the Prime Minister and Lord Bathurst to review his appointment after three years – which never seems to have happened – Lowe had no idea how long his onerous tour of duty would last. As events turned out he had to wait until Napoleon's death in May 1821 before he was released. The ending of the direct contact with Napoleon during that period did not, however, in any way lessen the daily problems he still had to face.

EIGHT

NAPOLEON'S CONTINUING PROBLEMS

Napoleon's withdrawal from direct face-to-face confrontations with the Governor after August 1816 did not diminish the problems that each of them faced in trying to assert domination and moral authority over the other. In Napoleon's case the anger, bitterness and contempt he displayed at those meetings, and the wounding insults that he directed at Lowe, sometimes left him contrite – he regretted that he had lost his temper in a manner in which, he said, he would not have even treated a humble servant in his days of power at the Elysée, without at least apologizing afterwards. But the issues underlying those outbursts remained to be faced.

One of the most contentious issues that had not been resolved was that of the running expenses at Longwood. As noted earlier, Lowe had frequently tried to raise it with Napoleon and with both Bertrand and Montholon, but without eliciting any meaningful response. The British Government had laid down an annual cash limit of £8,000, but actual spending was running at more than twice that amount. Hudson Lowe, in what for him was a daring and unaccustomed departure from his instructions, had offered to go to £12,000 (his own annual salary as Governor). Napoleon, however, simply refused to discuss this on the grounds that trivial administrative matters like this were not an appropriate subject for discussion between great men like emperors and generals. This was a bit rich of him since, like the Duke of Wellington, much of his own success had been based on meticulous attention to small detail, both in relation to the welfare and supply of his armies and the management of the French Government's finances, and in less grand matters of domestic economy. Josephine, a notoriously big spender, sometimes complained that when Napoleon was at home she saw little of him because he spent so much time looking into the minutiae of household business, like the kitchen accounts at the Tuileries. During his time as sovereign of Elba he was not too grand to intervene directly in a range of relatively minor expenditure matters – a letter of 15 October 1814 to General Bertrand, for example, addressed in detail such matters as garden and stable costs, stores accounts and transport costs.[1] Costs at Longwood should not have been beneath his attention, but it was the principle, of course, and not the substance that stuck in his throat.

Although conditions at Longwood were in many respects squalid, the household maintained a high standard of living so far as their table was concerned. In addition to breakfast they had two main meals a day and Forsyth, in his 1853 history of Napoleon's stay on St Helena, claims that they consumed three to four times as much meat – which was particularly scarce and dear on the island (no-one was allowed to slaughter a cow without the Governor's express permission) – as any English family.[2] The British Government, through the official purveyor, William Balcombe, provided them liberally with all the basic commodities such as beef and chicken, eggs, cheese, milk, sugar, coffee, fruit and vegetables and the other essentials for a reasonable cuisine. The amount of wine that they were supplied with and consumed was astonishing. From the records it has been possible to establish that, for example, from 1 October to 31 December 1816, no less than 3,716 bottles of wine were delivered to Longwood, including 830 bottles of Bordeaux, 2,030 of wine from the Cape and 36 bottles of champagne.[3] The totals slipped a little in the next two quarters, to 3,336 and 3,252 respectively, but although there were plenty of sorrows to drown at Longwood, this was an extraordinary amount of wine to consume. There were only normally seven people dining at the high table, so to speak, plus any guests, and even the extended household – there were two separate tables for the senior servants – could not reasonably have imbibed so much. Reports that there was a thriving black market trade of sales at the back door of Longwood to thirsty soldiers and other local residents ring true.

Lowe's starting point with Napoleon was that if he wished to exceed his cash limit he was free to do so provided he met the excess from his own pocket. He knew that Napoleon still had substantial sources of finance available in Europe, and we saw earlier that before he left Malmaison for Rochefort he had deposited a large sum with his banker in Paris. Napoleon readily accepted this on condition that he could write to his banker confidentially about this in a sealed letter. We now have another absurd 'Catch 22' situation. Lowe would not agree to the transmission of any sealed letters, even allegedly purely on business matters, and insisted that they were sent under open seal through him. This in turn was unacceptable to Napoleon, who claimed the normal right of confidentiality in any communications with his banker, and the situation became a stalemate.

Napoleon's way through the impasse was a typical bleeding stumps ploy, familiar to any treasury official facing pleading against expenditure cuts. He instructed his staff to sell the family silver.[4] They were ordered to start breaking up the silver plate he had brought out with him and take it down for sale in the market in Jamestown, but not before General Montholon had taken care to select a sufficient amount of the good plate to continue to meet Napoleon's future dining needs. Cipriani, wielding an axe, fell to it with a will, but also removed the imperial insignia before taking it for sale in Jamestown. The purpose of Napoleon's ruse was obvious. It was designed to shame Lowe and the British Government before the world by showing that he was so deprived by them of the basic necessities of daily living that he even had to sell the very plate off his own table in order to survive. As Forsyth put it, it was a 'manoeuvre of Napoleon to create sympathy for himself and draw public odium on Sir Hudson Lowe.'[5]

The ruse worked, at least initially. The sale was a great success and immediately brought in more than £400, and the townspeople were duly shocked. Marchand reports Cipriani returning from Jamestown and saying of the townspeople at the sale: 'L'indignation et la honte se peignaient sur leur figure' (You could see the sense of indignation and shame painted on their faces).[6] Lowe knew that he had been outmanoeuvred and after the sale of the first lot he ordered that subsequent ones were not to be displayed for public sale. After this dramatic episode the argument rumbled on for some time until Lord Bathurst finally approved Lowe's offer to raise the annual limit to £12,000 – but not a penny more. To give Napoleon his due, despite his refusal to discuss the matter with Lowe, he did take some time to go over the accounts with Montholon and order some economies at Longwood. In practice, however, he was by this time able to communicate reasonably freely with Europe and to tap such additional financial resources as he needed.

As stated earlier, one of the assumptions underlying the original figure of £8,000 was the expectation that Napoleon's entourage would diminish as some of his staff could not bear the situation and asked to leave. This did not immediately happen and Lowe was accordingly instructed to reduce the Longwood establishment by four. Since Napoleon was now unwilling to receive him, Lowe had to send his senior staff officer, Sir Thomas Reade, to Longwood on 4 October 1816 to convey this order.[7] Reade duly went over and met Napoleon in the garden. Napoleon was shocked and disturbed by the news. His most deep-seated fear was that he would be progressively deserted by his companions and left on his own. On returning into the house he complained bitterly and emotionally to Las Cases that the Governor was determined to leave him with no-one around him.

The issue was quickly settled. Napoleon was powerless to prevent the expulsions happening. Reade was less hesitant than Lowe in demanding action. The four chosen by the Governor for expulsion were the servants Rousseau, Santini, one of the two Archambault brothers, and a somewhat strange figure, Captain Charles Piontkowski.[8] He had been a member of Napoleon's Polish guard on Elba, and had followed him to Rochefort, but had literally missed the boat there. After successfully persuading the British to allow him to follow Napoleon to St Helena he had arrived there at the end of December 1815 and had been admitted into Napoleon's household.

They were all sent away at the end of December 1816 and Marchand relates that their departure left those who remained in great fear that a similar fate might in due course overtake them also. The morale of the household was also further depressed by Lowe's insistence, on instructions from Bathurst, who had never been satisfied with Lowe's earlier concession on the wording of the text, that everyone should sign a new declaration in the terms originally put to them.

On this occasion, Lowe rode off to Longwood to interview them personally and make them sign the new statement. He did so by the simple and brutal means of making it quite clear that anyone who refused to do so would be sent off to the Cape within twenty-four hours. Napoleon, who was, as before, torn between fundamental opposition in principle to the terms of the declaration and the desperate wish not to lose any more members of his household, could only sit a powerless spectator in his own room. In the event everyone signed except for Santini, who was to be expelled anyway. When Napoleon learned this he said that he understood their situation and interpreted it as a sign of their continuing loyalty to him. In Marchand's words, 'Il y vit un nouveau témoignage de notre attachement' (He saw in it a new proof of our attachment to him).[9]

One of the principal causes of Napoleon's objection to the terms of the declaration was that it referred to him as General Bonaparte and denied him his imperial title. This issue was, in the judgement of Lord Rosebery, 'not merely the source of half the troubles of the captivity, but it operated as an almost absolute bar to intercourse and as an absolute veto on what might have been an amicable discussion of other grievances.'[10] Although it seems unlikely that even if this issue had been removed there would ever have been much amicable intercourse between Napoleon and his jailor, so much did Napoleon come to detest him, it certainly added a high dose of extra poison to the relationship. The retention of the title 'Emperor' was fundamental to Napoleon's battle to maintain his status and dignity. After all, he had been recognized as Emperor by almost every power in Europe, and crowned as such by Pope Pius VII in the famous ceremony in Notre Dame in December 1804 – although he had in the event, in order to demonstrate his independence of the Catholic Church, placed the crown on his own head with the Pope, as it were, watching idly by.

When Napoleon had first come into British hands it had been decided by the British Government that he should be known as General Bonaparte and not the Emperor Napoleon and treated with the same formality and protocol as a British general not in full-time employment. Unlike most of the continental European powers, the British Government had never formally accepted him as Emperor of the French, although when he was exiled to Elba, of which he was the sovereign, he had been allowed to retain the title of Emperor, and the British representative on the island, Sir Neil Campbell, officially signed documents in which Napoleon was designated as 'Sa Majesté l'Empereur'.

This decision led to both bitterness and farce. For example, letters sent to the Governor from Longwood referring to 'His Majesty the Emperor' were returned on the grounds that the Governor was not aware of the existence of any emperor on the island. Equally, letters from the Governor addressed to General Bonaparte were sent back on the grounds that no person of that title was known at that address. On the famous occasion in May 1816 when Lowe, soon after his arrival, tactlessly sent the invitation to 'General Bonaparte' to attend a dinner at Plantation House in honour of Countess Loudoun, Napoleon, with a rare flash of perhaps grim humour, instructed Bertrand to return it with the words, 'Send this card to General Bonaparte; the last I heard of him was at the Pyramids or Mount Tabor.'[11] There were also numerous silly disputes about packages or other articles sent to or from Longwood that were rejected, returned or confiscated because the imperial insignia appeared somewhere on them.

Lowe was clearly embarrassed by this issue and on occasions tried to find a compromise. At their later meetings he had begun to fudge the question by addressing Napoleon simply as Monsieur rather than General, and he subsequently started to avoid the word 'General' altogether and refer to him in correspondence without any title, as plain Napoleon Bonaparte. Napoleon at one time also curiously floated the idea of using as a pseudonym the name of a Colonel Meuron, a fellow officer who had been killed at his side many years previously at the battle of Arcola, where Napoleon had first made an impact on public and political opinion in Paris.[12] It was an idea he had earlier put forward for use if he had been allowed to settle down in England as a quiet-living country gentleman who had renounced any future involvement in politics. However, this nonsensical idea came to nothing and the issue festered on. Poor Lowe had little room for manoeuvre. It seems obvious that he would have liked a way out, if only for a quieter life. But in June 1817, for example, he was again reminded by Lord Bathurst that he should not accept any letters referring to the Emperor.

Although Montholon, in discussing the problem later with Lowe, admitted that it was 'enfantillage' (childishness) to give the title of Emperor to someone who no longer had a throne, Napoleon's wish to cling on to the last vestiges of his imperial status is understandable, if perhaps a little pathetic. It symbolized the very essence of his outrage at his treatment by the British. He told Dr O'Meara that he retained the title 'parce que j'ai abdiqué le trône de France mais non le titre de l'Empereur. Je ne m'appelle pas Empereur de France, mais l'Empereur Napoléon' (because I have abdicated the throne of France but not the title of Emperor. I do not call myself Emperor of France, but the Emperor Napoleon).[13] His deepest resentment, however, was at having to accept the title of General from Lowe. Again, he told O'Meara on another occasion that he was not ashamed of the title of General, but he would not receive it from Lowe. Indeed, he went further in his general contempt for Lowe's treatment of him by saying that he was angrier at being placed in the hands of Lowe than in being sent to St Helena.

Although there was not the exodus from Longwood that the British had hoped for, Napoleon's dread of being deserted began to have some justification. Shortly after the expulsion by Lowe of the four servants, Napoleon's trusted amanuensis, Las Cases, was also expelled in dramatic circumstances.[14] Napoleon had just finished an interview with Admiral Malcolm at Longwood on 25 November 1816 and had returned to the salon where he called for Las Cases. As Marchand was going out through the garden, hoping to profit from an hour or two of freedom while Napoleon was closeted inside with Las Cases, he saw Lowe approaching the house accompanied by all the top brass of his staff, including Sir Thomas Reade, Major Gorrequer, the Commissioner of Police (in civilian dress) and two mounted dragoons. Turning back on his tracks he was surprised a short time later to see the cavalcade emerging from the house with Las Cases and taking him away in the direction of town. Marchand rushed into the house to alert Napoleon to what was happening and Napoleon was just in time to look through a window and see Las Cases being taken off towards Hutt's Gate.

What had happened was that, while Lowe waited outside, Reade and the others had gone into the house in search of Las Cases. When they could not find him in his own rooms, and heard that he was in the salon with Napoleon, they sent Ali in to ask him to come out to them. Napoleon, despite not knowing what it was about, somewhat surprisingly agreed that he could go out but asked him to come back soon. He never saw him again. As soon as Las Cases emerged he was arrested and taken away.

The precise circumstances and background to the arrest are still a mystery. There is evidence that Las Cases had volunteered to use a mixed-race servant to take a message to Europe to Napoleon's brother, Lucien, setting out the disgraceful conditions of his detention, but that Napoleon had dissuaded him from pursuing the project. Undeterred, however, Las Cases had persisted in writing a secret letter that was copied by his son onto a small piece of silk and concealed in the clothing of the same servant who was to take it to Europe. Somehow, 'soit par indiscretion, soit par trahison' (either by indiscretion or by treachery),[15] as Marchand put it, the Governor got wind of the plot, ordered Las Cases' arrest and seized the incriminating document. The hapless servant who was to be the carrier was shipped off in short order to Ascension Island.

Napoleon, taken completely by surprise, was outraged by Lowe's action. Of Lowe's conduct, he said: 'Il me parut voir les anthropophages des îles de la Mer de Midi, qui dansent autour de leurs victimes avant de les dévorer' (It looked to me like cannibals of the South Sea Islands dancing round their victims before devouring them).[16] The next day he sent Bertrand to the Governor to protest and find out the reasons for the arrest. Lowe simply replied that he regretted it but had been obliged to carry out his orders, since it was not the first time Las Cases had been involved in clandestine correspondence and he was well aware of the punishment if he was caught.

Las Cases and his son, who was allowed to join him, were housed at first in a cottage outside the Longwood boundary, and a few days later at Rose Cottage, further away. He had taken with him a good deal of the dictation he had taken from Napoleon, including that on his Italian campaigns, together with some of his own journals and personal documents. There was some argument about which documents properly belonged to Las Cases and which to Napoleon, but after carefully scrutinizing them for any possible security breaches Lowe handed many of them back to General Bertrand. Napoleon, wishing to see Las Cases back at Longwood, sent him a long and very affectionate letter, which included the following – 'Votre conduite à St Hélène a été, comme votre vie, honorable et sans tache. J'aime à vous le dire' (Your conduct on St Helena has been, like your life, honourable and without a stain. I want you to know this).[17] The letter also contained for the record the usual long complaints about the disgraceful treatment they were receiving from Lowe, who was described as 'cet homme hypocrite et méchant, que les vrais Anglais désavouerant pour Breton' (this hypocritical and unpleasant man, whom true Englishmen would not judge worthy of being British).

The letter from Napoleon led to another of the absurdities arising from Lowe's excessively petty and punctilious application of the restrictions. It was closed with the imperial seal. The orderly officer, Captain Poppleton, to whom it was given to transmit to Las Cases, gave it to Lowe instead, in accordance with his standing instructions. Lowe sent it back to Napoleon on the grounds that he could not accept sealed letters. On this occasion Napoleon swallowed his pride and broke the seal and the letter found its way to Las Cases.[18]

Between then and his deportation Las Cases showed no signs of wishing to return to Longwood to bid Napoleon farewell, despite agreement by Lowe that he could go there on condition that he then returned. Indeed some reports say that he actually asked Lowe to speed up his departure from the island. In a final meeting with Bertrand and Gourgaud, who came to see him in Jamestown, he said he thought he would serve Napoleon better by returning to Europe and publicizing his plight than by staying on St Helena. This was a clever line to take in order to justify his decision. He also returned to Bertrand the valuable diamond necklace, which had been given to Napoleon by his daughter-in-law, Hortense, at Malmaison and entrusted by him to Las Cases to bring to St Helena. Napoleon subsequently left it to Marchand in his will.

Napoleon genuinely missed Las Cases. He valued his company and his literary and linguistic expertise. He said of him that he was the only one who could speak English well, or explain it to his satisfaction, and that without him he could no longer read the English newspapers. He was also beginning to be concerned about being left by his companions. He said ruefully to Marchand that if his captivity lasted for a long time, 'les Anglais pourront bien n'avoir plus à garder que nous deux' (the English could well end up with only the two of us to guard).[19] But there is no evidence that Las Cases regretted his departure, and it may well be that he connived with Lowe in his arrest and deportation. Indeed he told Lowe that he did not want to return to Longwood and described life there in lurid terms. When he finally left on the sloop *Griffon* for the Cape it is perhaps significant that Lowe, of whom he now had kinder things to say, gave him handsome letters of introduction for various friends and contacts there. Gourgaud's earlier comment that Las Cases had only gone to St Helena to write a book surely had a good deal of truth in it. In 1823 Las Cases published the *Mémorial*, which became the *locus classicus* for Napoleon's early period on St Helena, and he made a small fortune out of it.

Las Cases' departure left the field freer for Gourgaud and Montholon. This was no doubt welcome to them and Napoleon now spent more time with them. It might have been expected that with fewer prima donnas to look after, Napoleon would have had an easier time. However, the ever sensitive, restless and anxious Gourgaud soon spoilt that and was the next to go. He began to be jealous of Montholon's relationship with Napoleon and became more and more irritable. He began to quarrel openly with Napoleon, answering him back in a manner that would have had him removed immediately for insubordination in Napoleon's heyday. Napoleon was normally absolutely insistent on the correct form of address when speaking to him. Ali was, for example, once given a very rough reprimand and a kick in the backside for daring to address him in a careless moment with the more familiar 'vous' instead of 'Your Majesty'.[20] Gourgaud was, however, given a little more licence. His jealousy of Montholon was clearly the dominant factor in his conduct, but boredom – the word appears time and time again in his diaries – combined with the claustrophobic atmosphere of Longwood, its unpleasant physical conditions and the absence of his own female companion all played their part. His health too was probably a genuine problem, whether for physical, or psychosomatic reasons.

Matters came to a head in July 1817 when he challenged Montholon to a duel – a ridiculous gesture, which Napoleon soon intervened to prevent.[21] In the end Napoleon could stand his petulance no longer and suggested he should seek a return to Europe. The Governor readily agreed to this and on 13 January Gourgaud left Longwood and reported to Plantation House. He was then lodged with Lieutenant-Colonel Basil Jackson, the engineer officer whom Lowe had brought out and made responsible for supervising the repairs to Longwood, the building of Bertrand's cottage, and the planning and construction of the proposed New Longwood House. Jackson was instructed not to let Gourgaud out of his sight until he left the island.

It was a month before a suitable East India Company vessel arrived to take Gourgaud to Europe and Marchand says that 'ses souffrances de corps et de l'esprit durent être affreuses pendant ce long mois sans pouvoir communiquer avec Longwood' (his suffering of both body and spirit must have been appalling during this long month when he was unable to communicate with Longwood).[22] However, it is doubtful whether at this stage the tortured and erratic Gourgaud really wished to communicate with them. He talked freely to Hudson Lowe – sometimes disparagingly of Napoleon. When he first approached Lowe to ask to be repatriated he told him that he could no longer live at Longwood, where he had been treated like a dog. He wanted out, and claimed that there had never been any difficulty, despite all Lowe's precautions, in sending messages to Britain and the rest of Europe. In one revealing comment, assuming it was genuine and not just said to ingratiate himself with Lowe, he said that even if an angel had been sent out to govern St Helena, it would have been just the same.[23]

The loss of Gourgaud was two-edged for Napoleon. In one respect it got rid of the turbulent priest who was causing such ructions in the household. On the other, it brought nearer the spectacle of desertion and isolation. It therefore served Napoleon well to represent Gourgaud's departure as due to health problems. The truth, however, is that Gourgaud simply could not tolerate any longer the boredom, deprivation and rigours of the closeted life they had to lead, and his naturally jealous temperament was tortured by the thought that anyone else could take precedence over him in Napoleon's affections.

Gourgaud's departure in turn put more responsibility and pressure on Montholon, especially since the faithful Bertrand did not live on the job in Longwood House. This was perhaps just as well as Bertrand and Montholon were never on really good terms. However, the Montholon relationship was itself complicated by the presence in the house of his wife, Albine, who became the next to leave, with her children, in July 1819.

Napoleon's approach towards women was fairly representative of general male attitudes of his time. Although he introduced some progressive, if limited, educational advances for females, whose academic education would largely stop at what we would call secondary level, his personal approach to sex and women was fairly crude. For him women were tools and there primarily to be at men's disposal. He is alleged to have once said 'J'ai mes saisons, comme les chiens. Une femme! Une femme! Tout de suite! Qu'on m'amène une femme' (I have my seasons, like dogs. A woman! A woman!

Quickly, someone bring me a woman!).[24] Another interesting, though more trivial, example of his attitude was a dismissive aside recorded by Bertrand in February 1821 that: 'women's clothes are a quite ruinous expense and a very bad investment. It is enough for a woman to be clean and decently garbed.'[25]

On St Helena he was starved of female company of his own. After his defeat in 1814 and exile to Elba, his second wife, the Empress Marie-Louise, and his infant son, the King of Rome, had been taken back to stay with her father, the Emperor Francis II, in Vienna and prevented from joining Napoleon. He had not now seen them for nearly two years. By contrast, two of his senior colleagues, Bertrand and Montholon, were married and had their wives with them, and his valet, Ali, slept with and eventually married the Bertrand children's governess, Mary Hill. In addition, another valet, Noverazz, married Madame de Montholon's maid; one of the two Archambault brothers had a mistress, Mary Foss; and Gentilini, a handsome footman from Elba, seduced several soldiers' wives. It was said that Montholon even complained about the noise made at Longwood by fornicating servants, soldiers and sailors and for this reason, to Napoleon's great anger, asked Lowe to increase the number of sentries round the house. Even the single Gourgaud had his amorous aspirations. He fell in love with Miss Wilks, the daughter of the popular Colonel Wilks, the Governor of the island when they arrived there, but this was not reciprocated and he is said to have uttered a despairing 'Adieu, Laure', when she sailed away, to be married in due course to General Sir John Buchan, and to live to the age of ninety-one.

Napoleon thus became increasingly sexually frustrated. Although there were from time to time disparaging rumours in circulation about his actual potency, he was a man of strong sexual demands and had played the field to the full during his earlier years. Although a slow starter, and shy with women as a young, thin, empty-pocketed and not very attractive artillery officer, he had a first sexual encounter with a young prostitute in the Palais Royal in Paris at the age of eighteen. Thereafter he was not slow in acquiring mistresses as his own reputation and career blossomed.[26] In conversation with Bertrand he admitted to seven mistresses but that is probably an understatement. His early mistresses included Eugénie Désiré, the first real love of his life, with whom he had a long and passionate affair, and in 1798, during the Egyptian campaign, he first seduced Pauline

Fourès, the wife of a young lieutenant of the 22nd dragoons, whom he conveniently dispatched on a far away mission, and then took to his bed Zenab, the beautiful young daughter of a sheikh. She became known as the 'General's Egyptian', but after Napoleon deserted his army in August 1799 she was executed for her relationship with him.

Back in Paris his most notable mistress was the famous Italian operatic soprano, Giuseppina Grassini, known as 'La chanteuse de l'Empereur', who, by a coincidental turn of fortune, became the mistress of the Duke of Wellington when in 1814 he was serving as British Ambassador in Paris. She was followed into Napoleon's bed by Marguerite-Josephine Weimer, a big, buxom and beautiful actress, whose stage name was 'Mademoiselle George' and who also was taken over by Wellington. Many years later, when asked to compare the two great generals' performances, she is reported to have said that 'Monsieur le Duc était de beaucoup le plus fort' (The Duke was much the more potent).[27] Napoleon's favourite and most constant mistress, however, was the Polish Countess, Marie Walewska, who was married to a much older man when he met her in Warsaw in 1806. He went to great lengths to attract and seduce her and she had a son by him, Alexandre Walewski – one of the two illegitimate children to which he admitted – who later became French Ambassador to London and Foreign Minister under the Second Empire. Marie was genuinely attached to him, as he to her, and was the only one of his paramours to visit him on Elba, where she stayed for twelve days.

The great love of his life, however, was always Josephine, whom he had married, initially for financial and career purposes, in 1796, and divorced in December 1809 because she could not give him a male heir to found a dynasty. Josephine, who was six years older than Napoleon, was a Creole from Martinique. Her real name was Marie-Josèphe Rose Tascher de La Pagerie, but she was soon called Josephine by Napoleon. She had become the mistress of the powerful Paul Barras, the leading member of the ruling Convention, who was probably tiring of her and happy to pass her on to his rising young protégé, General Bonaparte. She had two children, Hortense and Eugène, by her first husband, Alexandre de Beauharnais, an aristocrat who had been guillotined during the Revolution.

Anyone who has read any of the torrid and passionate correspondence between Napoleon and Josephine will know what a turbulent relationship it was. They both cheated on each other regularly, but each knew what the other was up to and reconciliation always followed, usually in bed. He was utterly besotted with her and once said to Bertrand: 'I really loved her, although I had no respect for her, as she was far too great a liar. But she had something, I don't know what, that attracted me. She was a real woman and had the sweetest little arse in the world, on which could be found the three Islets of Martinique.'[28] The image and memory of Josephine always haunted him and he reminisced frequently about her at Longwood. He was deeply distressed when informed of her death at Malmaison in 1814 when he was on Elba, and during the few days he spent at Malmaison before his flight to Rochefort in July 1815 he spent hours wandering and talking about her with her daughter, Hortense, in the gardens amid the flowers that Josephine had so loved and tended.

His lasting love for Josephine did not, however, mean that he did not develop a sincere respect and affection for Marie-Louise, whom he had married in April 1810 for dynastic reasons. He once said to Bertrand, 'I had much more respect for Marie-Louise, though I loved her perhaps somewhat less than I loved Josephine.'[29] The young and inexperienced bride, who had had little say in the matter, was terrified at being betrothed to the ogre of Europe whom she knew only by portrait and reputation. So far as Napoleon was concerned her primary role was to give him a male heir and he lost no time in introducing her to sex for the first time (according to him she liked it so much she asked for more, but he would say that, wouldn't he?). She duly did her duty in March 1811 by producing a son, the future King of Rome, after a particularly long and agonizing labour. Touchingly, at a crucial stage during labour, when it was thought that the mother and child could not both survive, Napoleon, on being asked to make a choice, told the doctor to save the mother.[30]

A real affection on both sides developed between them but after Napoleon was exiled to Elba and she was detained in Vienna he never saw her again, and this separation should be remembered when judging his behaviour and state of mind on St Helena. He knew that his wife was being alienated from him – she was assigned a handsome Austrian army officer escort, who soon became her lover – and that the future for his precious son was uncertain, but he could do absolutely nothing about it. His longing for his son was primarily his wish to perpetuate a Napoleonic dynasty, but there was genuine paternal affection too. He desperately wanted contact with them and until he died he kept portraits of them and a bust of the young boy in his small, cramped and damp room at Longwood. Ali comments on how much better Napoleon would have been if he had had his son with him.

On St Helena Napoleon had limited outlet for his sexual frustration. During the early weeks at the Briars he had had fun playing with the attractive and precocious adolescent, Betsy Balcombe, but although the relationship may have had sexual undertones it was probably no more than light-hearted relief after the tedium of the journey on the *Northumberland* and the prospect of the harsh realities of the life at Longwood to come. There are stories that in the early days at Longwood he also took a fancy to a pretty farmer's daughter of seventeen who lived in a quiet glen that he renamed the Valley of the Nymph. Dr William Warden – one of the surgeons on board the *Northumberland* who spent some time with Napoleon both on the ship and afterwards on St Helena, but whose self-important memoirs are probably the least reliable of all – tells how Napoleon often visited the farm until her relatives grew concerned and ordered her to stay out of the way when he visited.[31] He had also noted what a keen eye Napoleon had for pretty English girls on the sightseeing boats when they were anchored at Plymouth. There are also stories that in the early days at Longwood Napoleon induced into his bed Esther Vesy, a seventeen-year-old mixed-race girl employed as a nurse by the Montholons, and that, although Marchand offered to marry her, he refused this and ordered her to be removed from Longwood when she became pregnant in October 1816. She had a son, named James-Octave, in 1817, who was said to resemble Napoleon, and the widespread belief on the island was that Napoleon was his father.[32]

The only women at his own level with whom he had regular close contact were the wives of the two generals, Bertrand and Montholon. Fanny (Françoise-Elizabeth) Bertrand was the daughter of an Irish refugee, General Arthur Dillon, who joined the French army, rose to become Commander in Chief of the Army of the Ardennes and subsequently a member of the National Assembly, but fell foul of the Revolutionary authorities and was guillotined in 1794. Although a pamphlet ascribed to one Theodore Hook, who visited St Helena in November 1818, described her as 'long and lanky, and sallow and shapeless', though 'somewhat interesting,'[33] she is generally agreed to have been an elegant, proud, aristocratic-looking and certainly independent-minded woman who probably gave up more than anyone else in following her husband to St Helena. For example, an Eng-lish lady who met her on St Helena said that she was:

> a most engaging fascinating woman ... She spoke our language with a
> perfect fluency but with a slight French accent. Her figure was extremely
> tall and commanding: a slight elegant bend took from her height and
> added to her interesting appearance. Her eyes were black and sparkling,
> soft and animated: her deportment that of a young Queen, accustomed to
> command admiration.[34]

She was already related distantly to the imperial family as her mother was a cousin of Josephine. She had enjoyed a high social life in Paris as wife of the Grand Marshal of Napoleon's court – whose marriage had in fact been arranged by Napoleon – and the very last thing she wanted to do was to be exiled thousands of miles from anywhere and entirely deprived of the society she was used to. But after her dramatic protest at Plymouth, she stoically followed her husband and the call of duty.

Napoleon's relationship with her was not an easy one. To Napoleon's great irritation she insisted on living separately from Longwood and, with three children to look after, and the birth of another child on the island, she had plenty of good reasons for not attending at Longwood when Napoleon wanted her. Dr James Verling, the surgeon to the Royal Artillery contingent on St Helena, who, as their personal doctor, often visited Madame Bertrand and her children at home and was obviously on intimate terms with the Bertrand household, describes in his diaries her frequent illnesses. Although he refers disparagingly to her 'chimerical complaints,'[35] she had at least two miscarriages, and frequent vaginal discharges, so that not all her illnesses were imaginary or psychosomatic.

Her refusal to be at his beck and call annoyed Napoleon enormously. Whether it was a case of genuine sexual attraction, or the fact that her independent attitude simply made her a greater challenge and offended his masculine ego, there is no doubt that Napoleon tried hard to seduce her. There is plenty of evidence for this, not least in some of the remarkably frank and offensive admissions by Napoleon recorded in Bertrand's own memoirs. He once, shortly before he died, told Bertrand some abusive stories about his wife and said that he resented her refusal to become his mistress.[36] He also later taunted Bertrand with the unlikely claim that Fanny had become the mistress of his young Corsican doctor, Antommarchi. Bertrand does not tell us whether he responded to this as any insulted husband should have done. Napoleon, no doubt frustrated by Fanny Bertrand's refusal to yield to him, also told Bertrand during this period that Albine de Montholon had been cleverer than his wife, who had not known where her best interests lay, and that he was angry with her because for six years she had not played the role at Longwood that she should have done.[37]

When Napoleon was dying in April 1821 he also told Montholon, who later reported it back to Fanny Bertrand, that the reason he had declined to see her for many weeks was because he wanted to teach her a lesson for refusing to become his mistress. Finally, however, close to his death, he relented and allowed her to visit him, but only on the first occasion for about half an hour. Thereafter she was allowed to see him again daily. There is also an amusing incident recounted by Dr Warden, of when he was out for a ride in Napoleon's carriage with Fanny Bertrand and Napoleon some months previously. Napoleon put his arm round her and said in the little bit of English he knew, 'This is my mistress.'[38] It took some time for Dr Warden to explain to Napoleon that the word 'mistress' was perhaps not the appropriate term to use, whereupon he replied that he was sorry and really meant to say 'My friend, my friend'. Bertrand, who was also present, is said to have laughed, but perhaps rather grimly through his teeth. This may have been a Freudian slip – at any rate, Fanny Bertrand rejected his advances and he had to look elsewhere.

The other woman that Napoleon could set his sights on was the wife of General Montholon, Albine-Hélène de Montholon. She was thirty-six when they went to St Helena and a member of a royalist family ennobled by Louis XVI. Her father, unlike Fanny Bertrand's, had escaped the guillotine but had been arrested and imprisoned and died when she was only fifteen. She had been married twice before, the second time to a Swiss financier, Baron Roger, whom she divorced hurriedly to marry Montholon, who was then serving as French diplomatic representative in Würzburg. This incurred the great displeasure of Napoleon, who hypocritically did not approve of marriage with a woman who had been twice divorced, and in any case thought it was his job to arrange the marriages of his senior aides.

By all accounts Albine was a very attractive woman, with a sexy and coquettish manner. She played the piano and sang well and brought a breath of fresh air into the otherwise fusty atmosphere of Longwood. The relationship between her and Fanny Bertrand, however, deteriorated as time passed, and Dr Verling records that in January 1819 Madame Bertrand told him that Madame Montholon 'hated her and would not hesitate to say or do anything however false, however atrocious to injure her.'[39] This is more evidence, if any is needed, of the seething atmosphere of jealousy and unhappiness within the Longwood community.

The apartments allocated to the Montholon family at Longwood were very near to those of Napoleon and he was bound to come into close and frequent contact with her on a daily basis. The temptation must have been acute. She recorded her own account of that time in a secret journal that was only published for the first time in uncensored form in 2002, under the title *Journal Secret d'Albine de Montholon, Maîtresse de Napoléon à Sainte Hélène* (The Secret Journal of Albine de Montholon, Mistress of Napoleon on St Helena). The title, of course, begs the leading question. Reading the journal, however, it is very difficult not to believe that the star-struck and adoring language she uses is that of a lover. Even allowing for the tendency of diarists to exaggerate their own role, especially their relationships with famous people, the editor of the journal, a descendant of Albine de Montholon, is convinced that the diary shows that they went to bed together and talks about her 'passion sans pudeur' (shameless passion).[40]

Whatever the precise truth, and whether or not Napoleon was in love with her, it is clear that they developed a remarkably intimate relationship within the confines of Longwood and that she was besotted with him. They talked frequently, freely and frankly about a wide range of topics in a manner much less restrained and more challenging to Napoleon, in a flirtatious way, than anyone else would have dared to do. Marchand tells us how often Napoleon used to visit her in her bedroom, not only when she was ill or confined. In his own journal Dr Verling, who was her personal physician, relates that Baron Stürmer, the Austrian Commissioner, once said to him 'Madame Montholon was able to triumph over her rivals and climb into the imperial bed.' Bertrand also recalls in his memoirs remarks related to him by his wife in March 1821, which were clearly intended to insinuate that little Napoléone-Joséphine de Montholon, born at Longwood on 18 June 1818, was Napoleon's child.[41] There is no conclusive proof of this but there is at least a reasonable presumption that the child was Napoleon's. Sadly the child died in Brussels, where she was buried, shortly after Madame Montholon returned with her to Europe.

The relationship caused tension and friction among the other inmates at Longwood. Gourgaud in particular detested Albine, thought she was a whore and spoke openly of her as being Napoleon's mistress. He criticized Napoleon to his face for his relationship with her and Napoleon, suspecting that it was simply jealousy on Gourgaud's part, reacted sharply. It also further soured the already strained relationship with Fanny Bertrand, whom Dr Verling records as saying to him in October 1818 that the influence General Montholon now possessed with Napoleon was due to the complaisance of his wife; that the new child did not resemble him; and that Gourgaud had openly declared it was Napoleon's. Fanny Bertrand went on to add that for her part she could have been Napoleon's mistress many years back if she had chosen to be so.[42] Verling had, however, the decency to note also that this 'extraordinary conversation' followed a period of illness and mental anxiety on the part of Fanny Bertrand, 'whose mind is perpetually agitated by female jealousy'. He also later commented, however, that Albine de Montholon hated Fanny Bertrand.[43]

The outcome was another sad one for Napoleon. After the birth of Albine's second child on the island she became progressively less well and Dr Verling advised that she ought to move away to a more suitable climate. Napoleon was consulted and reluctantly agreed to her departure, which, Marchand says, 'allait priver l'Empereur d'une personne à laquelle il attachait du prix et sa vie en société allait être bouleversée' (would deprive the Emperor of a person on whom he placed great value and cause great upset to his social life).[44] When the final farewells before her departure came on 2 July 1819 they were emotional and tearful. Marchand claimed that Napoleon wept for her, perhaps for the first time in his life, but he was probably being tactful as Napoleon's immediate reaction after that was to rush off for yet another hot bath (perhaps he should have taken a cold one). To give him credit he did tell Montholon that it was wrong of him to let his wife and children go back without him. But he must have been mightily relieved that Montholon promised to stay, citing as the reason that his wife did not want to add to Napoleon's problems by depriving him of her husband's services. Perhaps she really meant it.

It should be added that Albine de Montholon was also notorious on the island for a suspected affair with a young British army officer,

Lieutenant-Colonel Jackson. He spent many of his evenings with the Montholons in their rooms at Longwood. It became quite a scandal: the Russian Commissioner, Count Balmain, apparently brought the matter to Bertrand's attention, and finally to Napoleon himself. Napoleon, whose motives were somewhat mixed, to say the least, summoned the Montholons and told them to break off the relationship. Albine, however, who claimed that Jackson was a 'fort bon jeune homme' (very good young man), and that there were few enough distractions at Longwood, simply ignored this and Bertrand reports that at the end of the month Albine and Jackson were still meeting regularly. When Albine left the island in July, Jackson, carrying dispatches for Lowe, left also six days later. However, there is no evidence that any serious relationship was continued in Europe.

Thus departed the last woman with whom Napoleon could hope to have any intimate relationship on the island, at least reasonably openly. It might be thought that with all the other problems and preoccupations – battling against Lowe and his restrictions, sorting out the jealousies and squabbles at Longwood, regulating the household expenses, coping with the depar-ture of his colleagues, dictating the great *apologia pro vita sua*, coping with his sexual frustration and the relationship with the two jealous wives – he would have had little time left to spare for anything else. But this was not so. For a man of his incredibly restless energy, whose life had been devoted to action and work, not having a proper full-time job in authority was killing him. He was faced with the plague that finally finished Gourgaud – sheer tedious boredom. The days were long and there was no end to them in sight. In the early days he was convinced that a change of gov-ernment or policy in England would secure his return to Europe. Even in September 1819, when any realistic hope of release must have been pretty well extinguished, Fanny Bertrand told Dr Verling that Napoleon still 'had great hopes some turn of affairs might remove him from St Helena.'[45] But as time progressed he had to face the reality that there was no escape, and that, like Prometheus, he would remain chained to the rock forever. This sapped his morale, made him even more depressed and perhaps even began to make him lose the will to live.

He nevertheless tried all sorts of ways to fill the time. Having long hot baths was one of them. Marchand says that he seldom spent less than an hour and a half in the bath. This infuriated Lowe, who once remarked that

1. Napoleon on HMS *Bellerophon*, July 1815

2. Sir Hudson Lowe entering Napoleon's study at Longwood

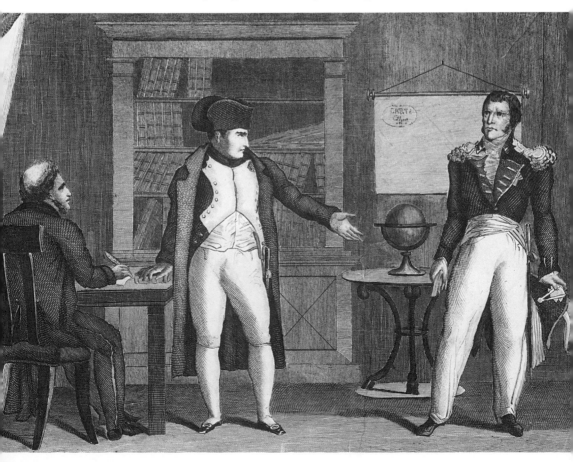

3. *(above)* Napoleon with his close companions on St Helena, Generals Bertrand, de Montholon and Gourgaud, and Count de Las Cases and his son
4. *(below left)* Betsy Balcombe (later Mrs Elizabeth Abell), 1816
5. *(below right)* The corpulent Napoleon on St Helena, with the Briars in the background

6. (*above*) General and Mme Bertrand, with their youngest son, at Napoleon's tomb in Geranium Valley
7. (*below left*) Fanny Bertrand
8. (*below right*) Albine de Monthalon

BRITISH FIGURES ON ST HELENA *(clockwise from top left)*

9. Lieutenant-General Sir Hudson Lowe, Governor of St Helena
10. Rear-Admiral Sir Pulteney Malcolm, naval Commander at St Helena, 1816–18
11. Major Gideon Gorrequer, Aide de Camp to Sir Hudson Lowe throughout his stay at St Helena
12. Dr Barry O'Meara, Napoleon's doctor from 1815 to July 1818

NAPOLEON'S COMPANIONS ON ST HELENA (*clockwise from top left*)

13. General Charles Jean Tristan de Montholon
14. General Gaspard Gourgaud
15. Count Emmanuel de Las Cases
16. Dr Francesco Antommarchi, Napoleon's doctor from September 1819 until his death

17. Mt Pleasant House, December 2007; the home of Sir William Doveton, to which Napoleon made his final excursion from Longwood in October 1820

NAPOLEON'S SERVANTS *(left to right)*

18. Louis Marchand (first valet)
19. Louis Marchand *(left)*, and Louis Etienne St-Denis *(right)*, known as Mameluke Ali (second valet)

20. A replica of the wooden aviary built for Napoleon in November/December 1819 by his Chinese gardeners at Longwood, from which all the captive birds escaped

21. Sketch by Captain Frederick Marryat of Napoleon on his deathbed, May 1821

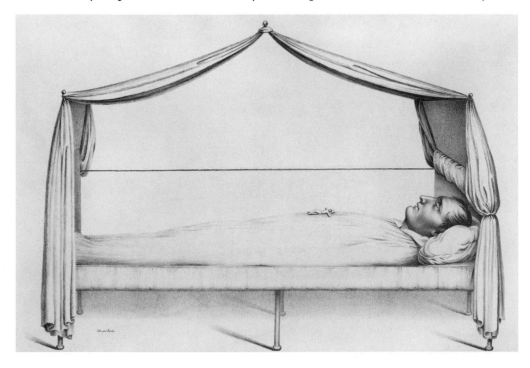

22. Napoleon's funeral cortège on St Helena, 9 May 1821

23. The triumphal return of Napoleon's remains to Paris, December 1840

'he did not know what business General Bonaparte had to stew himself in hot water for so many hours and so often at a time when the 53rd regiment could scarcely procure enough water to cook their victuals.'[46]

He could not, however, spend all his time in the bath. As we have seen, dictating and reading, or being read to, were other ways of passing time. However, there was a limit to the amount of dictation he could do, particularly after Las Cases had left him. The incentive perhaps began to wear off and in any case he did not have available all the reference books he needed, despite his prodigious, if selective, memory. Reading was, a great saviour. He had an extraordinarily wide and catholic range. The habit had started in his early youth: as a junior artillery subaltern at Valence he claimed over three years to have read almost all the library there. When on campaign he usually took a portable library of 3,000 volumes with him. He was even accompanied to Waterloo by a travelling library of 800 volumes in six cases, including the Bible, Homer, Ossian and all the seventy volumes of Voltaire. His powers of recollection were amazing and we even find him disputing on his deathbed at Longwood with Bertrand the respective merits of Homer and Virgil. He came down on the side of Homer because the author or authors clearly had actual battle experience, whereas Virgil's was second hand.

At Longwood some of his happiest days were when books arrived, often sent by his greatest sympathizer in London, Lady Holland. Sir Hudson Lowe also supplied books and newspapers regularly both to Napoleon at Longwood and to the Bertrands. When a consignment of books arrived, Napoleon would often open the crates himself excitedly and scatter the books on the floor or the billiard table. But as Lord Rosebery said, this and other diversions became somehow a futile exercise. He was like a caged animal, pacing restlessly up and down his cage, watching the outside world with the fierce glare of his wild eyes.

From time to time he developed other enthusiasms. In late 1819 he suddenly took to gardening.[47] There is a wonderfully bucolic portrait of him, looking benign and portly and wearing a wide-brimmed straw hat to ward off the sun, with a spade and flowerpots nearby. Some of them probably contained seedlings of the everlasting daisy that Lady Holland also sent from England, and which now proliferate all over the island. For a short time he threw himself into this new hobby. He had all his colleagues, even the generals, hard at work with the Chinese gardeners from five thirty in the morning until eleven o'clock, with only a short break for breakfast, toiling and sweating away constructing new paths and alleys, laying out flower and vegetable beds, and transplanting trees and shrubs where they would offer the most shade and protection. There are delightful descriptions of him at work by Marchand, wearing a nankeen farmer's jacket, red trousers of the same material and his broad-brimmed hat. Ali and Noverazz were made to wear the same outfit to confuse any English onlookers. It must be very doubtful whether his conscripted colleagues enjoyed all this as much as he did.

Much as he liked this new distraction, often joining in himself and holding a hose pipe to water the plants, the novelty began to wear off. Some of the transplanted trees and shrubs failed to take, mainly as a result of lack of water, and Ali tells us that the vegetable garden produced practically nothing. Napoleon was, however, proud of what he had achieved. It kept him occupied for a few weeks, and the mounds and embankments they had built did at least serve to act as screens to keep the English sentries a little more distant. His health also temporarily improved.

He also caused the Chinese gardeners to construct two fish basins, supplied by a new irrigation system, and a beautiful and elaborate wooden aviary. He filled the basins with goldfish bought in Jamestown and obtained some serins to keep in the aviary. Alas, again, all the fish in the basins died, presumably poisoned by an inappropriate lining; and most of the birds in the aviary either died, were killed by cats or escaped after a couple of months. Even some pigeons that Napoleon caused to be put in flew away as soon as the aviary door was opened. In the end the only occupant was a pheasant which was kept for a time as a lone prisoner. A full-scale model of the wooden aviary can still be seen in the services area at Longwood House today – sadly empty, just as it was soon after Napoleon installed the original one.

The failure of his brief gardening venture somehow symbolized Napoleon's own condition. It is impossible not to feel sympathy with his despairing *cri de coeur* when, according to Antommarchi, he exclaimed: 'Everything I love, everything that belongs to me, is immediately struck; heaven and mankind unite to persecute me.'[48] An echo of the suffering Prometheus, chained to his rock, can clearly be heard in this cry.

At one time he decided to fill the time with hunting. He had been allowed by Lowe to keep small-arms weapons. This too soon ended in disaster, if not absolute farce. He started with a few chickens, which had strayed into the vegetable garden. He had some success with this and shot three birds which he triumphantly told Ali to take to the chef to make a good soup. He then more dubiously moved on to a young kid, which he wounded in the shoulder when it followed its mother into the garden. The climax came when he shot a piglet and then killed with a single shot a valuable Company cow – absolute sacrilege on the island – which by some chance also found itself in the Longwood enclosure. This was the last of his hunting. The Governor was becoming anxious and Marchand says that neither chickens nor cows ever appeared in the garden again.

A very important means of passing the time was to receive visitors. Napoleon welcomed this, partly out of sheer interest and also because it could always offer an opportunity to win over a sympathizer who might take back to Europe news of the appalling treatment to which he maintained he was being subjected. He particularly welcomed captains and sailors and set out to impress them. He generally got on well with them and they were particularly well placed to act as messengers for him. Dr O'Meara records, for example, that a Captain Stanfell, who had been introduced to Napoleon by Admiral Malcolm, said afterwards that 'instead of being a rough, impatient and imperious character I found him to be mild, gentle in his manner, and one of the pleasantest men I ever saw.'[49] Gourgaud also noted that a group of English visitors whom he received on 15 May 1816 went away amazed. They had expected to see a tiger but found a man. With his legendary ability to charm, Napoleon knew how to put it on. For their part, visitors staging at St Helena were always flattered to secure a prestigious interview with the great man and although there were some heated spats with Lowe about the procedures involved – Bertrand officially issued visitor permits, but Lowe's prior approval was also required – Napoleon seemed to have little difficulty in seeing anyone he wanted to. His charm did not, however, always work. Some of his callers were not impressed and reported back to Lowe that they thoroughly approved of the way he was treating Napoleon.

The last significant diversion for Napoleon was exercise. In the earlier days he frequently went out walking, riding or for a drive in his carriage, usually with one of his senior colleagues and often with one or both of the two wives. But as time passed, except for the short gardening phase when his health improved, he took less and less exercise and consequently put on more weight. The chief obstacle was his fundamental objection to the rule that he had to be accompanied by an English officer if he went outside the prescribed bounds. This was the subject of row after heated row with Lowe (always, of course, after August 1816, conducted through intermediaries) until Napoleon took the view that unless he was free to go out unaccompanied, he would not go out at all.

Lowe's growing concern for Napoleon's health – although he would gladly be rid of him, neither he nor his Government wanted to incur the odium of being accused of neglecting Napoleon or hounding him to his death – led him to offer in October 1817 to extend the areas where Napoleon could roam unrestricted and unaccompanied by the orderly officer. By this time, however, relations between them had sunk to such a low and unpleasant level that Napoleon rejected the offer, which he described as mere *tracasserie*, or harassment.[50] The situation became a stalemate and, when he was not in the bath, Napoleon began to spend more and more time sitting and lying in his bedroom or study, despite constant medical advice telling him he should take more exercise. The consequences were two-fold. First, his health deteriorated and he put on even more weight. Second, he made it virtually impossible for the orderly officer to carry out his duty of reporting to Lowe that he had seen him twice a day. When the hapless orderly officer, despite all kinds of ruses such as peering in at the windows from the garden and even planning to bore a hole in the ceiling of Napoleon's room, reported that he simply could not catch a glimpse of him, Lowe exploded. He threatened to use force to break in to see him, but Napoleon, who kept five loaded pistols at hand, said that if anyone tried to force their way in it would be over his, and probably their, dead bodies.

Napoleon did, however, take the advice to take more exercise seriously enough in January 1821, only four months before his death, to get the carpenters to make a wooden seesaw and install it in the billiard room.[51] He probably remembered having seen one that the children played on in the Balcombes' garden when he was staying at the Briars in his early days on the island. He summoned Bertrand and asked him if he knew what this novel contraption was. The great military engineer suggested it might be some kind of war machine and asked whether it could be used to scale a rampart. Napoleon explained that it was a seesaw, but at first pretended he had got it in for the children. He then confessed it was for his own use and that he intended to exercise on it for quarter of an hour each day.

The normally staid and dignified Bertrand entered into the spirit and on the next day he and Napoleon entertained his son, Arthur, to whom they first said it was a gun, by taking their places on each end of it. The image of the now portly victor of Ulm and Austerlitz sitting down at the bottom end of a seesaw, and the builder of the bridges over the Berezina up in the air at the other, must have been one of the great comic sights of history. Bertrand caught the mood when he said that there ought to have been a cartoon with Napoleon weighing the seesaw down at one end and all the crowned heads of Europe up at the other, unable to lift him off the ground. Alas, however, the novelty soon wore off and although Montholon was conscripted to exercise with Napoleon and sit on one end of it – which had to be weighed down with lead to offset Napoleon's greater weight – after a fortnight Napoleon grew tired of it and it was quietly dismantled and put away The seesaw diversion, like so much else at Longwood, was not a great success.

All these activities and pastimes helped to eke out the days and stave off boredom. But Napoleon could not escape the brutal reality of his position. Two of the four 'evangelists' had left him; Albine de Montholon had gone too and his relationship with Fanny Bertrand had seriously deteriorated; and there was no sign of any change in policy in London that might reprieve him and allow him to return to Europe. He probably knew too that any hope of a rescue or escape was now a pipe dream. It must have been extremely difficult for him to stave off serious depression. He had in a sense got the better of Lowe by insulting and patronizing him, sending him off and refusing to receive him again. But this did not change the reality. However unpleasant an atmosphere he had created for him, Lowe still held all the cards.

NINE

SIR HUDSON LOWE'S PROBLEMS

IN PRINCIPLE THE PROBLEMS facing Hudson Lowe should have been much less severe than those facing Napoleon. He was, after all, Governor and Commander in Chief, and Napoleon was his prisoner. He had unchallenged authority on the island, with a hand-picked staff and nearly 3,000 troops to back it; and he was comfortably housed in the Governor's spacious and elegant residence, Plantation House. He also had a newly acquired wife and two attractive step-daughters to supply his domestic comforts. With luck, all he had to do was to hold his nerve, ensure that Napoleon did not escape, and in the end a grateful nation and government should recognize and reward the outstanding service he had rendered. In addition, after those first six increasingly unpleasant personal encounters, he would no longer have to go face to face with Napoleon again. But in practice it did not turn out quite like that.

In the first place, although he had been assured in London by the Secretary of State, Lord Bathurst, that many matters would be left for local decision at his own discretion, in practice – even allowing for the lengthy delays in physical communication – his every action was minutely scrutinized in Whitehall. He was constantly at the receiving end of the most detailed instructions, often on the most trivial issues. Moreover, despite the Government's overall mantra that Napoleon should be treated as indulgently as possible, compatible with maintaining total security,[1] the instructions as often as not veered in the direction of tightening the security screw, for which Lowe incurred the odium of Napoleon directly. For example, it was Bathurst who required Lowe to take back and tighten up the wording of the written declaration that he had, with some difficulty, persuaded Napoleon's colleagues and servants to sign shortly after his arrival. It was also Bathurst who, as an economy measure, insisted on the removal of four of Napoleon's staff from the Longwood household and was initially reluctant to agree to Lowe's personal agreement – a rare occasion when he dared to exceed his instructions – to raise the annual cash limit from £8,000 to £12,000. He regularly harassed Lowe on the subject of reducing Longwood expenses and it was Bathurst again who absolutely insisted on maintaining the practice that was such a red rag to Napoleon: the requirement to address him as 'General' rather than 'Emperor', and who in January 1817 told Lowe that in future he must only ever write to Napoleon himself, and leave it to his subordinates to write to members of Napoleon's staff. He also was the one who insisted on Napoleon being sighted twice a day, which led to farcical hide-and-seek games with the orderly officer, and bitter recriminations. No wonder Lowe said somewhat plaintively in a letter to Bathurst in December 1816: '... wherever I deviate from the letter of my instructions I feel my responsibility to be a very painful one.'[2]

Lowe cannot have been so obtuse as not to realize that the Government in London were concerned to cover their backs and keep their options open. Although they had no sympathy for Napoleon, whom they would have preferred dead, and hoped that he would soon become a faded memory in Europe as he steadily wasted away on that far-off isolated island, they were faced with a significant body of influential pro-Napoleon sympathizers among the opposition at Westminster. They did not want to be held responsible either at the bar of the Houses of Lords or Commons, or of history, for his assassination – which was how an early death on the island from disease, neglect or ill-treatment would be represented. They therefore made a point of putting regularly on record their somewhat double-edged directions to Lowe that he should treat Napoleon as indulgently as possible, compatible with total security. Even the occasional commendations for his conduct that he received – for example, from the Prince Regent or the Prime Minister, Lord Liverpool – were somewhat two-edged and generally accompanied by a further reminder of the need to keep the security lid on tightly. No wonder Lowe became unnerved by this constant surveillance and tried to cover his own position also. He stressed to Bathurst his anxiety to 'yield every indulgence to General Bonaparte that my instructions can possibly admit.'[3] However, he must have suspected that if any disaster occurred, he and he alone would be held responsible for it and made the scapegoat.

Lowe's position was, therefore, a very difficult and delicate one, but he made it much worse then it need have been by his insistence on reporting every detail of his dealings with Napoleon and Longwood back to the Secretary of State – seeking endorsement of his action or further instructions. We have already seen how after each meeting with Napoleon he rushed back to Plantation House or his headquarters in Jamestown to compose and dictate to Major Gorrequer a long dispatch to London, which usually in time received an equally long, if not longer, reply. He was constantly nervous, suspicious and in need of being reassured and having his hand held – rather like those earnest and ambitious ambassadors who fire off long telegrams to London reporting how strongly they defended their country's interests in their latest meetings with the local foreign ministry in the hope of receiving a 'You spoke well' reply from the Secretary of State. Count Balmain, by far the best of the Commissioners, summed him up well when he described him as: 'Un homme que la responsabilité dont il est chargé étouffe, fait trembler, et qui s'alarme de la moindre chose' (A man who is suffocated and made to tremble by the responsibility with which he is charged and who takes alarm at the slightest development).[4]

There are many examples in the Lowe papers of letters to Lord Bathurst with unbelievable detail about matters which, as Commander in Chief and Governor, he should really have been capable of dealing with and resolving on the spot. For example, he allowed himself to become far too involved in the complicated and emotional arguments and negotiations over who should be Napoleon's physician after Dr O'Meara had been removed. Between November 1818 and the end of 1819 he sent a succession of letters to the Secretary of State about Dr Verling and his position in relation to both Napoleon and the Bertrands, to whom he had acted as personal family doctor.[5] He also engaged in an unnecessarily detailed correspondence with Verling himself, which should have been mostly delegated to his subordinates. It was a fraught and very sensitive subject, as Napoleon would not accept as his doctor anyone nominated by the Governor unless the doctor also signed up to a set of written conditions dictated by himself. Dr Verling thus found himself in a genuinely awkward position, but it was ludicrous of Lowe to refer every dot and comma of the disputatious dialogue to the Secretary of State. Lowe must at times have realized this, as he prefaced a long letter of 4 November 1819 to Bathurst with: 'The enclosed letter marked separate is on a subject which I should hardly think it necessary to intrude on your Lordship's consideration, except so far as circumstances might hereafter require me to refer to it.'[6] No indeed! Nevertheless he seemed at times to be unnerved by the responsibility laid on him, and the scrutiny to which he was subject; he was incapable of acting with the robustness and common sense with which his rank, experience and appointment should have endowed him. Perhaps there was something justified in Napoleon's insulting remark that he behaved more like a corporal or a company clerk than a general.

He also compounded his problems, particularly after Napoleon refused to receive him again after the final August 1816 meeting, by allowing Bertrand and Montholon – usually acting as intermediaries on Napoleon's dictation – to dispute with him in detail the very meaning and interpretation of his own instructions. He often rose to their bait and entered into a form of competitive textual criticism with them. This was again ludicrous and put him immediately on the defensive and undermined his authority. He should simply have notified them of the substance of the instructions he had received and the way in which he intended to implement them – not permitted himself to be drawn into a debate about them. It is inconceivable that Napoleon would have allowed any such debate on the part of his marshals or other senior subordinates, let alone a prisoner. Lowe's perpetual sense of insecurity and need to justify himself perhaps also stemmed, despite himself, from an inevitable feeling of awe in the presence of Napoleon, even as a prisoner (he modestly once described himself as the greatest monarch the world had known since Charlemagne). This is a little reminiscent of the later remark attributed to Field Marshal Lord

Montgomery who, when asked who were the three greatest generals in history, offered to name the other two.

Lowe's punctiliousness and attention to detail might have made him a good staff officer – and indeed he had demonstrated this in his earlier career – but combined with his nervousness and lack of confidence, and consciousness of 'Big Brother' in London looking closely over his shoulder, it soured his relationship with many of his own military and civilian subordinates. The most senior of these was the admiral commanding the naval squadron guarding the seas around St Helena. It was obviously most important that they should enjoy a close and cordial relationship. The first admiral was Sir George Cockburn who brought Napoleon over on the *Northumberland* and remained in command at St Helena until Lowe's arrival as Governor in April 1816. As we have seen, Napoleon on the whole liked and respected him, although he grew less enthusiastic as time went on, and, after Lowe arrived, constantly compared Lowe unfavourably with Cockburn, whom he would have preferred to remain as Governor. This rankled with Lowe, who was therefore probably not displeased when Cockburn left in June 1816, not long after the fiasco when he was excluded from Lowe's first meeting with Napoleon in April.

Admiral Cockburn's successor as Commander in Chief of the South Atlantic Station, and thus of the naval squadron at St Helena, was Rear-Admiral Sir Pulteney Malcolm, another tall, handsome and distinguished sailor, who had been promoted to rear-admiral in 1813 and had commanded the naval force that cooperated with Wellington's army during the Waterloo campaign. As noted in Chapter Six, he had the added attraction for Napoleon of having married an aristocratic wife, Lady Clementina Malcolm. Both she and her husband were well connected socially with leading Whig figures in London, such as the Hollands and the Lansdownes, who were generally sympathetic to Napoleon and critical of the decision to send him to St Helena.

Much of our knowledge of the relationship between the Malcolms and Napoleon comes from the memoirs of Lady Malcolm, *A Diary of St Helena, 1816–17*, published in London in 1899. Some of the contents are clearly derived from conversations with Napoleon at which she was present; others are probably based on accounts told or dictated to her by her husband. Even allowing for some inaccuracies and exaggerations, they constitute an entertaining and illuminating account of a series of amicable meetings with the great prisoner, of a kind that was never possible for Hudson Lowe, let alone for Lowe's wife, who never even met Napoleon at Longwood. At various times they discussed the battles of Waterloo and Trafalgar. Napoleon agreed that Nelson was the greatest sea officer ever, but, although in earlier years he had quite often showed appreciation of Wellington's qualities as a general, on St Helena his view of Wellington became increasingly jaundiced and he could no longer bring himself to praise him. This was partly because he still believed that Wellington was responsible for the choice of St Helena. They also talked about his own campaigns in Egypt, Spain and Russia; the attitude of the British people if he had invaded Britain or won at Waterloo (he was convinced that the British people would have welcomed him as their liberator from an oligarchic and aristocratic tyranny); his return from Elba and his views on a wide range of political, religious, moral and literary questions. He was particularly fond of the pseudo-poet, Ossian, and often discussed him with Lady Malcolm in view of her Scottish connections.[7] He frequently invited the Malcolms to drop in and see him when they were calling on the Bertrands in the house across the road; and he was free with gifts to them, such as a valuable china coffee cup and saucer, which he presented to Lady Malcolm in June 1817. He also played chess with her.

This was all very well as far as it went, and to some degree might have helped to offset the rancorous relationship with British authority in the form of the Governor, but there is no doubt that Napoleon set out to exploit it and drive a wedge between Malcolm and Lowe. As the almost gossipy relationship with the Malcolms developed, Napoleon began to criticize Lowe openly to Malcolm's face. He complained about the way in which Lowe imposed the restrictions on him, claiming that they went well beyond the instructions originally given to Cockburn, and at a meeting on 25 July 1816, which lasted for four hours – twice as long as any of the meetings that Lowe had with Napoleon – he told Malcolm, who had started to defend the Governor, that Lowe was a cunning man who deceived him. He also declared that he was angrier about being placed under Lowe than actually being sent to St Helena.[8]

It is clear that both Malcolm and his wife disapproved in many ways of Lowe's treatment of Napoleon and found Lowe a difficult man to deal with. Nevertheless, the evidence suggests that they remained loyal to Lowe when talking to Napoleon and generally sought to defend him, and that the Admiral genuinely tried to smooth over the differences between Lowe and Napoleon. During a conversation on 7 March 1817 Malcolm told Napoleon that Lowe had a 'good heart' and that he misunderstood his character.[9] Later on, on 19 June, when Napoleon bitterly attacked a speech by Lord Bathurst in the House of Lords defending the Government against accusations of mistreating Napoleon (in a motion moved by Lord Holland), Malcolm again stoutly defended Lowe and dismissed Napoleon's complaints.

Lowe's suspicious mind, however, could not dismiss the thought that Malcolm was seeking to undermine his position. As Lady Malcolm once put it, he doubtless believed that Napoleon was making 'a tool of the admiral'.[10] The relationship had not, of course, got off to a very propitious start when, at the first meeting with Napoleon, to which Malcolm had accompanied Lowe, Napoleon had studiously ignored Lowe and concentrated most of his attention and conversation on the newly arrived Admiral. Following an earlier spat between Lowe and Malcolm, in a tetchy exchange of correspondence about supplies and transport matters, when the latter returned to St Helena from a visit to the Cape at the end of November 1816, the deterioration of the relationship came to a head when Malcolm sent Lowe a long report of a conversation he had had with Napoleon at Longwood on 7 March 1817.[11] Malcolm had in fact been defending Lowe but in the course of his letter he made a tactless reference to Lowe's 'certain quickness of temper'. Lowe's hackles were immediately raised and in an unnecessarily long and pompous reply to Malcolm he said that he disputed and resented the reference to his temper and declared: 'I cannot be more desirous than I always have been to yield every indulgence to Bonaparte that my instructions can properly admit.'[12] This more or less ended any semblance of a good working relationship between them, although Malcolm replied to Lowe denying that he had actually used the offending words with Napoleon. When Malcolm left the island at the end of June 1817 Lowe was probably relieved to see the back of him. He then enjoyed a much more comfortable relationship with his successor, Rear-Admiral Robert Plampin, who was more supportive of Lowe's policies, less inclined to be lured into gossipy visits to the Bertrands or Longwood, or seduced by Napoleon's charm, and was therefore less of a threat. By the same token he was disliked by Napoleon.

If Lowe had an uncomfortable relationship with his most senior colleague, Admiral Malcolm, his relationship with his military and other staff at Plantation House and the Castle at Jamestown was not exactly the most cordial either. His most senior military aide was Lieutenant-Colonel Sir Thomas Reade, who strongly supported a tough line with Napoleon, and even thought Lowe too soft with him. This can hardly have induced Lowe to take a more relaxed approach. But the officer on whom he relied the most throughout the whole five and a half years of his Governorship was his Aide de Camp and acting Military Secretary, Major Gideon Gorrequer.[13]

Major Gorrequer was thirty-five years old and a bachelor when he went to St Helena with Lowe. He had served with him in Sicily and the Ionian islands and had accepted Lowe's offer to accompany him. Gorrequer was formally subordinate to the official Military Secretary, Lieutenant-Colonel Edward Wynyard, but he was in practice by far the most important member of Lowe's staff and Wynyard seems to have been content to let Gorrequer take the lead and do most of the work. He was a fluent French and Italian speaker, and thus an invaluable presence at the various meetings and communications with Napoleon and his staff, and he lived on the site at Plantation House. He was constantly at Lowe's side with his note book and pencil; his inside knowledge of Lowe's administration and of the personalities on all sides on the island was unrivalled. He took dictation from Lowe, sent out instructions, made minutes of meetings, copied and recopied letters and with the aid of his notes helped Lowe to draft the long dispatches he sent to Lord Bathurst as well as the letters to Napoleon or his generals. To outward appearances he was a discreet, loyal and supportive aide – the very model of a modern military secretary.

The reality, however, was somewhat different. The picture changes dramatically when we read Gorrequer's secret diaries. There can seldom have been a greater difference between the outer man, the busy and efficient staff officer, and the angry, repressed, resentful author of these almost venomous accounts of daily life at Plantation House with Lowe. They were not decoded and published until James Kemble completed the task in 1969. It was not an easy one: the diaries were written on various odd scraps of paper, often in minute scribble or crosswise over the original script, and Gorrequer devised an extraordinary and often very amusing, if offensive, series of pseudonyms for the principal characters. They give, however, an astonishingly close insight into the character of both Lowe and Gorrequer and many of the other principal actors in the drama.

The most striking feature of them is Gorrequer's seething anger and frustration at his treatment by Lowe, and his excoriating criticism of Lowe's conduct and character. He wrote the diary in the evenings after he had returned alone to his small room at Plantation House. It must sometimes have taken hours as many of the entries are extremely long and detailed. The image of the impeccably efficient Major getting his pent-up frustration and anger out of his system by pouring it vitriolically, in a stream of invective, into a secret journal (which was never meant for others' eyes) is both a saddening and fascinating one. As my wife and I were guided through the corridors of Plantation House in December 2007, and took coffee in Hudson Lowe's library after dinner with the Governor and Mrs Gurr in the very same dining room in which Gorrequer had often joined Sir Hudson and Lady Lowe, I could almost feel the phantom presence of the hidden Gorrequer scribbling away obsessively behind his locked door, trying to get his frustration and indignation off his chest.

On reading the diaries it is difficult to understand why Gorrequer stayed at his post with Lowe for so long, or why indeed he had ever agreed to go with him to St Helena. He must have known his character well from his previous service with him and there is more than an element of masochism in his behaviour. The diaries are full of bitter complaints about Lowe's irascible and inconsiderate temper, of which he must have felt the sharp edge many times before, and about the way in which he was, without appreciation or thanks, grossly overworked. He complained that 'with all my labour from morning to night it was impossible for me to do right'; and that 'there was not a black man nor a slave on the island who had not more relaxation than I had.'[14] Even when he was ill, but nevertheless continued working, Lowe showed no appreciation and simply told him he was 'out of humour' or 'extremely touchy and very subject to losing his temper'.[15]

He is impressively inventive in the number of different ways in which he describes Lowe's behaviour. Lowe has a 'rough scolding voice'; an 'angry, rude, violent manner of speaking'; his tone of voice is often 'most revolting'; on one occasion he became 'furious, foaming at the mouth and spluttering'; and in August 1820 when the orderly officer at Longwood reported that he had not actually seen Napoleon for three days, 'his gesture, his furious foaming at the mouth manners and the Billingsgate expressions . . . continued for a considerable time.' According to Gorrequer, Lowe was vain too, and when he was trying on a new uniform sent from London he describes him as 'strutting about like a peacock, admiring and looking at himself in specchio [mirror], buttoning and unbuttoning abito [coat] ... and admiring the reflexion of himself'.[16] Gorrequer was irritated above all by Lowe's habit of repeatedly redrafting the letters and dispatches, which he was forced to take down, amend, draft again and then transcribe in fair copy usually in great haste to catch an awaiting vessel bound for London. He refers in November 1819 to Lowe having altered a draft at least thirty times, while only composing six lines. He was also furious with Lowe for blaming him time after time for losing or mislaying papers, which were on Lowe's desk or in his office all the time.

Anyone who has worked for an unreasonable and unappreciative boss will recognize this kind of behaviour and these feelings. But they can rarely have been expressed with such bitter anger and resentment as Gorrequer achieved in his diary. He records plaintively that his only moments of ease were when Lowe went to town; and after a row in March 1819 – this time about matters relating to Gorrequer's own salary and military position – when he could not contain himself any longer, he told Lowe that in twenty-one years of service he had never been spoken to so unkindly by any officer under whom he had served. He offered to resign, but still stayed on and continued to discharge his official functions loyally and effectively.

Much of his anger and frustration was clearly a function of being so close to Lowe every day, both in the office and at meals, and on other social occasions at Plantation House. The tension might have eased a little if Gorrequer had lived separately, like the Bertrands from Napoleon, so that they occasionally got away from each other. As it was they brought out the worst in each other. It is rather surprising, therefore, that a later and more considered judgement of Lowe was less harsh. In a passage in his diaries probably not written until August 1823 Gorrequer wrote:

Mach [i.e. Lowe, presumably from Machiavelli] is but a machine – he is just what his nature and circumstances have made him. He slogs the machine which he cannot control. If he is corrupt, it is because he has been corrupted. If he is unamiable it is because he has been marked and spitefully treated. Give him a different education, place him in other circumstances, and treat him with as much gratefulness and generosity as he has experienced of harshness, and he would be altogether a different nature. A man who would be anxious to be loved rather than feared; and instead of having the accusation of being a man who was satisfied to spread around him anguish and despair, one who has an instinct for kindness.[17]

Although this is perhaps a little patronizing, it is a remarkably sympathetic statement from someone who expressed such contempt for him in his earlier commentaries.

Gorrequer's strictures on Lowe are also put into a more balanced perspective by his mockery of almost everyone else on the island. In the diaries Admiral Malcolm was a 'damned ass', and the Austrian Commissioner, Baron Stürmer, a 'damned shuffling ass'. General Bertrand was another 'damned ass'; Count Balmain, the Russian Commissioner, who married one of Lowe's step-daughters, a 'complete blackguard' and a 'mean dirty fellow'; and Dr O'Meara the 'greatest rascal that ever existed' (a sentiment that Lowe would have heartily endorsed). Almost everyone on both the British and French sides was given a comic or abusive pseudonym in his diaries. Sir Thomas Reade was 'Nincumpoop', or just 'Ninny'; the French Commissioner, Count Montchenu, was 'Old Frog'; General Bertrand was 'Shrug' and his wife 'Madame Shrug'; General Montholon was 'Buggiardo' and his wife 'Donna Veritas'; while Napoleon escaped lightly by merely being called the 'Neighbour'. The Prime Minister, Lord Liverpool, was 'Pond of Liver', and all the admirals were some variety of 'Polyphemes'. His immediate superior officer, Colonel Winyard, was 'Grape'. There are dozens of such inventions in the diaries. With such a bitter and cynical approach permeating the atmosphere, he and Lowe must have had some very bad days in the office together. But perhaps they deserved each other.

Apart from Lowe himself, Gorrequer's spleen was mainly directed against Lady Lowe, whom he generally called simply 'Donna' or 'Sultana'. He clearly detested her and complained often of the way in which she snubbed or ignored him, and above all of her unwillingness to allow him to have a decent room or furniture at Plantation House, when there were plenty of both available, or to have his laundry done with rest of the house's laundry. One entry in the diary also fumes about her unwillingness to let him have decent candles: he had to make do with broken or used ones (the Treasury would have applauded this!). He variously accused her of heavy drinking (an entry of 1 August 1818 claims that she consumed a bottle of brandy in two to three days, a whole bottle of sherry daily, and 'drinks grog every night and liqueurs'),[18] jealousy of Fanny Bertrand, an affair with one of the more junior aides de camp, and alleged that she once said that she would never have married Lowe if she had known that she was to have more babies ('Pickaninies') on the island. All this cannot have added to the congeniality of the atmosphere in which Lowe worked at Plantation House.

These observations add vivid colour and detail to our picture of daily life on St Helena, and particularly of the way in which Lowe operated and the problems he had to contend with. They are not very flattering to Lowe, but Gorrequer was not that sort of man and they probably exaggerate the unattractive side of Lowe's character. What is surprising is that although he stayed on to the very end and left St Helena with Lowe on 25 July 1821, his diary barely mentions the events surrounding Napoleon's death and funeral. He was no admirer of Napoleon and perhaps thought that if he ignored him at the end, others in the world would too. He was, however, upset when Lowe did not turn to him first to give him the honour of conveying the dispatch announcing Napoleon's death to London.

Difficult and unpleasant as Lowe's relationship was with Gorrequer and some of his other colleagues and subordinates, the man who gave him the greatest grief on his own side – and who was mainly responsible for the subsequent damning of his reputation in Britain – was Dr Barry O'Meara, the naval surgeon who became Napoleon's personal doctor at Longwood after winning his confidence on both the *Bellerophon* and the *Northumberland*.

Dr O'Meara, who was born in County Cork in Ireland, was only thirty-three when he arrived in St Helena. After service as assistant surgeon in the 62nd infantry regiment, he transferred after a minor regimental scandal to the Royal Navy and became surgeon to HM warships *Goliath* and *Bellerophon*. He was in the latter when Napoleon surrendered to it from the Ile d'Aix in July 1815 and, with his fluent French and Italian, soon won the confidence of Napoleon, who asked him to accompany him to St Helena when his own French doctor, Maingaud, decided to abandon ship and leave him. With the permission of the Admiralty and Lord Keith, O'Meara accepted but on the strict condition that he 'should always be considered as a British officer and at liberty to quit so peculiar a service, should I find it not to be consistent with my wishes.'[19] It was a peculiar service indeed, and one that was to have profound consequences both for O'Meara himself and Sir Hudson Lowe.

O'Meara was quickly installed in quarters in Longwood House itself, only a few damp doors and corridors away from Napoleon, and the relationship soon became an intimate one, going far beyond strictly medical matters. Marchand notes in his memoirs how O'Meara's influence with his master grew, and Albine de Montholon remarks on the familiarity of their conversations. There are numerous accounts of O'Meara's behaviour in the diaries, journals and official papers of the time, but a main source is his own massive volume, *A Voice from St Helena*, which he published in 1823 after the death of Napoleon. It contained a dedication to Lady Holland, whose husband was one of the fiercest critics of British Government policy and who frequently sent gifts of books and other items to Napoleon on St Helena. It is not difficult to guess, therefore, where O'Meara's sympathies in the book lay. The inside cover of the book also contains a quotation in Greek from Aeschylus' tragedy *Prometheus Vinctus*, with the fate of whose protagonist Napoleon often compared his own.

The views among historians on O'Meara's testimony in *A Voice* are mainly critical. Lord Rosebery regarded it as 'worthless' and his evidence 'impossible to accept'.[20] Another eminent champion of Hudson Lowe, Forsyth, in his monumental three-part volume of 1853, described O'Meara as 'a pest of literature', belonging to the class of writers 'who corrupt the stream of history by poisoning its fountains, and the effect of his work has been to mislead all succeeding authors and perpetuate a tale of falsehood'.[21] So far as Forsyth was concerned, O'Meara's book was mainly designed to 'avenge himself' on Hudson Lowe. This general view is also shared by the most recent French historian to write about Hudson Lowe, Jean-Pierre Fournier La Touraille, who in his remarkably sympathetic 2006 book, *Hudson Lowe, Le Géolier de Napoléon*, presents O'Meara as a double if not triple agent, playing 'un role ambigu et un double jeu'.[22]

The truth, as usual, is probably less one-sided. There is no doubt that O'Meara had absolutely unrivalled access to Napoleon and his senior colleagues at Longwood and was able to converse with him astonishingly freely and frequently on all manner of subjects. There is no obvious reason why he should have taken against Lowe in the early days of his tour of duty, but as a young and junior officer he must have been enormously flattered to be in such unique proximity to the great defeated former Emperor and gradually to have developed some sense of sympathy with and loyalty to him. However, as time went on he found himself, as Marchand also recorded, 'entre l'enclume et le marteau' (between the hammer and the anvil).[23] Lowe expected O'Meara to report back to him on Napoleon's behaviour and intentions at Longwood, and Napoleon saw in O'Meara an opportunity to discover what Lowe was up to and to spread a message about the outrageous treatment he was receiving to the outside world.

O'Meara was by no means uncritical of the Longwood household. He strongly condemned, for example, their 'lavish' lifestyle, with almost unlimited wine, two large main meals a day, and three to four times as much meat a day as any ordinary English family could afford. As time progressed, however, O'Meara's sympathies inclined more strongly to Napoleon. He began to feel the effects of and detest Lowe's brutish temper, and he genuinely believed that the strict security measures imposed on Longwood were detrimental to Napoleon's health and were in any case unnecessary given the impregnability of the island. He therefore urged Lowe to relax the rules on the positioning of sentries round the house and the requirement, which particularly irked Napoleon, that he could only make an excursion on foot or horseback outside the Longwood grounds if he first gave notice and was accompanied by an English officer. In doing this he cleverly used the argument most likely to carry weight with Lowe: that Napoleon could die prematurely from lack of proper exercise, and that Lowe would be held directly responsible for this.

After August 1816, when Napoleon refused ever again to meet Lowe, O'Meara's role as a go-between assumed much greater importance. In October 1816, for example, Napoleon gave him a paper to take to Lowe about his curious proposal, which he had once floated before, to be allowed to live in England as a private citizen under the assumed name of a Colonel Meuron, who had been killed at Napoleon's side at the battle of Arcola. This was in the context of the running dispute about the British decision to address him as General rather than Emperor. In November, in return, Lowe asked O'Meara to explain to Napoleon that he was only obeying his instructions, and on another occasion in December to tell him that 'It is fortunate for him that he has so good a man for governor over him and that others with the instructions I have would have put him in chains for his conduct.'[24] On yet a further occasion at the end of the year he also gave O'Meara a note for Napoleon with the somewhat pathetic plea that: 'The Governor is not conscious of ever having wilfully given to General Bonaparte just cause of offence or disagreement. He has seen with pain misunderstanding arise on points where his duty would not allow him to pursue any other course, and which might have been frequently removed by a single word of explanation.'[25]

None of this cut any ice with Napoleon, who must have been delighted to see Lowe rising yet again to the bait and seeking to justify to his prisoner his own interpretation and implementation of his instructions. It is inconceivable that he would ever have apologized in this way himself. It was very foolish of Lowe to allow himself to be drawn into this. By now O'Meara was more firmly in the Longwood camp. He had already made it clear to Lowe that, in his professional medical capacity, he was not willing to act as a spy. He further angered Lowe by subscribing to the Longwood view that Napoleon, and other members of his household, were suffering from acute hepatitis, caused by the unhealthy conditions and climate at Longwood – the inference from which was that they should be sent back to a healthier climate in Europe. Partly as a result of his anger and frustration, and of Lowe's refusal to listen to him, O'Meara – without the knowledge of either Lowe or his superior naval officer on the island, the Admiral – conducted a separate clandestine correspondence with a friend in London, Mr Finlaison, the Keeper of the Admiralty Records. Not surprisingly, Finlaison passed his letters on to his minister and through him they became known to other members of the cabinet, including Lord Bathurst. This put Lowe in an intolerable position. The letters were severely critical of him, even implying that the instructions O'Meara received from him were tantamount to ordering him to murder Napoleon. When Lowe became aware of this he confronted O'Meara, whom he now regarded as 'an instrument in French hands'. O'Meara was unrepentant and defended his conduct vigorously. He later referred in *A Voice* to 'the invincible repugnance that everyone at Longwood has to his (Lowe's) presence,'[26] and there is no doubt that at this stage he fully shared that sentiment.

Major Gorrequer, supporting his chief in this matter, urged Lowe to get rid of O'Meara. But Lowe, still nervous and lacking self-confidence, hesitated to do so. In the first place he wanted cover from Lord Bathurst, which was not immediately forthcoming, and secondly he was still frightened that if O'Meara left he would be held responsible for Napoleon's premature death from lack of proper medical care, since he knew that Napoleon would not accept any other British doctor nominated by Lowe, except on conditions that were unacceptable to him. So the duel continued and any number of issues gave cause for angry rows between the two men, adding to the already very unpleasant atmosphere between them and with Napoleon. One time in May 1817, O'Meara exploded and threatened to resign after Lowe had reprimanded him for giving newspapers to Napoleon before Lowe had seen and authorized them (Napoleon was always desperate to see the European press, particularly the British, although his ability to understand English was still very limited). Nothing further, however, immediately came of this.

On 18 July, after another violent quarrel, Lowe formally ordered O'Meara not to hold any further conversation with Napoleon except on strictly professional matters and to report personally to him twice a week at Plantation House and Jamestown. O'Meara responded by asking to be relieved of his post, but wrote in his journal that he had decided to confine himself to his medical duties and avoid 'all unnecessary communication with a man who could avail himself of his irresponsible situation to insult an inferior officer.'[27] Somewhat bizarrely, one of the bitterest disputes occurred when Lowe, who now described O'Meara as a 'jackal running about in search of news for General Bonaparte,'[28] was told by O'Meara that he refused to be treated as a 'mouton.'[29] Lowe, prone as ever to be waylaid into textual criticism, fell into an angry argument about the precise meaning of the curious expression 'mouton'. When O'Meara defined it as someone who insinuates himself into the confidence of another, for the purpose of betraying it, Lowe threw him out in a paroxysm of rage. During a later argument, in January 1818, Lowe almost threatened him with physical violence. Napoleon must have enjoyed this situation: he knew exactly from O'Meara what was going on between Lowe and O'Meara and he had the Governor on the perpetual defensive.

The situation could not continue. After further incidents, including a heated row about a request to O'Meara by Lieutenant-Colonel Lascelles, the Commanding Officer of the 66th regiment – at the instigation of Lowe, through Brigadier-General Bingham – to resign his membership of the 66th officers' mess[30] (a request that O'Meara not surprisingly regarded as a serious imputation on his personal honour), Lowe's wish to expel O'Meara was at last granted by Lord Bathurst.[31] The Secretary of State authorized him to withdraw O'Meara from attendance on Napoleon and to forbid all further intercourse with the inhabitants at Longwood. Admiral Plampin also received instructions from the Admiralty as to O'Meara's destination after he left the island; O'Meara's friend, Finlaison, had presumably been powerless to intervene in London.

Events then moved speedily. O'Meara, disobeying Bathurst's order 'for the sake of humanity and his professional duties,'[32] paid a formal farewell call on Napoleon – who presented him with a valuable snuff box and a miniature statue of himself. Not missing a trick, he also charged him with various messages for his family and asked him to try to recover from his brother Joseph a set of correspondence with Tsar Alexander and the King of Prussia, which he presumably wanted O'Meara to publish (in fact O'Meara did not succeed in this). Napoleon had suspected throughout that if O'Meara was expelled he would write and publish his memoirs in a way that was favourable to his cause. His comment when O'Meara told him of the decision to expel him was: 'le crime se consomme plus vite' (the crime is being committed so quickly).[33] O'Meara left St Helena on 2 August 1818 and soon after his arrival in England was dismissed from the navy. However, he took his revenge in the form of the publication in 1822 of *A Voice from St Helena*, which profoundly influenced public opinion against Lowe and his treatment of Napoleon and did much to establish him in history as the villain of the St Helena piece.

Dr O'Meara had been in an impossible position. He could not have lived cheek by jowl and in daily contact with Napoleon without being drawn into discussion of non-medical matters and he was under constant pressure to act as an agent for both Lowe and Napoleon. It was unreasonable to expect a relatively junior officer to resist the aura and charisma of Napoleon on the one hand and the gubernatorial authority and fierce temper of Lowe on the other without overstepping the bounds at some stage. But although he may not merit some of the adjectives applied to him by Rosebery and Forsyth, there is no doubt that his conduct was disloyal and unacceptable on the part of a serving British officer and there was an element of Iago about him. If he could not stand the heat he should have got out of the kitchen. His efforts to undermine Lowe behind his back in Whitehall by his separate correspondence with Finlaison were particularly discreditable and were damaging both to Lowe's position in relation to Napoleon on the island and his career thereafter. They must also cast some doubt on the reliability of his often bitter testimony in *A Voice*, particularly as there are some inconsistencies between that and his Admiralty correspondence, although it is by no means as 'worthless' as Rosebery claimed. It is perhaps significant that in a note regarding Dr Verling of August 1819, Madame Bertrand is said to have described O'Meara as a 'troublesome and mischief-making man' and that 'had it not been for him things would have gone on much better between Longwood and the Governor.'[34]

Lowe's primary task as Napoleon's jailor was to make sure that he did not escape. It became more complicated and less pleasant as time went on. Napoleon maintained his refusal to meet him again and began to confine himself to his room for long periods with loaded pistols at the ready to shoot anyone who forcibly tried to cross his threshold. Lowe blustered and made fruitless and often undignified visits to Longwood, sometimes circling the house and peering in at the windows, in the hope of catching a glimpse of Napoleon or meeting him by chance in the garden. Frustrated and angered by Napoleon's tactics he berated a succession of hapless orderly officers who had to resort to the most absurd, and hazardous, hide-and-seek tactics to try to see Napoleon, even surreptitiously when, as often, he was taking a bath. Lowe clearly passed an increasingly tense and miserable time, not sure of approval from his political masters in London and terrified that Napoleon might escape or even die without his knowledge.

The custody of Napoleon was not, however, the only responsibility he had to discharge. Although the British Government took over the island in 1815, he still remained accountable to the Court of Directors of the East India Company for the civil administration of the island. This was no sinecure. The arrival of over 2,000 troops in April 1815 added severely to the day-to-day economic problems, not least the supply and distribution of fresh water, the shortage of which was a constant complaint at Longwood. The presence of so much licentious soldiery, despite the curfew and other restrictions, also added to the law and order problems on St Helena and it is not surprising, if somewhat shocking, that in Gorrequer's diary entry of 24 July 1818 we find an almost casual reference to Lowe breaking off from his preoccupation with Napoleon to sign a death warrant for someone convicted in the island's criminal court.[35]

We have seen how Lowe's conduct was closely monitored by the Secretary of State in Whitehall, and how Lowe made his own life even more miserable than it need have been by his excessively detailed reporting to him. This close surveillance seems to have been matched by that of the directors of the East India Company. For the most part, especially in the early days, they seem to have approved of the way in which, through the island Council, Lowe managed their affairs. However, the papers of the time show a distinct deterioration in this relationship as Lowe, under increasing pressure from his commitments to Napoleon, became more offhand, if not offensive, in dealing with them. Matters came to an unpleasant head in 1819 when Lowe suspended a certain Thomas Breame, the Company's farmer, over an irregularity in the accounts. Lowe also around that time upset the directors by appointing a Major Hodson, his choice rather than theirs, to command the St Helena Artillery (the Company's troops). After tetchy exchanges of correspondence the directors sent an astonishingly long and detailed letter to Lowe – signed by all of them but, in the quaint fashion of the time, purporting to come from 'Your loving Friends' – severely reprimanding Lowe for his conduct.[36] It contained such statements as that his remarks were 'neither consistent with propriety or respect', 'we cannot suffer ourselves to be thus dictated to as to the manner in which we may choose to seek the information relative to our affairs at St Helena', and 'the tone and temper in which you have indulged in discussing [our affairs] are as unsuitable to the relative situation in which you stand towards the Court [of directors] as they would be incompatible with a due regard to the authority we possess.'

This was a rocket indeed, and the directors must have been at the receiving end of Lowe's hot temper and abrasive style in just the same way that the poor Gorrequer had been. But such was the time it took to compose their letter – one can just imagine the repeated drafting sessions around the company board table – that it was not signed until 2 May 1821, a few days before Napoleon died and Lowe was then free to leave the island.

Among the other issues that Lowe addressed was that of slavery. Slavery flourished on St Helena during the captivity of Napoleon and most of the island's labour force, apart from the Chinese workers, was recruited in this way. For the most part the slaves were treated reasonably well, but some of the slave owners had a bad reputation for inhumanity and brutality. Lowe raised the issue many times in the island Council, but without any effect. An incident in August 1818, in which Brigadier-General Sir George Bingham witnessed the ill-treatment of a young slave girl, however, brought matters to a head.[37] Sir George summoned the owner, a Mr Charles de Fountain, before him at the Magistrate's Court and inflicted the statutory fine of £2 on him, adding that he wished he could have made it £40. Mr de Fountain complained of Sir George's conduct before the island Council, but Bingham was unrepentant and Lowe, supporting him, gave notice that he would bring up the question of slavery again at the next Council meeting. Soon after, on Lowe's proposal, the island agreed voluntarily – in a resolution put to the assembled slave proprietors on 17 August 1818, and later in the same day passed into law by the island's Council – to end the practice of slavery. Lowe deserves great credit for this and on this occasion the directors of the East India Company thoroughly endorsed his action and wrote to him accordingly to say so.

It was an achievement of which he could be rightly proud and it was recognized as such in the fulsome testimony given to him on his departure by the inhabitants of the island. It stands in marked contrast to the ambiguous behaviour of the essentially racist and colour-prejudiced Napoleon, who by a decree of 20 May 1802[38] had carried against a significant minority opposition in the Assembly the 'Loi relative au traite des noirs et au régime des colonies' (Law relating to the slave trade and the administration of the colonies). Contrary to Napoleon's earlier moves to abolish it, this had effectively restored slavery and the slave trade in Martinique and most of the other French West Indian colonies.

Burdened by both the military and civil issues of his office, Lowe must have passed an increasingly anxious and miserable time, never knowing when his vigil would finish. He faced a number of dilemmas. After August 1816 he was spared the unpleasantness of direct meetings with Napoleon, at which it was obvious that there was a growing personal antipathy between them. Napoleon clearly could not stand him, not simply as his jailor but as a person. On the other hand it meant that without direct access he had to rely on others to verify that Napoleon was still indeed where he was meant to be. Napoleon was well aware of this, hence the games he played by staying in his rooms or the bath and refusing to appear for long periods. Again, Lowe must have prayed that Napoleon's life would end sooner than later. But at the same time he was terrified of being accused of ill-treating him and being branded as his assassin. In the event, however, Napoleon's deteriorating state of health meant that the drama had to come to an end.

TEN

THE ROAD TO THE END

ALTHOUGH CONTEMPORARY SOURCES COVER the whole period of Napoleon's captivity on St Helena, we know rather less about the later years than the earlier period of settling in at Longwood – except for the last few weeks and months before he died, on which Bertrand, Marchand, Ali, Antommarchi and others have left almost daily detailed accounts. The account of the most prolific diarist, Las Cases, in his mammoth *Mémorial* ended when he left the island in December 1816, and similarly O'Meara's detailed journal on life at Longwood only went up to his departure in August 1818.

The drama also progressively lost some of its other principal actors with the departures of Gourgaud and the Balcombes in March 1818, and the sudden and mysterious death on 26 February 1818 of Napoleon's trusted Corsican maître d'hôtel, Cipriani.[1] Cipriani was buried in the country church near Plantation House in a Protestant service conducted by the

Senior Chaplain on St Helena, the Rev. Richard Boys, who became notorious for his violent denunciations from the pulpit of Admiral Plampin for bringing out a lady to St Helena who was not his wife.[2] In June 1818 Napoleon also lost his valued personal chef, Lepage, who deserted the cause by marrying a fellow chef allocated to Longwood by the Governor, and was replaced by Pierron who had only just taken over the maître d'hôtel duties from Cipriani. As we have seen, the next to depart, with particular significance for Napoleon, was Albine de Montholon, with her children, in July 1819.

After he had broken off direct relations with the Governor, conducting them thereafter mostly through Bertrand and Montholon, and using Dr O'Meara as long as he was able to, Napoleon attached great importance to receiving visitors at Longwood. He particularly welcomed visiting captains and naval officers, in the hope both of engaging their sympathy for the way in which he was being treated by the Governor and using them to take letters and messages back for him to Europe. Thus in the earlier years of Napoleon's stay at Longwood a succession of captains and officers of naval ships and East Indiamen turned up at Longwood to meet him.

A celebrated naval visitor towards the end of Napoleon's captivity was Captain Frederick Marryat, of popular sea story and novel fame, who had served his naval apprenticeship as a midshipman under the celebrated frigate captain, Thomas Cochrane, whom Napoleon much admired. Marryat had played a heroic and exceedingly dangerous part on one of Cochrane's explosion vessels on 11 April 1809 in the destruction of part of the French fleet at the famous 'battle of Aix Roads', or the 'Basque Roads'. This was the very place from which Napoleon had surrendered in July 1815 to Captain Maitland of the *Bellerophon*, who had himself also commanded the frigate *Emerald* in that daring fireship attack. Marryat was sent to St Helena in early March 1821 in command of the 10-gun brig *Beaver* to form part of the flotilla guarding the approaches to the island.[3] An amateur artist, he was later invited by Hudson Lowe to be present at Napoleon's lying-in-state on 6 May and drew a sketch of Napoleon and of the subsequent funeral procession.

Napoleon was willing also to receive army officers, either when they were formally taking their leave at the end of their tour of duty, or officers newly arriving to replace them. Like the naval officers they were flattered to be received by the great man and many of them succumbed to his persuasive

charm and were sympathetic to his complaints about the way in which he
was being treated. Napoleon exploited his visitors as far as he could, but
even in his desperate situation he could sometimes see the irony, if not the
humour, of his position. According to O'Meara he once remarked: 'It is
difficult to distinguish those who come to look at me as they would an elephant or some other wild beast from those who come with other motives.'[4]
The constant access to him by others was, however, dirt in the eyes of the
Governor, who, after August 1816, was reduced to prowling round the exterior of Longwood in the hope of catching a glimpse of his prisoner. An
amusing incident took place in August 1819 when Lowe and Napoleon
unexpectedly came face to face in the garden. It was the first time Lowe had
seen him at close quarters for three years, but Napoleon quickly made off
through the bushes into the house before the Governor could utter a word
to him.

Not all Napoleon's visitors swallowed his story. In July 1817 he was visited by Lord Amherst, a British emissary to China, who was on his way
back to Britain after leading a delegation there. In his account of the meeting, Marchand says that: 'l'Empereur paraissait satisfait de l'audience' (the
Emperor seemed satisfied with this interview) and that Amherst offered
to try to mediate between him and the Governor.[5] Napoleon, however,
refused this offer on the grounds that it would serve no useful purpose.
He commented: 'Ce serait inutile; le crime et la haine de moi sont dans la
nature de cet homme; il a besoin de me torturer, comme le tigre d'enfoncer
ses griffes dans la proie dont il prend plaisir à prolonger l'agonie' (It would
be useless; such is the criminal intent and hatred of me in the nature of
this man; he needs to torture me, just as a tiger needs to embed its claws in
its prey whose agony it enjoys prolonging).[6] These words are perhaps the
most bitter and dramatic expression of Napoleon's view of Lowe, but they
show how much he had come to loathe him. Amherst, however, afterwards
reported to Lowe that he thought Napoleon's complaints about his treatment and the conditions at Longwood were unfounded. The rest of their
conversation was mainly devoted to Lord Amherst's notorious refusal to
kowtow to the Emperor of China, which Napoleon thought was a political mistake, arguing that he should have conformed to the customs of the
country to which he was accredited.

After 1817 the number of visitors at Longwood began to drop off. This
was partly due to the departure of the Malcolms, who had been constantly

in and out of Longwood or the Bertrands' cottage, and had presented many (especially fellow naval) visitors to Napoleon, and partly due to Lowe's tightening of the rules about receiving visitors, which aroused Napoleon's bitter indignation and opposition. Routine presentations of newly arrived officers continued, though less often, and there was much coming and going of medical staff, but fewer official or social calls overall. An exception in April 1819 was Mr C.M. Ricketts, a relation of the Prime Minister, Lord Liverpool, who spent no less than four hours with Napoleon, who for obvious reasons was keen to impress him.[7] In spite of this, as with Lord Amherst, there is no evidence that this paid off in terms of sympathetic reporting to high authority in London. Mr Ricketts does not appear to have been convinced by Napoleon's complaints about his treatment or the alleged state of his health.

With the steady decline in the number of visitors and the gradual seepage of his staff at both senior and junior levels, Napoleon became increasingly terrified of being deserted and left alone. He was not the only one at Longwood to suffer the physical and mental effects of the climate and the claustrophobic isolation, and there are suggestions that some of his companions – notably Montholon, who was often ill himself and badly missed his wife and children – were not displeased at his deteriorating state of health since it might accelerate the departure of all of them from the island. There is no reliable evidence, however, that Montholon, who in the event stayed with him right to the end, and was the principal beneficiary of his will, was complicit in his death, either by poison or any other means. We shall return to this later when discussing the cause of Napoleon's death.

Napoleon's greatest single fear was that the Bertrands might leave him. Although he tended to take the loyal and steadfast General Bertrand for granted, and had fallen out with Fanny Bertrand, he would have been absolutely devastated by their departure. That would have meant relying on Montholon alone, who could not be guaranteed to be always at his side. Bertrand himself was under continual pressure from his wife to leave, or to let her and the children do so. She was frequently ill on the island, with false pregnancies, vaginal bleeding and at least one genuine miscarriage. She was also under pressure from the breakdown of her relationship with Napoleon, having refused to become his mistress.

In October 1820 Bertrand told Napoleon that, for the sake of his wife's health and the education of their children, he wished to have permission to send them back to France or England, and moreover to have nine months' leave of absence himself to settle them in and sort out some of his own affairs.[8] He promised, however, that he would then return to St Helena in order to 'se consacrer entièrement à l'Empereur' (dedicate himself entirely to the Emperor).[9] Napoleon was shocked. Bertrand's departure would create 'un vide immense' (an enormous hole)[10] in his existence. He gave no immediate response, but the likelihood of imminent departure of the Bertrands was apparently common talk in Jamestown, and Lowe, who knew what was going on, decided not to try to intervene. He had no love for Bertrand, with whom his relations had deteriorated badly, and would probably have been glad to see the back of him. Matters dragged on indeterminately for a while and Napoleon even seemed to accept a rapprochement with Fanny Bertrand which temporarily raised his health and his spirits.

Fanny Bertrand still, however, longed to leave. According to Marchand, she even said that she would go with or without her husband, but when Napoleon would not give agreement to his departure with her the proposal was eventually dropped, even though at one stage some of her luggage was taken aboard a ship waiting to depart.[11] Bertrand was torn between acquiescing in his wife's plan, and remaining true to Napoleon, whom he knew in his heart he would never see again if he left the island. His loyalty was truly remarkable, particularly during the last weeks of Napoleon's life when he abused Bertrand's wife to his face, uttering obscenities, calling her a whore and improbably accusing her of having an affair with Dr Antommarchi.[12] Bertrand bit his lip and said nothing, making allowance for the almost deranged rantings of his dying master's mind.

As the months passed, the tedium at Longwood was occasionally relieved by incidents that either temporarily raised Napoleon's spirits or achieved the reverse. His health was also now steadily deteriorating. He maintained his unyielding opposition to the restrictions imposed on him by Lowe, but at the same time refused to accept concessions. Lowe, for example, offered to reduce the number of sentries close to Longwood, and to grant to Napoleon's companions the same freedom of movement as himself, but Napoleon would have none of it and sent an insulting reply. A similar performance was repeated on other occasions. Napoleon, while complaining, could not bring himself to accept concessions from a man he so detested.

In March 1817 Napoleon's hopes had been raised by the intervention of Lord Holland, who introduced a motion in the House of Lords condemning the Government's treatment of Napoleon on St Helena.[13] He was, however, angered and depressed by Lord Bathurst's vigorous speech of rebuttal on behalf of the Government, when in due course a copy of it was sent to him by Lowe. O'Meara said that he felt ashamed of it. But Napoleon's supporting lobby in the British Parliament was not quite as strong as he had hoped.

The next year, 1818, saw the departures of Gourgaud, the Balcombe family, O'Meara and also the Austrian Commissioner, Baron Stürmer, who had spent a frustrating time on the island, never meeting Napoleon, and had now had enough. As the year drew on the increasingly depressed Napoleon also ceased dictating his memoirs. This was a significant development. With hopes of a change of policy and return to Europe now almost completely faded, it was critically important for him to 'spin' the story of his career in his own terms if he was to leave to posterity his version of his legacy. But the effort of maintaining the narrative without the proper records and facilities must have been increasingly frustrating and debilitating, particularly when Las Cases was no longer there to support him.

In January 1819, however, he paid a visit to New Longwood House, which was under construction for him next door.[14] He did so on a Sunday, when there were no workmen there, in the hope that his visit would not be known to Plantation House (a vain hope, as the Governor soon got to hear of it). Marchand, who accompanied him, reports that Napoleon found the house completely unsatisfactory. The layout of the rooms was wrong – Marchand's bedroom was too far away from his – and Napoleon commented that the flagstones on which he trod would in due course be used to build his tomb. He said that he would never occupy it. His real objection, however, remained that of principle. To take an active interest in the house and make suggestions on its layout would imply that he accepted that he was on St Helena for good. To move to it would also remove his basic cause for complaint about the state of his accommodation on the island.

It is difficult to know exactly when Napoleon finally gave up hope of returning to Europe. In a sense he could never allow himself to do so, even when he knew in his heart of hearts that St Helena was the end. In July 1816 he had told Dr O'Meara that he was confident that as soon as the affairs of France were settled and things were quiet, the English Government would allow him to return to Europe and finish his days in England. However, the prospect had become progressively bleaker since then with no sign of a change of government or of government policy in London. A further heavy nail was driven into the coffin by the outcome of the meeting of the allied powers at the Congress of Aix-la-Chapelle early in 1819. The Russian Government – in which Napoleon had placed particular faith because of his mistaken belief, following the Treaty of Tilsit in July 1807, in his personal influence with the young Tsar Alexander (an extraordinary self-delusion in view of his subsequent invasion of Russia in 1812) – submitted a note that, as Lord Rosebery comments, might have been drafted by Lord Bathurst himself.[15] It demanded continuing rigorous treatment of Napoleon, including that he should be compelled to show himself twice a day to the Commissioners and to the Governor. The news of the outcome of the Aix conference, which in essence decided that he should remain on St Helena, was a fearful blow to Napoleon. It was formally conveyed to him by Lowe in March, but he almost certainly got wind of it earlier. One of his reactions was to start preparing the first draft of his will.

A further significant date for Napoleon was the arrival in September 1819 of the party sent out by his uncle, Cardinal Fesch, at the instigation of his mother, Madame Mère, who was living in Rome. It consisted of two priests, the Abbés Buonavita and Vignali, Dr Antonio Antommarchi and two servants for the kitchen and household, Chandelier and Coursot. The idea of sending them had been long in gestation, and the purpose was to comfort Napoleon by providing him with his own proper Catholic priest (there was hitherto no Catholic priest on the island), and a doctor whom he could trust (i.e. one who was not appointed by the Governor). The result, however, was near disaster.

Abbé Buonavita was sixty-six when he arrived and his main experience was as a missionary in South America, though he had served for a time as Madame Mère's chaplain on Elba. Napoleon took one look at him and summed him up. He told Bertrand that they had sent him 'un homme déjà cassé par l'âge et dont la vie s'est passée au Paraguay. De quelle resource voulez-vous qu'il soit pour moi?' (a man already broken by age, whose life has been passed in Paraguay. What use do you expect him to be to me?)[16] He also remarked later to Antommarchi that he feared that the Cardinal had only sent out the good old man so that he could be buried on St Helena! Poor Buonavita had a miserable time on the island. He contributed very little – certainly to either Napoleon's spiritual or physical comfort – and left on 17 March 1821, before Napoleon's death.

Abbé Vignali was a young Corsican, whose credentials, apart from his youth, were scarcely more impressive. He was said to be low born, ill-educated and almost illiterate – hardly very good qualifications for dealing with the immensely well-read and subtle-minded Napoleon. Ironically, however, although we know little else of his contribution, he conducted Napoleon's funeral service. The third member of the trio was Dr Antommarchi, whom we shall consider more fully later. He had studied at Pisa and Florence and was a well-trained academic anatomist and pathologist, but had limited experience of practical general medicine. He made a very poor impression on Napoleon to begin with, and hardly improved on this by his display of medical prowess later. Napoleon found him on first acquaintance 'un peu jeune et présumptueux'[17] (he was just thirty when he arrived) and later on, when he had had more experience of Antommarchi's bedside manner, he remarked that he would readily give him his horse to dissect, but would not trust him with the cure of his own foot.

Napoleon's disappointment with this curious caravan was such that he refused to receive them at Longwood on the first evening. Hudson Lowe filled the breach by inviting them for dinner, no doubt wishing to size them up and get his retaliation in first. Napoleon contented himself with calling in the far more useful Chandelier, who had been cook to his sister, Pauline, in Rome, and Coursot, who had been in service in Madame Mère's household. He quizzed them eagerly about his mother and Pauline and other members of the family. The next day he was in better humour and agreed to receive Buonavita, Vignali and Antommarchi. He subjected them to a similar interrogation, fixed their salaries, and then arranged for their accommodation – Antommarchi in O'Meara's old rooms, Buonavita in General Gourgaud's, and Vignali in the apartment of the Captain of the Guard, to which was added later a room that was now vacant from the Montholon suite.

As time progressed the most critical issue was obviously that of Napoleon's health. It became a political as much as a medical issue. The political dilemma arose on both sides. The British authorities did not want to believe or accept that the deterioration of Napoleon's health was due to endemic hepatitis exacerbated by an unhealthy climate and the conditions at Longwood. To do so would have led to the conclusion that he should be moved to a healthier place, presumably back in Europe. They were therefore averse to the hepatitis diagnosis, or to any doctor who subscribed to it. On the other hand they did not want to be open to a charge of, in effect, assassinating Napoleon by neglect. One of Lowe's main problems with O'Meara was that he stuck to this diagnosis and frequently warned Lowe that he would be guilty of murdering Napoleon unless he moved him from Longwood. For his part Napoleon made their dilemma more acute, after O'Meara's removal, by refusing to accept any other doctor proposed to him by Lowe, except on conditions that were unacceptable to both the Governor and the military surgeons concerned. He was thus without regular professional medical care until the arrival of the doctor, Antommarchi, chosen by his family, and as we have already seen, he valued Antommarchi's expertise as practically nil.

Napoleon several times remarked that he would have liked to have the services of the great Dr Dominique Larrey, who had been his principal army doctor on many of his military campaigns, including the Russian disaster and Waterloo. Larrey was commonly regarded as the most out-standing surgeon of the Napoleonic era and had made major advances in battlefield surgery and care. He was, for example, the inventor of mobile field ambulances: horse-drawn carriages used to evacuate the wounded from the battlefield, which the French army introduced years before the British. Napoleon described him to O'Meara as 'the most honest man and best friend to the soldier I ever knew.'[18] However, Larrey was not available, and although he would certainly have been an improvement on the doctors who did attend Napoleon on St Helena, it is doubtful whether any doctor, with the state of medical knowledge at the time, could have done much for Napoleon, given the nature of the disease that caused his death. Better and more constant medical care might, however, have alleviated some of his suffering.

As discussed in Chapter One, at only forty-seven years of age when he went to St Helena Napoleon was in reasonable physical shape. He had put on weight, and the cramped and unhygienic voyage on the *Northumberland*, with limited scope for exercise, together with the immense physical and mental strains of the previous months, could hardly have helped to keep him in top condition. Nonetheless, the descriptions of his early stay with the Balcombes at the Briars, where he took long walks and played childhood games with Betsy Balcombe, and the energy he displayed in sorting out his household and seeing off Hudson Lowe during his first months at Longwood do not suggest he was a particularly sick man at that stage. But thereafter it was a steadily downhill progression, with occasional remissions.

The diaries and journals of the time describe the symptoms from which he suffered. Apart from his increasing corpulence, early in 1817 he developed swollen legs and ankles, which further restricted his mobility.[19] He also regularly suffered from inflamed gums, probably a scorbutic condition associated with vitamin deficiency, and for the first time in his adult life he had to have teeth extracted. It was during this time that Dr O'Meara gave Lowe a strong warning that, unless he relaxed the restrictions on Longwood, allowing Napoleon to take more exercise, he would not survive for more than another year or two. In September 1817, during a period of bad weather, Napoleon was in great distress with his legs and with bleeding gums. O'Meara's diagnosis, unpalatable to Lowe, was acute hepatitis. By the middle of 1818 his condition was much worse and O'Meara records that on 7 June when he extracted two of Napoleon's teeth he had been confined to his room for nearly six weeks.[20] Marchand also tells us that Napoleon was spending more and more time in the bath, seldom for less than an hour and a half, and he was eating, reading and working there with the aid of a small mahogany tray that he had made to fit on each side of the bath. Napoleon made the claim that is familiar to many of us, that the hot soaking eased the pains that he was increasingly feeling in his abdomen and side.

In January 1819, well after O'Meara's departure, Bertrand and Montholon, alarmed at Napoleon's condition, which may have been aggravated by the disappointing news of the outcome of the Aix-la-Chapelle Congress, made an urgent request to Dr John Stokoe, the surgeon on the *Conqueror*, to come and see him.[21] Napoleon had already refused to see the Governor's nominee, Dr John Verling, the young Irish surgeon to the St Helena artillery detachment. Stokoe arrived at Longwood on 17 January, and Napoleon agreed to be examined by him. Stokoe paid several visits between then and 21 January and, to Lowe's disgust, endorsed O'Meara's hepatitis diagnosis. Lowe believed, or wanted to believe, that this was nonsense and merely a ruse to support O'Meara and give Napoleon an exeat. Stokoe prescribed several forms of treatment, including bleeding, various pills (unspecified) and friction of the limbs. The latter seemed to do him some good and his condition improved. Stokoe also seemed ready to accept a more permanent post with Napoleon if the Governor and his own chief, the Admiral, agreed. As we shall see later, this brought him into serious conflict with Lowe and the Admiral.

During the rest of 1819, Napoleon's condition remained reasonably stable, with ups and downs. On better days he was able to resume some walking or other form of excursion and towards the end of the year, and in the early part of 1820, he coerced the whole household into a serious blitz on gardening. It was at this time, however, that Napoleon showed that he suspected his ailment was something more serious and fundamental than hepatitis. In discussion with Antommarchi he referred to hereditary disease, noting that his father died at an early age from sclerosis (a tumour) in the pylorus (the entrance of the stomach into the duodenum).[22] As the year progressed the pains in his stomach grew worse, extending to the right costal region and shoulder, and he was often short of breath. By the late autumn, when he was not in the bath, he was spending more time in bed, sometimes resting for twelve to fifteen hours a day. He once said pathetically to Antommarchi: 'What a delightful thing rest is. The bed is become for me a place of luxury. I would not exchange it for all the thrones of the world. How fallen am I.'[23] How fallen indeed.

In October 1820 he made his last real excursion outside Longwood, travelling about five miles in a *calèche* to Mount Pleasant, a delightful family house in the south of the island which he had previously visited in June.[24] It was not far from Sandy Bay and had a glorious view across to Diana's Peak and the other highest points of the island. This visit was impromptu but he was welcomed by the owner, Sir William Doveton, a member of the island Council and one of its leading grandees. He was persuaded to stay for breakfast, which was set out on the lawn, and enjoyed meeting Sir William's daughter and young children. Napoleon much enjoyed the visit but the return journey, on bumpy roads, was too much for him and he was very tired and drowsy when he got back. Soon afterwards the symptoms of his fatal disease began to worsen, in the form of frequent vomiting and stomach pains, and he had difficulty in keeping any food down. He found some relief from taking salt-water baths but he had no faith in the various medicines and pills prescribed by his doctors, especially Antommarchi, and often refused to take them. He summed his approach up well by once remarking: 'I will not have two diseases; the one given to me by nature and the other by the physician.'[25] He also received a severe blow to his morale when he heard in December 1820 the news of the death of his sister, Elisa. She was the first of his brothers and sisters to die, and Ali records that by this time he had lost all hope and was looking only to death.[26]

The disputes over doctors obviously aggravated Napoleon's problems. He adamantly refused to accept Lowe's nominees, whom he regarded as spies, unless they accepted his terms of employment, which were impossible for a serving British officer. He thus went for long periods without a regular doctor in attendance. In 1816 the Governor had wished him to accept the services of Dr Alexander Baxter, the senior and experienced surgeon who had served with him in the Corsican Rangers and at Capri, and accompanied him to St Helena to take up the position of Deputy-Inspector of Hospitals. He remained on the island until 1819 but Napoleon would never allow him to attend him in a medical capacity. All Baxter could do was to provide Lowe with reports based second-hand on oral briefings by O'Meara. Another doctor involved was the surgeon to the *Conqueror*, Dr John Stokoe, referred to earlier in this chapter. After being summoned urgently to Longwood by Bertrand and Montholon, he eventually paid five visits to Napoleon between 17 and 21 January 1819, and evidently grew quite close to Napoleon and the Longwood household. However, with the support of Admiral Plampin, he was charged and sent home by the suspicious Lowe on various charges relating to attending and conversing with Napoleon without permission. He was later summoned back to St Helena to be court-martialled and dismissed from the service. It was an extraordinarily severe and vengeful act by Lowe, demonstrating his acute nervousness and near paranoia about Napoleon's security, and merits a more detailed investigation elsewhere. One of the main factors weighing against Stokoe in the eyes of Lowe was his previous close association with Dr O'Meara.

It is no surprise, therefore, that Dr James Verling, the surgeon to the Royal Artillery, also got into a terrible tangle when ordered by the Governor, after O'Meara's removal, to be ready to give medical assistance to Napoleon if required. He was lodged at Longwood but Napoleon simply refused to see him. The vivid account of that period in Verling's diaries records the events of his stay at Longwood until, to his great relief, he was allowed to leave the island on 25 April 1820. He had become very close to the Bertrands, particularly Fanny Bertrand who was always calling for his services for herself or her children, and to Montholon who was also frequently unwell. A feature of his diaries is his account of the extremely detailed and fraught exchanges he had with the Governor about his personal position and his activities at Longwood. Verling was in a difficult and delicate position, and many of his letters were obviously designed to ensure that his own version of events was on record, but the correspondence is yet another example of the way in which Lowe felt it necessary to intervene personally in great detail when much could have been delegated to Reade, Gorrequer or another subordinate. At least Verling escaped, however, without being disciplined by Lowe, and when the latter was subsequently engaged in a lawsuit with O'Meara after his return to England, Dr Verling was among those who were willing to testify in his favour.

The other principal personage in the drama worth mentioning is Dr Archibald Arnott, surgeon to the 20th foot regiment. Although he was strongly recommended to Napoleon by both Bertrand and Montholon, who trusted him, and was in regular contact and consultation with Antommarchi, he was not admitted to see Napoleon until early in April 1821 when he was already dying.[27] Although for a time he stuck to a diagnosis of hypochondriasis – in other words that Napoleon was shamming serious illness – which was comforting to Lowe, he finally reached the conclusion that Napoleon was suffering from a hereditary sclerosis or cancer. He did not subscribe to the hepatitis or liver disease diagnosis, thus disagreeing with Antommarchi on this. He remained in attendance at Longwood until Napoleon's death, and was present at the post mortem. The Governor at least allowed him a free hand and did not complicate his task by bureaucratically insisting on receiving regular formal medical bulletins at Plantation House. Dr Arnott luckily escaped the fate of Dr Stokoe, although he too became involved in a ludicrous spat with Lowe when he accepted for his regiment's mess a gift from Napoleon from his Longwood library – a book about Marlborough, which had a letter 'N' inscribed on it, allegedly by Napoleon himself.[28] Lowe's view was that he should not have accepted any gift from Napoleon, particularly an inscribed one, without explicit prior permission. Once more Lowe's obsession with the slightest possible infringement of the rules got the better of common sense and judgement.

With this plethora of doctors involved in one way or another it is hardly surprising that Napoleon was prescribed an astonishing range of treatments, which probably exacerbated his condition rather than the reverse. It was perhaps fortunate for him that he resisted taking many of them, especially those prescribed by Antommarchi. The treatments, in addition to salt baths, which perhaps did help him to relax, included bleeding, blisters, mercury ointment (probably for swollen gums), quinine and quassia (to reduce fever), magnesium sulphate (as a wash for the mouth or to put in the bath to help soothe muscle pains) and a range of enemas and laxatives, such as castor oil, calomel and mercurous chloride (sometimes known as 'horn quicksilver'). In addition to his stomach and side pains Napoleon frequently suffered from constipation and the laxatives were presumably intended to get his bowels working and clear his system of noxious substances. The result, however, often was prolonged suffering, so much so that Bertrand tells us that sometimes near the end he was shouting with pain. It is impossible at the human level not to feel great compassion for him. The constant daily devotion of not only his two valets, Marchand and Ali, but also of Bertrand and Montholon is also truly remarkable. The Grand Marshal of the Court, General Henri Gratien Bertrand, whom Napoleon had often taken for granted and sometimes disgracefully abused, did not shirk from carrying out the most intimate and unpleasant physical tasks to help his suffering master.

Although he was now clearly dying, Napoleon still rallied from time to time between January and April 1821. With an amazing effort of will, memory and concentration he dictated to Montholon during April – or even, according to Bertrand, wrote parts of the codicils under Montholon's dictation himself – an incredibly long and detailed will, of which Montholon was the principal executor and beneficiary.[29] Marchand says that it occupied him for eight to ten days, and this is not surprising in view of his condition and the amount of detail contained in it. In addition to the bequests for his family and his senior companions and servants on St Helena, there were provisions for numerous of his former colleagues in arms, including individual veterans, some of them crippled from wounds, who had served with him both long ago and more recently at the battles of Ligny and Waterloo.

The only sour note – from a British point of view – was a grant of 10,000 francs to a Lieutenant Cantillon, who had unsuccessfully tried to assassinate the Duke of Wellington when he was British Ambassador to Paris in February 1818.[30] Napoleon claimed that Cantillon had as much right to assassinate the 'oligarch Wellington' as Wellington had to send Napoleon to perish on the rock of St Helena. This action had a significant effect on

Wellington's assessment of Napoleon's character, which, in contrast to his admiration for him as a general, he had never estimated very highly. In 1826 Wellington told his friend, John Croker, that it was further proof of Napoleon's 'littleness of mind'.[31] Cantillon eventually received some money from Napoleon's executors, in small instalments between 1823 and 1826, but in many cases, because of difficulties in accessing and releasing the funds, it took years before the legacies in the will were received, and in some cases the legatees remained disappointed. Again, Wellington strongly criticized Napoleon for making what he called 'high-sounding legacies' when 'there was not a shadow of a fund', and observed that 'I think one who could play such tricks but a shabby fellow'.[32]

Although Napoleon was now desperately ill there were still moments when he was sufficiently revived to revert briefly to old habits. Bertrand even records that on 25 February he drank three glasses of Burgundy at 6am, a glass of Armagnac at 8am – not bad for a dying man – and was taken for a short drive round the Longwood grounds in a carriage on the following day.[33] This exhausted him and he had to be supported back to his bed. He also occasionally asked to read or be read to, and this was not just, as it were, light hospital reading. Bertrand mentions among other authors: Virgil, Polybius, Livy and Caesar, reflecting Napoleon's lifelong love for, and familiarity with, the classics. He was especially pleased when another consignment of books arrived from his favourite champion in London, Lady Holland, on 2 March. There was also happily a touching reconciliation with Fanny Bertrand, who had been virtually ostracized from Longwood for a long time because of her insistence on living separately and not yielding to Napoleon's advances. It was a moving, if brief, visit by Fanny Bertrand, but it cleared the way for her to resume visits to him most days until his death.

By the end of April 1821 Napoleon was often losing his memory and sometimes raving or delirious.[34] On Hudson Lowe's instructions, Dr Arnott, who had been admitted to see Napoleon for the first time earlier in the month, consulted two other doctors, Dr Charles Mitchell, surgeon on the *Vigo*, and Dr Thomas Shortt, principal medical officer on the island. They supported Arnott's recommendation that Napoleon should be given a strong dose of the cathartic medicine calomel. Accordingly, despite the objection of Antommarchi – who probably rightly thought the shock to Napoleon's now very weak system would be too great – a dose of ten grammes was administered at 6pm on 3 May. When the calomel had not worked by 11pm Arnott spoke of repeating the dose, which Antommarchi again sensibly opposed. By 11.30pm, however, the calomel had produced its violent results on Napoleon's system and shortly afterwards he accepted a few spoonfuls of whipped-up eggs, sugar and wine.

Napoleon slept for much of 4 May, waking only occasionally to mutter a few largely incoherent words, but showing signs of recognizing Bertrand. He had now been moved from his small bedroom to the larger salon. During the evening the whole retinue of doctors was in attendance – Antommarchi, Arnott, Shortt and Mitchell. Lowe had been in the house, but he was not admitted to see Napoleon, and he finally decided to return to Plantation House, but asked to be kept closely informed of Napoleon's condition. During the evening Napoleon slept fairly soundly, occasionally waking to be given sips of orange-flower water, but his pulse was erratic, his skin very cold to the touch and his eyes only half open. The doctors doubted whether he would survive the night.

On the following day, 5 May, Napoleon rallied a little in the early morning. He was clearly, however, in great pain and he uttered his last recognizable words. According to Marchand, they were: 'France, mon fils, l'armée, Joséphine.'[35] Bertrand's version is simply: 'A la tête de l'armée.'[36] Whatever the truth, they reflected three of the things in his life most dear to him – his son, the army and Josephine. For the rest of the day he alternated between sleeping and occasionally opening his eyes, which seemed glazed and half closed. Dr Arnott was amazed that he clung to life for so long. The end was clearly imminent and as the day drew on sixteen people had crowded in a vigil around his bed in the salon, including, in addition to the doctors, Bertrand and his wife, Montholon, Marchand, Ali and his wife, Noverazz, the Abbé Vignali and the young Napoleon Bertrand, who at one time was sick and had to leave the room. At 5.30pm his breathing became short and difficult and at 5.49pm, just after the sun had set, Napoleon breathed his last. Ali says that 'il s'est éteint comme s'éteint la lumière d'une lampe' (his light went out like that of a lamp).[37] That solemn and dreaded moment is immortalized in the painting by Steuben. The very elements seemed to echo to the awful occasion, as a severe storm raged outside, shaking the huts and tents of the troops camped on Deadwood Plain, and tearing up many of the surviving trees and shrubs that Napoleon had planted at Longwood, including the favourite willow tree under which he liked to rest and find shade. In the salon the faithful and grieving Marchand covered his Emperor's corpse with the cloak that the young general had worn at the battle of Marengo, over twenty years before.

Events then moved swiftly. During the night of 5 May, at the request of Montholon, Dr Arnott watched over the body. On Sunday, 6 May, it lay on the bed in sleeping attire, with a crucifix on the breast. It was formally viewed in the morning by the Governor, Admiral Robert Lambert (who had succeeded Plampin in the previous July), the French Commissioner, Montchenu, and various senior military and civil dignitaries. It was the Governor's duty to verify that the corpse was indeed that of Napoleon, and Montchenu performed perhaps his one useful service on the island by confirming this to him. Lowe must have had mixed feelings of relief that his own sentence had now come to an end, and awe at seeing the giant at last on his deathbed.

During the afternoon a post mortem took place. It was performed by Antommarchi. Despite his mistrust and disparagement of him as a general physician, Napoleon had asked that he should undertake it and that no British doctor should be allowed to touch his body, although he agreed that Dr Arnott could be in attendance to help if necessary.[38] He had several times expressed a wish that an autopsy should be performed to verify the nature of his disease, which he believed was the same as his father's. In fact Dr Arnott and six British doctors were present, together with Sir Thomas Reade, the Abbé Vignali, Marchand, Ali and two other British officers.

After this grisly procedure was completed, the body was sewn up again and washed and dressed in Napoleon's favourite green uniform of colonel of the Chasseurs de la Garde, with his famous tricorn hat on and the crucifix still at his breast. Napoleon's heart had been removed and put in a silver vase filled with wine, there being no embalming spirit available. There was an argument about what should be done with it. Napoleon had instructed that it should be sent to his wife, the former Empress, Marie-Louise, who was still in Vienna, and Fanny Bertrand had also laid a claim to it. Perhaps she wanted to achieve literally what Napoleon, when living, had been unable to obtain metaphorically from her. Lowe, however, ordered that it should be sealed with the body in the coffin. He did not want to leave behind any relics that could form the basis of a Napoleonic cult. The diseased stomach was similarly extracted and sealed in a container to be placed in the coffin.

Lowe had also informed Montholon that his orders were not to allow the body to be buried outside St Helena.

The corpse lay in state for the rest of the day and large numbers from the military garrison and the civilian population came to Longwood House to file past and view it, some out of respect to pay tribute, others from sheer curiosity. The awe they felt at seeing the corpse of Britain's greatest enemy, the legendary Bony, must have overcome any feelings of triumph they might have had at seeing him brought so low. On the following morning, 7 May, the carpenters finished constructing the strong mahogany, lead and tin-plate coffins and the body was placed inside the last one – none too soon given the rate of decomposition in that climate. Meanwhile a deep grave was being excavated, lined and reinforced down by the freshwater spring in the green isolation of Geranium Valley. On 9 May the funeral took place, with all the pomp and ceremony that the island could reasonably muster, short of according to Napoleon the honours that would have been due to a head of state. Lowe, no doubt so relieved to see the back of him, at least gave him a decent send-off. We have now come back full circle to the scene described in the introduction of this book.

There has always been debate about the cause of death. The majority view is that it was a form of cancer of the stomach. Many of Napoleon's symptoms, such as the pains in his abdomen and the referred pains in his side, were consistent with this. The autopsy showed that although the liver was a little enlarged, which is not unusual in association with cases of stomach cancer, much of the internal surface of the stomach was occupied by a cancerous ulcer, which can be caused by the affected glands in the stomach lining ulcerating the surface and leaving raw areas that can bleed. Whether it was hereditary, which Napoleon suspected, is uncertain, though possible. Although modern research has shown that the bacteria that contribute to cases of cancer can be passed down within a family, most stomach cancers are not so and the rare type that can be hereditary, sclerosis carcinoma, or 'leather bottle' stomach, is not normally associated with an ulcer.

Dr Shortt, as the island's principal medical officer, was required to draw up the official autopsy report, which he signed first, followed by Drs Arnott, Burton and Mitchell. Antommarchi refused to do so, partly on the basis that as he had conducted the autopsy, he should be the principal signatory, and partly because Bertrand was unhappy with him signing a document drafted by English doctors. He therefore prepared his own statement, so that there were two autopsy reports.[39] In any case, he disagreed with the conclusion of cancer, which ruled out hepatitis as the primary cause of death. The Governor also perversely objected to Dr Shortt's report, and unsuccessfully tried to amend it. This was on the grounds that the reference in the report to an enlarged liver did not represent the view of the majority of the doctors present. He was still anxious to avoid giving any credence to the hepatitis theory. Even at this solemn moment he clung to the old arguments and the dispute was depressingly reminiscent of the constant squabbles about doctors and diagnoses that had bedevilled Napoleon when he was alive.

There has been much dispute and speculation, and many studies undertaken, on the possibility that Napoleon was deliberately poisoned. The usual theory is that arsenic was steadily administered to him, either by the British or by a member of his own household, or by both in complicity, in order to accelerate his death. The finger is usually pointed at Montholon, who stood to gain the most from Napoleon's will and was eager to return to Europe to see his wife and children again. But although Montholon no doubt wished to get his hands on Napoleon's money as soon as possible, there is no specific evidence to prove that he was planning or prepared to commit murder. It is difficult also to see why the British, or Lowe in particular, who were anxious not to be vulnerable to public accusations of murdering Napoleon, should have taken the risk of deliberately administering arsenic to him.

Studies by the Canadian businessman, Ben Weider, have claimed that Montholon progressively administered arsenic to Napoleon over the whole period of his captivity on St Helena.[40] The intention was not to kill him by arsenic poisoning but to weaken his system so that the *coup de grâce* could eventually be administered by a combination of less obviously noxious and lethal drugs, which produced deadly mercurial salts in his already weakened stomach. This theory was supported by research, using irradiation testing procedures at the University of Glasgow, which revealed high arsenic content in samples of Napoleon's hair. It is also argued that the almost perfectly preserved state of Napoleon's still corpulent body on exhumation was consistent with a high arsenic level.

There can be no certainty about this. However, a more recent study in 2008 by Italian researchers has dismissed the arsenic-poisoning theory.[41]

Their tests suggested that the poison was gradually accumulated throughout his whole life and that the concentration by the time he died was no higher than among his contemporaries generally. By using a small nuclear reactor at Pavia to subject hairs – said to have been taken from Napoleon at different stages in his life, from boyhood on Corsica to his death on St Helena – to eight hours of irradiation, they found arsenic levels 100 times the average found in hair today. However, by testing other samples, including locks of hair taken from Josephine, they concluded that the levels were normal for the time. They commented: 'The environment in which people were immersed at the start of the 19th century led to the ingestion of quantities of arsenic that we would consider dangerous today.' Possible sources included dyes, glues and the smoke from wood fires. We know from other previous tests that there were traces of arsenic in the green dye used to colour the wallpaper at Longwood, and it is quite possible that some of this was absorbed into Napoleon's system in the damp conditions of the house. There were often also smoky wood fires in the billiard and other rooms at Longwood. Arsenic might also have been put down occasionally to help kill the rats, although it is most unlikely that it was used in large quantities or without close control in view of the obvious dangers to the human occupants, especially the children, and the resultant stink of putrescent rats. Moreover, if Napoleon's system was affected seriously or even mortally by the casual absorption of arsenic in this way, it would be very surprising if he was the only one among the inhabitants of Longwood so to suffer.

As stated above it is difficult to believe that throughout the five and a half years of Napoleon's captivity, or even only during the later years, Montholon was steadily planning to murder Napoleon in this way. In any case he had no more control over Napoleon's food and drink during the final weeks of his life than General Bertrand or Marchand and Ali, who were constantly at his side and regularly performed the most personal, disagreeable and intimate services for their dying chief. No-one has accused them of poisoning him. Moreover the majority of the drugs, misguided and harmful though many of them may have been, were specifically prescribed and administered by Antommarchi and the other doctors.

Two studies published in 2009 have also critically examined and rejected the assassination by poisoning theory. They are *La Mort de Napoléon* by Thierry Lentz and Jacques Macé, and *Napoleon's Poisoned Chalice: The Emperor and his Doctors on St Helena* by Dr Martin Howard. The former concludes that the cause of death was 'une maladie de l'estomac' (a disease of the stomach)[42] and the latter that Napoleon died from cancer of the stomach (gastric carcinoma).[43] Lentz and Macé also demolish the fanciful theory, espoused by several French historians, that the remains in the tomb at Les Invalides in Paris are not those of Napoleon but of his servant Cipriani, who died mysteriously in 1818 and was allegedly exhumed by Lowe and his corpse substituted for that of Napoleon when Lowe called at St Helena en route from Ceylon in 1828.

The question of the precise cause of death must remain open. There was no second exhumation or autopsy after Napoleon was transferred in 1840 to his final resting place at Les Invalides in Paris and it is unlikely that there will ever be one. In my view, although some of the drugs administered to Napoleon during his final days, especially the huge dose of calomel on 3 May, may well have accelerated the end, the probability, accepted by most historians, is that Napoleon, after five and a half years of increasingly miserable captivity on the island, died in great pain from a form of the terrible disease that had killed his father. Bertrand, who was ever present during the final stages, later accepted this, and in his very detailed account of the post mortem and its aftermath Marchand, who would have been among the first to have suspicions of any foul play, does not question it. Napoleon certainly did not get the medical treatment he needed, which might perhaps have alleviated his suffering – but this was to a large extent his own fault in refusing medical attention, and in any case no doctor could have significantly arrested his condition. There may well also be a lot of truth in Chateaubriand's verdict – after Napoleon had accepted that there was to be no escape from St Helena – that he died of 'melancholy', in other words that he lost the will to live. It was a sadly squalid and miserable end to his life, but perhaps no more so than the agony and suffering of the hundreds of thousands who had died as a result of Napoleon's pursuit of his destiny during the previous three decades.

ELEVEN

A JUDGEMENT

HISTORY HAS FOR THE most part marked Sir Hudson Lowe as the out and out villain on St Helena, the brutal jailor who treated Napoleon, to use his own words, like a Botany Bay convict. This is not just true of the understandable French tradition, with the notable recent exception of Fournier La Touraille, but also of some leading British historians. Lord Rosebery, in his 1900 study, though not totally critical, in general had little time for Lowe. Admittedly Rosebery was dismissive of many of the actors in this drama. Dr Warden's journal was 'valueless',[1] O'Meara's diaries 'worthless',[2] General Gourgaud a 'fretful porcupine',[3] and Napoleon, although he respected his enormously wide range of competences, a 'self-deluding egoist'.[4] But poor Lowe, whom Rosebery did not regard as a 'gentleman', perhaps the ultimate Victorian censure, was described as a 'narrow, ignorant, irritable man, without a vestige of tact or sympathy'.[5] Even Forsyth, who in his massive three-volume history of 1853 is generally regarded as one of Lowe's stoutest champions, had to admit that 'his manner was not prepossessing, even in the judgement of favourable friends'.

The Duke of Wellington, who had been reasonably tactful about Lowe on previous occasions, although he had not chosen to have him on his staff at Waterloo, said in a letter to Lord Ellesmere in 1820, after hearing a report that Lowe was mistreating Napoleon on St Helena, that: 'I always thought Lowe the most unfit person to be charged with the care of Napoleon's person.'[6]

How far does Lowe merit these harsh judgements? There is no doubt, especially on the evidence of Major Gorrequer's diaries, and even allowing for Gorrequer's somewhat paranoic obsessions, that Lowe was an irascible, irritable, insecure and short-tempered man, quick to blame others for his own errors, and often petty minded and inconsiderate of his subordinates. He could also be brutal when it suited him, as in the case of Dr Stokoe, who had been placed in an almost impossible position in relation to Napoleon and probably never understood fully why he had been arrested and brought back to the island for court martial and dismissal. Lowe was also prone to offend those who should have been his staunchest friends. Admiral Sir Pulteney Malcolm and Lady Malcolm were a case in point. They found him very difficult to get on with, partly because they considered him unreasonable in the way he applied the restrictions on Napoleon, but they remained remarkably loyal to him in their conversations with Napoleon, despite his jealous touchiness and his letters bordering on the offensive to such a senior colleague.

As described in earlier chapters, he was under very strict and precise instructions from Whitehall and, even with the slow communications of the time, under constant surveillance. But he positively invited such attention by his unnecessarily frequent reporting, which betrayed his lack of confidence and anxiety not to put a foot wrong. He was always seeking reassurance that what he had done met with the Secretary of State's approval. He had been given authority by Lord Bathurst to use his local discretion within his overall instructions. However, although Bathurst was a powerful and experienced minister, to whom far grander figures than Lowe reported, he was very nervous about taking advantage of this: 'whenever I deviate from my instructions I feel my responsibility to be a very painful one.'[7]

His anxiety to comply exactly with his instructions led him to many unnecessarily petty measures. Cases in point were: the affair in 1817 of Dr Stokoe and the book on Marlborough given to him for his regiment by Napoleon; the withholding in June 1817 for two weeks of a bust of

Napoleon's son, the King of Rome, which had been brought out to St Helena for Napoleon by a gunner on a British warship (it was claimed at Longwood that Sir Thomas Reade wanted to throw it into the harbour);[8] his objection in July of the same year to the presentation to Napoleon of an ivory chess set sent out by Fanny Bertrand's well-connected relative, the Hon. Mr Elphinstone – to thank him for saving his wounded brother's life at Waterloo – because it was engraved with the letter N and the imperial crown;[9] and other examples where letters or packages for or from Longwood were returned or rejected because they carried some kind of imperial reference or symbol. The final insult was when he refused to accept the form of words proposed by the French to inscribe on Napoleon's tombstone in Geranium Valley, even though it did not contain the word 'Emperor'.[10] The French wanted simply to have the word 'Napoleon' on it, whereas Lowe insisted on adding 'Bonaparte', which the French rejected, leaving the stone blank.

All these actions were strictly compliant with Lowe's instructions, but in many cases the application of a little more common sense, robustnesss and discretion by the man on the spot could have avoided or at least mitigated unnecessary friction and unpleasantness. A particularly ludicrous argument arose in April 1820 when the hapless French Commissioner, Montchenu, was upbraided by Lowe for accepting from General Montholon some haricots verts and haricots blancs from the newly resuscitated Longwood vegetable garden.[11] Lowe apparently saw in them some sinister political ruse, the green beans allegedly representing the defunct Napoleonic Empire and the white ones the restored Bourbon monarchy. He suggested that acceptance of them in some sense compromised Montchenu, but simply made himself look ridiculous.

As we have seen in Chapter Eight, by far the most contentious issue, which irritated and insulted Napoleon beyond measure, was the denial by the British to him of his imperial title and the use of the form of address 'General Bonaparte'. The more the British used this, the more Napoleon insisted on being addressed as 'Sa Majesté l'Empereur'. There was no dispute that he was now a former emperor. Nonetheless, to go some way to conceding the post-abdication title or the dignity of it to him, or at the very least not causing a fuss over every trivial situation where the imperial insignia appeared in some form or other, would have been a common-sense and generous gesture that might have softened a gratuitous insult and removed at least some of the friction between Lowe and his prisoner. Nowadays Europe is still full of ex-sovereigns, in reference to whom the 'ex-' is often dropped, and American former presidents have for many years retained their title after leaving office. Indeed, after Napoleon's death it did not take long for the British Government itself to revert to according him his imperial title. For example, the 1858 Ordinance conveying to the then French Emperor title to the ownership of the land on St Helena where Napoleon's original tomb was sited, referred to 'the site of the tomb of His Majesty Napoleon the First, late Emperor of the French'.

For his part Napoleon would simply not concede the point. As he once said to Dr O'Meara, 'The people of England want to know why I call myself Emperor, after having abdicated ... It was my intention to have lived in England as a private person incognito, but as they have sent me here, and want it to appear that I was never Chief Magistrate or Emperor of France, I shall retain the title.'[12] In spite of his instructions from London – in June 1817 Lord Bathurst again reminded him that he should not accept letters from Longwood referring to 'Emperor' – it is hard to believe that Lowe could not have done more to contest the original decision, or find some way of turning a blind eye on occasions locally, but he did not choose nor dare to argue the matter seriously with London further.

Although at a somewhat less-eminent level than the imperial grandeur of Napoleon, Hudson Lowe was equally desperate to maintain his own gubernatorial authority and dignity. He must have been an imposing sight, particularly on horseback, in his scarlet general's uniform, with the plumed cocked hat and sword, followed by a retinue of officers and orderlies in similar military and naval splendour. However, he constantly let himself down, prowling round Longwood in an undignified way like a burglar casing the joint, and even on one occasion creeping up to the walls to measure out the intervals that sentries had to observe after dark. Napoleon once described him to O'Meara as patrolling round Longwood like a 'gendarme'.[13] He sensibly restrained his temper in the earlier meetings with Napoleon, and was even commended for this by some of Napoleon's colleagues, who thought Napoleon had gone too far in his insulting treatment of him (a feeling which Napoleon himself somewhat guiltily shared on at least two occasions). But thereafter he could not resist the bait and rose immediately to Napoleon's provocation, involving himself in often minor disputes that should have been dealt with by his subordinates. This brought him into frequent and unpleasant conflict with the hapless intermediaries, Bertrand and Montholon, as well as with Napoleon. His strong words of reproof to Bertrand on one occasion were the reason why Napoleon told him that he acted like a corporal or a company clerk instead of a general, unlike Bertrand who had seen proper service and behaved like a real general, and therefore deserved suitable respect.

It must be remembered, however, that underlying Lowe's behaviour throughout his period on St Helena was his perpetual fear that Napoleon might escape. If he did, Lowe's career and reputation were in shreds, and he could expect severe retribution in London. On the face of it the fear of escape was unfounded. With hardly any practicable landing places, and a rocky ring of steep, bare and often jagged cliffs surrounding it, protected by guns at regular strategic points, and over 2,000 troops, St Helena was virtually impregnable to attack. One of the few places where a landing might have been contemplated was the so-called Sandy Bay in the south, but as we have seen this is no more than a shallow gravelly beach, surrounded by high rocky cliffs, and heavily defended. When I visited it in December 2007 the fortifications were still largely intact and a row of rusting cannons stretched across the top of the beach. It was for this reason that Napoleon and his sympathizers argued that the tight physical restrictions imposed on Longwood and within the island were unnecessary. Nevertheless, the fact is that, despite the presence (or rather temporary absence at the time) of a resident British Commissioner, sent there to keep a close eye on him, Napoleon had escaped from Elba.

There were also many reports of plots to assemble a force to invade St Helena and mount a rescue operation. Lowe was several time warned about these from intelligence sources by London and urged to remain vigilant. Most of them linked the plots with exiled Bonapartists in the United States or South America; in July 1816 he was informed of a plot discovered by French intelligence, and passed on to the British Ambassador in Paris; the plot involved equipping a fast ship in the Hudson River that was to sail to St Helena and pick up Napoleon.

One of the most dramatic plots is that related by Robert Harvey in his entertaining biography of Thomas Cochrane (*Cochrane, The Life and Exploits of a Fighting Captain*),[14] who was the model for both C.S. Forester's Captain Hornblower and Captain Aubrey in Patrick O'Brian's celebrated series of Napoleonic War novels. Cochrane was a friend of Admiral Sir

Pulteney Malcolm, who had left St Helena on strained terms with Lowe, and had also in April 1809 captained the 74-gun ship *Donegal* at the famous Aix Roads battle. After being dismissed from the Royal Navy on a trumped-up Stock Exchange fraud charge (like Aubrey), Cochrane was invited in 1818 to take command of the Chilean navy in order to help Chile gain its independence from Spain by destroying the Spanish navy's domination of the long coast line of their country. Cochrane, an outstanding and daring frigate captain, as well as an outspoken radical politician who was unpopular with the government of the day, was regarded in some quarters as a second Nelson and had spent most of his naval career fighting against Napoleon. But as a fellow fighting man he still admired him and he conceived a plan to sail to Chile via St Helena, snatch Napoleon away and place him on the throne of a new South American confederation to match the United States in the north. It sounds utterly fanciful, but we know from other sources that there was a more significant plot by a group of exiled Bonapartist officers in the United States, which envisaged Cochrane commanding an invasion force consisting of a 74-gun warship, two gunboats, and a force of 800 marines and 200–300 officers and soldiers. In the event the plot came to nothing, but if there was any man in the world who could have carried it off, it was Cochrane. Napoleon had the highest regard for him – he was known by the French as 'le loup des mers' (the sea wolf) – and once said that if he had been properly supported by his admiral he would have taken every one of the French ships at the Aix Roads battle where half the French fleet was destroyed by fireships in April 1809.

Perhaps the most bizarre and improbable plot was a report that some Bonapartists had offered £40,000 to a certain Thomas Johnstone, a former Channel pilot and smuggler who had collaborated with the American inventor, Robert Fulton, to build a submarine to be towed to St Helena.[15] The idea was that it would slip into St Helena unseen, take Napoleon off from a beach, and then return to the mother ship, which would convey Napoleon to South America. According to other reports a submarine was actually completed at a yard on the upper Thames, but, when being brought downriver, got stuck under an arch of London Bridge and was discovered by the authorities and destroyed.

Although we may believe that there was no real risk of a successful escape attempt, least of all by a submarine, Lowe, confined on the island, and with relatively little information about the outside world, was not to know this and had to remain on his guard. It is doubtful, however, whether Napoleon would in any case have attempted to escape. He once told O'Meara that he had no intention of trying to do so, although he would not give his word of honour on this, because by so doing he would implicitly accept that he was a prisoner.[16] There were a number of reasons why he was unlikely to try to escape. In the early days of his captivity he still had hopes of being allowed to return to Europe or America as a result of a change of government or policy in England. The physical risks of an escape attempt were high, and it would have been humiliating to be captured like some ordinary criminal fugitive, or even blown up at sea. This was one of the reasons why he had not favoured an attempt at a breakout through the British naval blockade at Rochefort in July 1815. It was not clear either what he would do if he found his way safely to the United States or South America. The idea of ruling a new confederation of Latin American states seems very far-fetched, and it is most unlikely that he would have been content to pursue for long a quiet life as a farmer or rancher. He also on occasions expressed a fear of being assassinated in the United States. Finally, as time passed, he increasingly saw his destiny and the road to immortality resting in ending his life as an unjustly persecuted victim on the rock of St Helena. This was the only further legacy he could now hope to leave to the world – the death of a martyr – so shamefully treated by the British, who would be condemned for their barbarous treatment of him by future generations.

In spite of this Lowe simply dare not take a risk, and his fear, combined with his growing personal antipathy towards Napoleon, ensured that he kept the screw on the Longwood household tightly turned. He was not, however, totally devoid of humanity and consideration. In the early days he told Lord Bathurst that he did not think Longwood a suitable residence for a former emperor, and he did what he could, but without success, to engage Napoleon in the plans for the New Longwood House. He chanced his arm in authorizing an increase in the Longwood cash limit from £8,000 to £12,000 and there are many recorded instances of his thoughtfulness in arranging for books, plants or other welcome deliveries to be sent to Longwood – even on one occasion some good coffee and almonds, of which he believed Napoleon was fond. Montholon, who was supposed to be in charge of the commissariat at Longwood, even volunteered the following testimonial to Major Gorrequer: 'Nous n'avons aucun reproche à faire au

Gouverneur; nous ne nous plaignions de rien et nous avons abundance de tout ce qui est nécessaire' (We have no reproach to make against the Governor; we had nothing to complain about and we have plenty of all the things we need).[17] It is less certain, however, that Napoleon would have endorsed this tribute. Even Antommarchi, during the final stressful days of Napoleon's illness, described Lowe as 'ever humane, compassionate and sincere'[18] – perhaps in contrast to the dismissive and insulting treatment he himself now seemed generally to receive from Napoleon.

Over the period of the captivity Lowe also offered to relax some of the physical controls on Longwood, but his relationship with the increasingly bitter and ailing Napoleon was now such that his offers were generally rebuffed. Napoleon would not, and for his own self-respect could not, accept any favours from his jailor. When it was really already too late Lowe did what he could, if only in his own self-interest, to provide Napoleon with proper medical attention, and the day after Napoleon's death he paid him the following tribute: 'He was England's greatest enemy, and mine too, but I forgive him everything. On the death of a great man like him, we should only feel deep concern and regret.'[19] This may perhaps have been intended more for public consumption than a genuine reflection of Lowe's real feelings, but within Lowe's irascible exterior there was sometimes a decent man trying to get out. It is a pity he was too frightened and unsure of himself to display it very often.

Lowe's problems were, of course, nothing compared with those facing Napoleon. It is impossible to exaggerate the extreme and dramatic depth of his cataclysmic fall from power, and the deeply depressing psychological effect it must have had on him. After Waterloo and the hostile reception he received on return to Paris, where he was simply not wanted any more, he must have realized that the game was up and that he would never ascend the imperial throne again. But in his wildest nightmares he could never have envisaged the complete emasculation and impotence that incarceration for life on St Helena would inflict on him. In his *Poetics* Aristotle defines the perfect tragedy as the fall of a great man from high to low estate, passing through peripeteia, or sudden reversal of fortune, to catharsis, or cleansing.[20] Napoleon's peripeteia was the crushing defeat at Waterloo and transportation to St Helena. His catharsis was his final agony and death on the island. His was a truly Aristotelian tragedy. To be stripped of his crown and title, rejected by his fellow countrymen, deprived of his wife and child and transported by the British, his life-long enemies to whom he had voluntarily surrendered, must have been an inconceivable humiliation.

Napoleon was an egoist and megalomaniac who had survived, and later tamed, the French Revolution and established his domination over first France and then most of the rest of continental Europe. After a relatively modest and inauspicious start – he had only passed out forty-second out of fifty-eight at the École Militaire in September 1785 – he fought his way up the dangerous ladder of power to become one of the greatest commanders in history by a combination of hard work, extraordinary intelligence, ruthlessness, taking risks and sheer genius. From the start he had decided to dominate in every sphere, and as his power grew, so it began to corrupt. In February 1806 he even proposed to the Minister of Public Worship that his birthday, 15 August, should be celebrated as the Feast of St Napoleon – almost an attempt at self-deification.[21] This need to dominate even applied within his own family. He had made it clear that, though only the second son, he intended, after his father's death, to be the head of the Bonaparte family. His brothers and sisters were made to feel this in later life as he bestowed titles and kingdoms on them, whether they liked it or not, arranged their marriages, and dealt with them at times with little short of contempt. His critical letters to Louis in particular, during his unhappy reign as King of Holland, were brutal and insulting in the extreme.[22] Even his elder brother, Joseph, felt the lash of his tongue, above all when he was being defeated and driven out of Spain by Wellington.[23] Members of his family were never allowed to forget that he was now His Majesty on the imperial throne. He was always insistent that he alone was right and knew what should be done. All had to be subject to 'mon bon plaisir'.

By the time of his first abdication in 1814, he already had to his credit massive achievements in the civil governance and administration of France. He had reshaped its laws through the new Code Napoléon, which became, and still remains, the basis of the legal systems of much of continental Europe; reorganized the structure of local government by establishing the network of départements; set up for the first time a universal system of primary and secondary education, for both sexes; reformed the relationship between State and Church and put the Pope in his place; founded the University and Bank of France, and the Légion d'Honneur; and by his military daring and genius, albeit at huge cost in terms of the lives sacrificed, redrawn the map of Europe and extended France's frontiers for a time to form an empire greater than that of Charlemagne. At its height in 1812 it ranged over the western half of continental Europe, comprising nearly forty-five million people in 130 *départements*, not counting four Catalan *départements*, six Illyrian dependencies and the twenty-four *départements* of the Kingdom of Italy. With just a modicum of extra luck and, so he maintained, more competent support from his subordinate commanders, he might have reasserted his mastery after the return from Elba and even brought his most resolute and bitter enemy, England, to terms.

However, all this had ended in disaster and there was a danger that as he steadily rotted away on St Helena this legacy would be eroded and his role in creating it forgotten. From the pinnacles of power he was now reduced to occupying a damp, rat-infested, hastily converted wooden house on a windy and often cloud-covered plain on a godforsaken British island thousands of miles from anywhere. He was deprived of his wife and son, who were steadily being alienated from him, and all he had to command was a squabbling and jealousy-ridden household consisting of three generals, a counsellor of state, and a mixed retinue of servants. Even in exile on Elba he had still enjoyed nominal sovereign status, even though over a miniature state, and command of more than 1,000 loyal troops.

In such circumstances, for his own pride and self-respect, and to keep going, he simply had to try to preserve to the utmost the dignity and outward show of an emperor. For this reason he insisted on the observation of strict protocol at Longwood, which must have become tedious in the extreme to his companions, and which in time even he could no longer maintain. He also, while he had the capacity to do so, had to ensure that he placed his own version of his legacy on record. This is why both on the voyage to St Helena and in the early months and years on the island he feverishly dictated his memoirs to Las Cases and Gourgaud. Unless he now set in tablets of stone his account of his career and achievements, the true history of his glory years might fade away into the St Helena mists, as the British no doubt hoped.

He never ceased to seethe with indignation at his treatment. In some sense this perhaps helped to keep him going. At the Congress of Vienna in March 1815 the allied powers had declared, following his escape from Elba, that Napoleon 'is placed out of the pale of civil and social relations' – in other words, is a public outlaw – and that 'as an enemy and a disturber of the world he is delivered up to public vengeance.'[24] But Napoleon, by the act of surrendering voluntarily at the Ile d'Aix to Captain Maitland on the *Bellerophon*, persisted in regarding himself as the guest of the British Government, and not as a prisoner. In any case, he argued, if he was to be regarded legally as a prisoner, prisoners of war were normally released and allowed to return home on the cessation of hostilities. His famous letter to the Prince Regent in July 1815 seeking asylum in England, like Themistocles at the court of the Persian King, exemplified this. There may have been some legal force in his contention, and it is arguable that if he had been formally designated a prisoner of war, the British Government had no right to deport him and treat him as they did on St Helena, their early 19th-century equivalent of Guantánamo. The British Government's anxiety to get him on board the *Northumberland* and away from British shores was a sign of their doubts about the legality of their action. Nevertheless, on any realistic assessment of the situation, in view of his record Napoleon could not have expected anything much less severe. Indeed, since there were no war crimes tribunals or international courts at the time, he was lucky not to have been executed summarily after his capture. Marshal Blücher, who hated him, would not have hesitated, and was only prevented from carrying this out by the Duke of Wellington – a fact that Napoleon never acknowledged.

He talked sometimes of committing suicide and professed to wish that he had been killed in battle at Waterloo. He had once made a somewhat botched attempt to poison himself at Fontainebleau, prior to his first abdication, but suicide would not have suited the Napoleon legacy that he was now so anxious to leave behind him. In her memoirs Hortense Beauharnais records that Napoleon said to her at Malmaison, before his flight to Rochefort, 'On se tue pour échapper à la honte. On ne se tue pour échapper au Malheur' (People kill themselves to escape shame; they do not do it to escape misfortune).[25] Napoleon could do little about his misfortune, but he was still determined to avoid shame and dishonour.

It has to be accepted – as Lowe himself did on occasions in his dispatches to Lord Bathurst – that Longwood was not 'fit for purpose'. For someone who, despite rigorous campaigning in extremes of climate, had for many years enjoyed palatial luxury right across Europe, it was a relative hovel. But as a prison, it could also have been worse. Given the tight supply situation on the island, provisions were plentiful – the amount of wine and meat consumed was amazing (even O'Meara admitted this) – and Napoleon had ample scope for recreation within Longwood's grounds or outside them if he was prepared to stomach the presence of an accompanying British officer. Contact with outsiders was relatively free. There was a continual stream of visitors, both to Napoleon and his companions, including the Bertrands across the road. We know from General Gourgaud's testimony after he left the island and from other sources that there was in practice no problem in communicating with Europe and the outside world – there were plenty of volunteers willing to act as couriers and take messages. It is difficult to imagine that Napoleon would have allowed such relative comfort and amenities to a major political prisoner – that is, if he had allowed him to live.

It was also Napoleon's own choice, as a matter of principle, that he did not take full advantage of many of the opportunities for exercise open to him, with serious detriment to his health. So he stuck to the view that he was not a prisoner and that Lowe had no right to treat him as such, from which it followed that he would not compromise his position by accepting any favours from him.

Napoleon's view of the English was ambivalent. They were his greatest enemy who, by their naval and maritime power, had frustrated his ambition to control the whole of Europe. He could not read English fluently but he once told O'Meara that he employed no fewer than thirty clerks to translate the English newspapers and journals and report anything of moment to him.[26] He was never short of views on how the British Government should manage both its civil and military affairs and he had remarkably detailed opinions on the changes he would make in British society and the constitution if ever he successfully invaded England. In spite of this the English remained his greatest enemy and source of frustration. They had organized and financed the coalitions against him. Secure in their naval and commercial power, they had, except for the short-lived Treaty of Amiens in 1802, refused to make peace and had thwarted his ambition to control the whole of Europe. From this stemmed paradoxically his admiration of the Royal Navy, which constantly, and with relative ease, defeated his own fleets and guaranteed British control of commerce and the seas. Crucially, they never gave him even twenty-four unguarded hours to allow his huge invasion army and fleet assembled at Boulogne to cross the Channel. Like Hitler, who also deluded himself that if he successfully invaded England the English would welcome him as a liberator, Napoleon would have preferred to have England as a partner rather than an enemy, provided it was compliant with his policies. He once said that he would perish or plant his flag on the Tower of London. Sadly for him only the first half of this prophecy came true.

This love–hate relationship was well illustrated by a remark he once made that: 'The British nation would be incapable of contending with us if we only had their national spirit.' He once also interrupted Lady Malcolm, when he thought she was saying he hated England, by exclaiming that he did not hate the English – on the contrary, he said, he had the highest opinion of their character, but 'I have been deceived, and here I am on a vile rock in the middle of the ocean.'[27] It was this sense of betrayal and deception that made him so bitter and intransigent on St Helena. And for him Hudson Lowe personified that treachery.

The reader must make their own judgement on whether Lowe deserves the condemnation of history that has generally fallen on him. Measured by the main task assigned to him, Lowe did not fail. Napoleon did not escape and he almost certainly died from natural, if horrible, causes. After his disappearance there was no further major war in Western Europe for another fifty years and France and Britain fought shoulder to shoulder in the disastrous Crimean War. Lowe was a competent soldier and a good administrator of the island who received a warm tribute from the islanders when he left and also a warm welcome when he subsequently called in on his return to England from Ceylon in 1827. He showed liberality and humanity by his abolition of slavery on the island, and he was by no means always insensitive to the indignity and unpleasantness of Napoleon's situation. However, he was by nature an ill-tempered, often inconsiderate and petty-minded man, whose perpetual sense of insecurity and fear of not complying strictly with his orders led him to discharge his duty in an unnecessarily cautious, pedantic and sometimes vindictive way. He did not deserve to be dropped, treated shabbily and made a scapegoat by the British Government on his return, but a little more courage and common sense on the spot might have eased the situation and secured for him a better reputation and treatment by the Government when he went back.

But we must always remember that, *pace* Tolstoy, he was facing a master tactician and one of the giants of history. It was really a mismatch. Since he was now powerless to do much else Napoleon never missed an opportunity to insult, frustrate and discredit his jailor, and when all hope of returning to Europe had gone he was determined in the end to die a martyr. A less rigorous and obedient jailor than Lowe might easily have succumbed completely to Napoleon's influence and lost control on the island. Lowe undoubtedly had many faults, but Gourgaud may well have been right when he said that 'even if an angel had been sent out as Governor, it would have been all the same.'[28] This sentiment was also echoed by Mrs Abell, the former Betsy Balcombe, at the end of her memoirs, with the words: 'I have often doubted whether any human being could have filled the situation of Sir Hudson Lowe, without becoming embroiled with his unhappy captive.'[29]

EPILOGUE

FOR FIVE AND A half years the imprisonment of Napoleon and his companions at Longwood had dominated the island of St Helena. The economic and social life of the colony had been severely disrupted by the sudden arrival of over 2,000 soldiers and sailors and by the security restrictions that applied throughout the island. Prices rose, many basic commodities were in short supply, and freedom of movement was constrained. When I visited the island at the end of 2007 I had the feeling that some atavistic memory of this uncomfortable period still lay behind the apparent indifference of many of the present islanders to their unique Napoleonic heritage. It was all very exciting at the time, but it made daily life for the islanders much more difficult.

After Napoleon's death and the completion of the funeral obsequies all the principal actors left the island after a very short time. On the day after the funeral, 10 May 1821, Sir Hudson Lowe returned to Longwood to carry out a formal inventory of Napoleon's effects and *en passant* to select some items of furniture that he fancied.[1] The fine crystal chandelier, which still dominates the dining room at Plantation House, was removed from Longwood and placed there by Hudson Lowe. He was accompanied at Longwood House for the very first time by Lady Lowe, who was warmly greeted by Madame Bertrand, on whom she had sometimes called at the Bertrands' cottage across the road.[2] Relations between Hudson Lowe and General Bertrand, which had deteriorated badly while Bertrand was acting as an uncomfortable go-between and fighting Napoleon's corner, also began to thaw. On 27 May, after dining at Plantation House[3] and paying a final visit of homage to Napoleon's tomb in the silence of Geranium Valley on the previous evening, the exiles embarked on the transport vessel, the *Camel*, to return to Europe. It was a crowded and uncomfortable ship, with squalid conditions, but they were relieved to be away, and they reached Spithead on 31 July 1821.[4]

The future for most of them was a surprisingly successful and happy one. Bertrand remained in London for a while with Montholon to sort out their affairs and to ensure that his own return to France would be a safe one (he had initially been on the proscribed list by the restored Bourbons and under threat of death after fleeing from Waterloo with Napoleon and accompanying him into exile). The way for his return was now cleared and he was allowed by Louis XVIII to retain his rank. He eventually became a deputy in the National Assembly in 1830 and was a leading member of the party under the Prince de Joinville that went to St Helena in *La Belle Poule* to recover Napoleon's body in 1840. He also took a prominent part in the magnificent ceremony in Paris when Napoleon's coffin was returned. After his death in his proud hometown of Chateauroux on 31 January 1847, his body was placed alongside the tomb of Napoleon under the great dome of Les Invalides – a fitting resting place for the most loyal and devoted of Napoleon's senior companions.

Napoleon's two astonishingly faithful and devoted valets, Louis-Joseph Marchand and Louis-Etienne St Denis, alias Mameluke Ali, also went on to live full lives after their vigil on St Helena. Marchand, who had been named an executor of Napoleon's will, together with Bertrand and Montholon, returned quickly to France after arriving in England and in 1823, in accordance with a wish expressed by Napoleon on his deathbed, married the daughter of General Brayer, in the presence of Generals Gourgaud and Montholon and other senior officers. Napoleon's role as a marriage broker thus continued beyond the grave. Marchand was also chosen to accompany Bertrand and Gourgaud to St Helena in 1840 and, again in accordance with a wish expressed in Napoleon's will, he was moved up the social scale and made a count in 1869. He became a revered figure in his local community and lived on to see the fall of the second Napoleonic Empire after the disaster at Sedan, and remained faithful to the exiled Napoleon III just as he had to his uncle after the defeat at Waterloo. He died at Trouville on 19 June 1876, and his funeral in Paris was attended by a large crowd of faithful friends.

Marchand's close colleague, Ali, lived a more discreet life after returning to France. Having obtained part of the legacy left to him by Napoleon, he settled in Sens in 1827 but still kept in close touch with Marchand. He also accompanied the 1840 expedition to recover Napoleon's body but devoted much of his time at home to assembling the papers relating to the period of captivity. He compiled his own *Souvenirs* of his service with Napoleon, but they were not published until 1926. They form an affectionate, touching and valuable account of his long and devoted service.

The future of the Montholons was less happy. Albine de Montholon had departed with the children in July 1819, but soon after her return to Belgium (she was not allowed to disembark in Britain) the infant Napoléone-Joséphine, Napoleon's presumptive child, died as a result of the hardships of the voyage and was buried in Brussels. In Albine's journal we have a moving account of this sad event.[5] Montholon himself left the island with the rest of the French party on the *Camel* and as first executor of Napoleon's will had the triumph of formally opening it on the ship in the presence of the other two executors, Bertrand and Marchand. After reaching England he soon moved back to France and was reunited with Albine. Thereafter his career went downhill. The relationship with Albine soured as he ran into financial difficulties – it took some time before they were able to lay their hands on the cash element of Napoleon's legacy – and the marriage broke up after Charles had had an affair and a child by a young housemaid, Hélène Gordon. In 1840 he became involved in the failed coup of Louis-Napoleon Bonaparte and was imprisoned for six years with him at the fortress of Ham. He died in Paris in 1853, Albine having predeceased him in March 1848.

Although he had left the island before the others, in fraught circumstances in March 1818, a word about General Gourgaud is also appropriate. After spending some time in London and passing on to the Secretary of State, Lord Bathurst, a great deal of information about Napoleon and life at Longwood, he returned to France. He was accepted back by Louis XVIII and in 1830 made commander of the artillery. In 1832 he became an aide de camp to King Louis-Philippe, and in 1840 he was a leading – if still touchy and temperamental – member of the expedition to bring Napoleon's body home to France and was given a role of honour in the ceremony at Les Invalides. In 1841 he was put in charge of the new fortification of Paris and made colonel of the 1st legion of the National Guard. He died in July 1852, just in time to see another Napoleon on the French throne. All in all, Lord Rosebery's 'fretful porcupine' did not do too badly from his switches of temper and allegiance.

The remains of Napoleon (in French always called 'Les Cendres') returned to the soil of his beloved native country in triumph in December 1840 after the exhumation described in the introduction to this book. This final act dramatically revived the Napoleonic legend and the process is brilliantly depicted in detail in Gilbert Martineau's account in his book *Napoleon's Last Journey*.[6] Napoleon could not have devised a better script if he had dictated it himself in advance on St Helena for his memoirs. After the voyage back from St Helena, the frigate *La Belle Poule* reached Cherbourg on 29 November 1840. Following a final Mass aboard, the heavy coffin was transferred to *La Normandie*, which was to transport it to the mouth of the Seine. As the *Normandie* could not navigate the Seine a flotilla of smaller ships escorted the black-painted *Dorade 3*, on which the coffin now stood, still guarded by the King's youngest son, the Prince de Joinville, and Napoleon's former companions.

The journey down the Seine was a triumphal passage past unprecedented displays of loyalty and rejoicing by packed crowds on the river banks at places such as Rouen, Elbeuf, Les Andelys, Vernon and Nantes, until on the evening of 12 December the flotilla halted at the Poissy bridge, where it was guarded by troops of the line and the National Guard. After Mass on the following Sunday morning the convoy started off again and in the evening reached Courbevoie, the end of the river voyage. The banks were covered with soldiers of every unit and formation, including veterans from the old imperial Grande Armée. Silence fell on the crowds as in a moment of great emotion the Minister of War, the ageing Marshal Soult, Duke of Dalmatia, a veteran of the Peninsular War and Napoleon's Chief of Staff at Waterloo, knelt to pay homage to the return home of his former Commander in Chief and Emperor.

At 9am on 15 December the sailors from *La Belle Poule* lifted up the coffin, carried it ashore and, straining under the weight, placed it under an open Greek temple where the enormous hearse was standing, drawn by sixteen black horses, harnessed four by four, and caparisoned in gold. The hearse was surmounted by a cenotaph, weighing thirteen and a half tonnes and standing ten metres high. It was supported on fourteen statues, representing Napoleon's victories, and other ornaments of every description. The coffin was placed carefully in the undercarriage.

The procession began its slow journey towards its final resting place at Les Invalides in the heart of Paris. It was accompanied by the pealing of the great bells of Notre Dame and other churches in the city. Despite the intense cold, said to be fourteen degrees below zero, dense crowds had been gathering throughout the night, occupying every possible vantage point. Windows and balconies along the route had been let at extravagant prices. Lining the roadside were detachments of the National Guard, the Seine gendarmerie, battalions of infantry, squadrons of lancers and cuirassiers, and many veterans who had found again and donned their tattered and threadbare uniforms, and faded bearskin bonnets, to honour their former chief. Some of them froze to death as they waited stoically throughout the bitterly cold night to get a glimpse of the coffin of their Emperor. It was one of those moments in history of which all Frenchmen would try to recall where they were and what they were doing at the time.

Among the many high dignitaries accompanying the catafalque were some of Napoleon's former marshals and generals, including Marshal Gérard, Commander in Chief of the National Guard, and hero of the battle of Ligny fought against the Prussians a few days before Waterloo. The Prince de Joinville, at the head of the sailors from La Belle Poule, accompanied the hearse, and the pall was carried by General Bertrand, Marshals Molitor and Oudinot, and Admiral Roussin. The cortège moved agonizingly slowly along the crowded Champs Elysées, under the Arc de Triomphe, heralded by a twenty-one-cannon salute, across the Place de la Concorde and on towards Les Invalides. On the Esplanade facing the church, now covered in swirling snow, more than 40,000 guests were massed on temporarily erected banks of seats, sitting shivering as they awaited the arrival of the coffin. Inside the church, in a deconsecrated chapel, the King and Queen were waiting too, Louis-Philippe wearing the ceremonial uniform of a lieutenant-general.

The matelots from La Belle Poule handed over the coffin to a team of non-commissioned officers who carried it to the gateway, where the Archbishop of Paris received it and entered the church, followed by the cortège headed by General Bertrand. The King descended from his throne and moved down towards the Prince de Joinville, who said: 'Sire, I present you with the body of Napoleon.' The King replied simply: 'I receive it in the name of France.' Marshal Soult then presented the King with a sword, which he in turn handed to Bertrand, saying 'General, I charge you to place the Emperor's sword on his coffin.' Overcome with emotion, tears streaming down his face, Bertrand came forward and at the same time General Gourgaud was invited to place on the coffin the cocked hat that Napoleon had worn at the bloody battle of Eylau. The two former companions in exile now stood united in both joy and grief at the fulfilment of their Emperor's wish 'to repose on the banks of the Seine in the midst of the French people I have loved so much'. Then came the funeral service, led by the Archbishop, and a performance of Mozart's *Requiem* by some of the greatest singers of the time, accompanied by a choir of 600 voices. It was a resurrection and apotheosis of the Emperor. There was no talk of General Bonaparte now. As someone is reported to have said as he left the ceremony, 'It is more than the glorification of a great man, it is like the restoration of his dynasty.'[8]

It was also the relaunch, with a vengeance, of the Napoleonic legend. Contrary to the hopes of the British Government, it had never really faded. Writing in April 1835 about her stay of several months in Paris, Fanny Trollope, the indomitable mother of the more renowned Anthony, said that 'it would, I think, be difficult to find a Frenchman, let his party be what it might, who would speak of Napoleon with disrespect.'[9] And later: 'This gratitude and affection [for Napoleon] endures still – nothing will ever efface it; for his military tyranny is passed away, and the benefits which his colossal power enabled him to bestow upon them remain, and must remain as long as France endures. The only means by which another sovereign may rival Napoleon in popularity is by rivalling him in power.'[10] With the return home of his body the Eagle now soared even higher than ever, nineteen years after that burial ceremony in lonely Geranium Valley on St Helena, which, although lacking head-of-state honours, was the most magnificent the island could offer – but nevertheless a pale sideshow compared with the triumphal pomp at Les Invalides in December 1840. And what a triumph the resurrection was, compared with the fate of Sir Hudson Lowe after St Helena.

Sir Hudson and Lady Lowe and their family, with Major Gorrequer and other members of his staff, left St Helena on the *Lady Melville* on 25 July 1821. Before embarking, Lowe received an exceptionally warm and appreciative testimonial of thanks from the inhabitants of the island.[11] Before arriving in England he also received on board a dispatch dated 10 July from Lord Bathurst, which conveyed his appreciation to Lowe and that of the recently crowned King George IV for his conduct as Governor on the island. It concluded by praising him for 'combining the secure detention of General Bonaparte's person, which was of necessity the paramount object of your attention, with every practicable consideration and indulgence which your own disposition prompted and your instructions authorized you to show to his particular attention.'[12] This was perhaps a little double-edged praise, with the unnecessary reference once more to Lowe's instructions. However, it seemed to augur well for Lowe's prospects on return and on 14 November Bathurst presented Lowe to the King, who shook his hand and congratulated him warmly, if rather briefly.[13] Lowe was soon afterwards granted the colonelcy of the 93rd Highland regiment, the first such vacancy to occur after his return to England.

But thereafter it was steadily downhill for Lowe all the way. A groundswell of criticism of his treatment of Napoleon on St Helena gathered steam, and attacks on Lowe began to appear in the press and elsewhere. It was even said that he was booed in the street. The situation was enflamed by the publication in July 1822 of Dr O'Meara's *Napoleon in Exile: A Voice from St Helena*. This became a popular bestseller and contained a vengeful attack on Lowe's conduct, depicting him as a brutal and tyrannical jailor. Lowe sought support from Lord Bathurst and the Prime Minister, Lord Liverpool, to rebut this but they were cool and evasive, and obviously intent on dropping him and making him a scapegoat. He therefore decided to seek redress at law, and retained the services of the Solicitor General, Sir John Copley, and a distinguished lawyer, Mr Tindal, to present his case.[14] They failed him completely. They took so long to compile the evidence against O'Meara, which involved gathering some twenty-one separate testimonies in Lowe's favour – including statements from Sir Thomas Reade, Brigadier-General Bingham, Dr Verling and, surprisingly in view of the contents of his diaries, Major Gorrequer – that by the time they brought the case before the judge in June 1823 it was declared out of time.

Hudson Lowe was angry and disappointed and considered bringing a civil action against O'Meara. When appealed to, however, neither Bathurst nor the Prime Minister would support him. Bathurst suggested that as a counter to O'Meara's book he should publish his own version of the events of his governorship of St Helena, but Lowe decided not to do this. This was perhaps an error of judgement because it would at least have given his supporters some material to deploy on his behalf. However, it is always a difficult question as to whether to reply publicly to public criticism or to keep silent. It can sometimes serve only to keep the issue alive, and Lowe may also have felt that he did not want to dignify O'Meara's extreme remarks by responding in writing to them.

Frustrated in his attempts to seek legal redress, Lowe lobbied Bathurst for a new post commensurate with his seniority and experience. The response was an insult. He was offered the governorship of the small dependent territory of Antigua, at a salary reduced from £5,000 to £3,000, a post much inferior to that which he had held on St Helena. He declined it and was then offered a slightly better post, that of commander of the British military forces in Ceylon, with the possibility of succeeding the current Governor when he retired. He accepted this and spent much of the following year travelling to Ceylon via Paris and other places familiar from his previous career.

He finally reached Ceylon and took command of some 2,000 troops and a small military headquarters staff – a smaller force than he had commanded on St Helena. In March 1827, however, he sought leave to return to Britain to defend himself against strong criticism in a new biography of Napoleon by Sir Walter Scott. Scott was a friend of Admiral Sir Pulteney Malcolm, with whom Lowe had quarrelled in St Helena, and had probably, with Malcolm's help, obtained improper access to official papers. Lowe was angry and hurt and wished to obtain support in London to rebut Scott's criticisms.

Lowe was granted leave and on the return journey to Britain he called in at St Helena and was again given a very warm welcome by the islanders. He visited Longwood House and was shocked to see how neglected and dilapidated it had already become. On reaching London he once more sought Lord Bathurst's support, but Bathurst was again unwilling to help and urged Lowe to return to Ceylon so that he would not miss the opportunity to be on the spot to succeed the incumbent Governor when he stepped down. Lowe also saw the Duke of Wellington, but failed to get his support for obtaining the governorship.[15]

Disappointed, Lowe returned to Ceylon, but fate betrayed him again. The expected vacancy as Governor arose at the end of 1830, but in the meantime the Government in Britain had changed, bringing in a Whig administration, with Earl Grey as Prime Minister. The Whigs had always been more sympathetic to Napoleon, and they appointed their own man, Sir Robert Wilmot Horton, as Governor. Lowe returned to Britain in 1831 and was never to hold public office again or receive the pension that was his due.

The rest of Lowe's life was one of sad decline. Bitter salt was rubbed in his wounds by having to read the triumphal accounts in the British press of the return of Napoleon's body to Paris in December 1840. *The Times* sent no fewer than seven reporters to cover the occasion. If Lowe got a mention, it was only as Napoleon's erstwhile brutal jailor. Some consolation came to the now-ailing septuagenarian in the belated bestowal of a GCMG in 1843 (the Grand Cross of St Michael and St George, known in diplomatic circles as 'God Calls Me God', but, alas, this hardly applied in Lowe's case) and his appointment to the colonelcy of his original regiment, the 50th of foot. He died, however, in relative poverty on 10 January 1844, in a small flat in London, and was buried without great ceremony in the crypt of St Mark's Church, in North Audley Street.

It was a sad end. Lowe was a difficult man, with many faults, who could have been a better custodian of Napoleon on St Helena. But he did what the Government had asked of him, and he did not deserve to be treated so shabbily and made a scapegoat when public opinion turned against them. This is unhappily not unusual behaviour in politics, and perhaps it said more about the politicians of the day than about Lowe. But Aesop's sick and fallen lion had certainly risen from the floor and kicked back at the ass.

NOTES

~~~

Introduction

1 Markham, *To Befriend an Emperor, Betsy Balcombe's Memoirs of Napoleon on St Helena*, p. 188.
2 Morgan, *Wellington's Victories*, pp. 117–18.
3 The account of the exhumation is based on Gourgaud's memoir of the 1840 expedition, *Le Retour des Cendres de l'Empereur Napoléon*, pp. 48–57.
4 *Ibid.*, p. 72.
5 The following account of the funeral is based largely on the eyewitness accounts by Marchand (pp. 589–91), Mameluck Ali (pp. 279–84) and Bertrand (pp. 267–7) in the memoirs cited in the bibliography and in Forsyth, *The Captivity of Napoleon at St Helena, from the Letters and Journals of Lieutenant-General Sir Hudson Lowe*, Vol. III, pp. 296 ff.

Chapter One

1 O'Meara, *Napoleon in Exile, A Voice from St Helena*, Vol. 1, p. 200.
2 Barbero, *The Battle, A History of the Battle of Waterloo*, p. 389.
3 *Ibid.*, p. 412.
4 Morgan, p. 112.
5 Roberts, *Napoleon and Wellington*, p. 163.
6 *Ibid.*, p. 152.
7 O'Meara, Vol. 1, p. 385.
8 Latimer, *Talks of Napoleon at St Helena with General Baron Gourgaud*, p. 191.
9 O'Meara, Vol. 1, p. 464.
10 Houssaye, *Waterloo 1815*, p. 410, n. 2.
11 Marchand, *Mémoires*, p. 227.
12 The following account of Napoleon's move to and stay at Malmaison, and the subsequent journey to Rochefort, is based largely on the accounts in Marchand, pp. 231 ff; Pincemaille, *La Reine Hortense, Mémoires*, Ch. 18,

pp. 373 ff; Latimer, pp. 9–12; and Mameluck Ali, *Souvenirs sur l'Empereur Napoléon*, pp. 120–9.

13   Marchand, p. 235.

14   Pincemaille, *La Reine Hortense*, p. 380.

15   Marchand, p. 246; and Mameluck Ali, p. 121.

16   Marchand, p. 253; Mameluck Ali, p. 121; and Cordingly, *Billy Ruffian; the Bellerophon and the Downfall of Napoleon*, pp. 228–9.

17   Marchand, p. 260.

18   From Montholon, *Récits de la Captivité*, quoted by Cordingly in *Billy Ruffian*, p. 234.

19   Much of the account of Napoleon's transfer to the frigate *Saale*, then to the Ile d'Aix and the subsequent surrender to the *Bellerophon* is based on Cordingly, *Billy Ruffian*, Ch. 16 and Pincemaille, *Napoléon et l'Ile d'Aix*, *passim*. There are also valuable eyewitness accounts in Marchand, pp. 255 ff; Mameluck Ali, pp. 129–32; and Las Cases, *Mémorial de Sainte Hélène*, Vol. 1, pp. 59–66.

20   Las Cases, Vol. 1, p. 62.

21   Cordingly, *Billy Ruffian*, p. 240.

22   Pincemaille, *Napoléon et l'Ile d'Aix*, pp. 114–15; Mameluck Ali, p. 130; and Marchand, p. 257.

23   Pincemaille, *Napoléon et l'Ile d'Aix* , p. 115; and Marchand, p. 257.

24   Marchand, pp. 257–8.

25   Cordingly, *Billy Ruffian*, pp. 236–8.

26   *Ibid.*, pp. 242–3; and Las Cases, Vol. 1, pp. 62–3.

27   O'Meara, Vol. 2, p. 392.

28   Las Cases, Vol. 1, p. 64.

29   Marchand, p. 258.

30   Latimer, p. 18.

31   The French text (see Marchand, p. 259) is: 'Altesse Royale, en butte aux factions qui divisent mon pays et à l'inimitiè des plus grandes puissances de l'Europe, j'ai consommé ma carrière politique, je viens comme Themistocle m'asseoir sur le foyer du people britannique, je me mets sous la protection de ses lois que je réclame de Votre Altesse Royale, comme celle du plus puissant, du plus constant, du plus généreux de mes ennemis.'

32   Roberts, p. 244.

33   The voyage on the *Epervier* is described in detail in the short monograph, *Napoléon à Bord de l'Epervier*, by Emile de Perceval, based on the eyewitness account of Gédéon Henri Pelletreau, an ensign on the *Epervier*.

34   Pincemaille, *Napoléon et l'Ile d'Aix*, p. 122; and Marchand, p. 260.

35 Marchand, p. 259.
36 Mameluck Ali, p. 132.
37 Las Cases, Vol. 1, p. 66.

Chapter Two

1   Cordingly, *Billy Ruffian*, p. 2.
2   Marchand, p. 264.
3   *Ibid.*
4   Cordingly, *Billy Ruffian*, p. 256.
5   *Ibid.*
6   Roberts, p. 195.
7   O'Meara, Vol. 1, p. 466.
8   Cordingly, *Billy Ruffian*, pp. 259–62, quoting Shorter, *Napoleon and his Fellow Travellers*, p. 295.
9   *Ibid.*, p. 263.
10 *Ibid.*
11 Marchand, p. 266.
12 Pincemaille, *La Reine Hortense*, p. 381.
13 O'Meara, Vol. 2, p. 184.
14 Lord Rosebery, *Napoleon, The Last Phase*, p. 58.
15 *Ibid.*, p. 60.
16 *Ibid.*
17 *Ibid.*, p. 57.
18 Marchand, p. 267. The French text of this passage is: 'Il serait peu d'accord avec notre devoir envers notre pays et les alliés de Sa Majesté que le général Bonaparte conservât le moyen ou l'occasion de troubler de nouveau la paix de l'Europe. C'est pourquoi il est absolument nécessaire qu'il soit restraint dans sa liberté personelle, autant que peut l'exiger ce premier et important objet. L'Ile Sainte-Hélène a été choisie pour sa future residence; son climat est sain et sa situation locale permettra qu'on l'y traite avec plus d'indulgence qu'on ne pourrait ailleurs, vu les precautions indispensables qu'on serait obligé d'employer pour s'assurer de sa personne.'
19 *Ibid.*, p. 268.
20 *Ibid.*, p. 269.
21 *Ibid.*, p. 271; Cordingly, *Billy Ruffian*, p. 272; and Mameluck Ali, p. 135.
22 Warden, *Letters Written on Board HMS The Northumberland and St Helena*, p. 5.
23 Marchand, p. 270.

24 Cordingly, *Billy Ruffian*, p. 274.

25 The customs inspection is described by Marchand, pp. 274–5.

26 Reported by Marchand, p. 275.

27 *Ibid.*, p. 277.

28 *Ibid.*

29 *Ibid.*, p. 278.

Chapter Three

1   Rosebery, p. 64.

2   *Ibid.*, p. 62.

3   *Ibid.*, p. 63.

4   Marchand, p. 279; Las Cases, pp. 92–3; Mameluck Ali, pp. 139–40.

5   The crossing the line ceremony is described vividly by Marchand, p. 283; Mameluck Ali, p. 142; and Las Cases, p. 160.

6   Marchand, p. 284; Mameluck Ali, p. 142; and Las Cases, pp. 116–17 and 184–5.

7   Las Cases, p. 115.

8   *Ibid.*, p. 129.

9   Rosebery, p. 21.

10 Mameluck Ali, p. 172; and Las Cases, p. 159.

11 Marchand, p. 280; and Mameluck Ali, p. 138.

12 Las Cases, p. 103.

13 Warden, p. 28.

14 Las Cases, p. 104.

15 *Ibid.*, pp. 103–4.

16 This is recorded in Chaplin, *Napoleon's Captivity on St Helena, 1815–1821*, p. 42.

17 Las Cases, p. 189.

18 *Ibid.*, pp. 189–90.

19 Marchand, p. 284.

20 Las Cases, p. 190.

21 *Ibid.*

22 Attributed to Madame Bertrand in Chevalier et al., *Sainte Hélène, Ile de Mémoire*.

23 O'Meara, Vol. 1, p. 8.

24 Marchand, p. 285.

Chapter Four

1 There is an excellent description of the island, covering its history, topography, geology and flora and fauna in the 2007 Bradt Travel Guide by Sue Steiner and Robin Liston.

2 Moorehead, *Darwin and the Beagle*, pp. 239–40.

3 Rosebery, p. 62.

4 Marchand, pp. 285–6.

5 *Ibid.*, p. 286.

6 *Ibid.*

7 The account of Napoleon's arrival and his subsequent stay with the Balcombes at the Briars is based on the detailed description in Betsy Balcombe's memoirs, *To Befriend an Emperor*, published in 1844. See Markham, *To Befriend an Emperor*, pp. 35–7, 42–71, 74–7, 79–91.

8 Marchand, p. 287.

9 *Ibid.*, p. 288.

10 Mameluck Ali, pp. 145–6.

11 Marchand, p. 291; and Mameluck Ali, p. 146.

12 Roberts, pp. 215–16.

13 Las Cases, Vol. 1, p. 195.

14 Marchand, p. 295.

15 Rosebery, p. 42; and Markham, *To Befriend an Emperor*, pp. 49–50.

16 Markham, *To Befriend an Emperor*, p. 44.

17 *Ibid.*, pp. 14 and 34.

18 *Ibid.*, p. 42.

19 Marchand, p. 305.

20 Las Cases, p. 284; and Markham, *To Befriend an Emperor*, p. 88.

Chapter Five

1 Markham, *To Befriend an Emperor*, pp. 111–12.

2 Tulard, *Itinéraire de Napoléon au Jour le Jour, 1796–1821*, p. 625.

3 O'Meara, Vol. 1, p. 312.

4 *Ibid.*, Vol. 2, p. 200.

5 De Candé-Montholon, *Journal Secret d'Albine de Montholon, Maîtresse de Napoléon à Sainte Hélène*, pp. 151–2.

6 Wilson, *Lady Malcolm, A Diary of St Helena, 1816–17*, p. 19.

7 Martineau, *La Vie Quotidienne à Sainte-Hélène au Temps de Napoléon*, p. 49.

8 Marchand, p. 428.
9 Martineau, *La Vie Quotidienne*, p. 53.
10 Forsyth, Vol. 2, p. 246.
11 O'Meara, Vol. 1, p. 270.
12 Rosebery, p. 8.
13 A particularly vivid and comprehensive account of all aspects of daily life at Longwood is to be found in Martineau's *La Vie Quotidienne*, particularly Ch. 2, pp. 46–82.

Chapter Six

1 Rosebery, p. 66.
2 There is an excellent account of Sir Hudson Lowe's background and career prior to St Helena in Forsyth, Vol. 1, pp. 85–137.
3 Fournier La Touraille, *Hudson Lowe, le Geôlier de Napoléon*, p. 13.
4 O'Meara, Vol. 1, p. 93.
5 Fournier La Touraille, p. 18.
6 Forsyth, Vol. 1, p. 99.
7 Fournier La Touraille, p. 21.
8 Rosebery, p. 66.
9 Las Cases, Vol. 1, p. 528.
10 Fournier La Touraille, p. 22.
11 *Ibid.*, pp. 24–5.
12 *Ibid.*, pp. 28–9.
13 Forsyth, Vol. 1, p. 270.
14 *Ibid.*, Vol. 1, p. 15.
15 O'Meara, Vol. 2, p. 118.
16 Chaplin, pp. 222–3.

Chapter Seven

1 Fournier La Touraille, p. 35.
2 *Ibid.*, pp. 37–8.
3 A plaque commemorating these annexations can be seen in the Naval Museum at Simon's Town in South Africa.
4 Detailed accounts of this non-meeting and of the subsequent first meeting between Sir Hudson Lowe and Napoleon on 17 April 1816 can be found in Marchand, pp. 330–3; Las Cases, Vol. 1, p. 524; O'Meara, Vol. 1, pp. 27–8; Forsyth, Vol. 1, p. 138; and Fournier La Touraille, pp. 39–44.

5 Marchand, p. 331.

6 *Ibid.*, p. 332.

7 Fournier La Touraille, p. 44; and Forsyth, Vol. 1, p. 147.

8 Fournier La Touraille, pp. 44–5.

9 The second meeting between Lowe and Napoleon on 30 April 1816 and the events that preceded it are described in Las Cases, Vol. 1, pp. 560–64; and Forsyth, Vol. 1, pp. 158–62.

10 Marchand, p. 333.

11 *Ibid.*, p. 336.

12 Las Cases, Vol. 1, p. 564.

13 *Ibid.*, Vol. 1, p. 564; and O'Meara, Vol. 1, p. 47.

14 Malraux, *Vie de Napoléon par Lui-Même*, p. 347; and Las Cases, Vol. 1, p. 658.

15 The Countess of Loudoun incident is described in Marchand, p. 338; Las Cases, Vol. 1, pp. 629–30; Forsyth, Vol. 1, pp. 169–70; and Fournier La Touraille, pp. 56–8.

16 Fournier La Touraille, p. 59.

17 Tulard, p. 611.

18 Marchand, p. 365.

19 Forsyth, Vol. 1, p. 179.

20 *Ibid.*, p. 190.

21 The text of the Paris Convention is set out in French on pp. 339–40 of Marchand.

22 Wilson, p. 41.

23 There are accounts of the fourth meeting between Lowe and Napoleon on 21 June 1816 in Marchand, pp. 347–8; O'Meara, Vol. 1, p. 65; Forsyth, Vol. 1, p. 195; and Fournier La Touraille, p. 71.

24 Marchand, p. 348.

25 The fifth meeting between Lowe and Napoleon on 16 July 1816 is described in O'Meara, Vol. 1, p. 78; Forsyth, Vol. 1, p. 220; and Las Cases, Vol. 1, pp. 658–61.

26 There is a full discussion of the Longwood expenses issue in Martineau, *La Vie Quotidienne*, p. 84ff.

27 O'Meara, Vol. 1, p. 89.

28 The sixth and final meeting between Lowe and Napoleon on 18 August 1816 is well covered in accounts by Marchand, pp. 353–4; O'Meara, Vol. 1, pp. 93–5; Forsyth, Vol. 1, pp. 245–55; and Fournier La Touraille, pp. 91–4.

29 Forsyth, Vol. 1, p. 255.

30 The full text is given by Marchand, pp. 354–60.
31 Forsyth, Vol. 1, p. 276.
32 *Ibid.*, p. 297.
33 O'Meara, Vol. 1, p. 99.

Chapter Eight

1 Thompson, *Napoleon's Letters*, pp. 309–10.
2 Forsyth, Vol. 1, pp. 360–2.
3 These figures are taken from the estimates in Martineau, *La Vie Quotidienne*, pp. 94–5.
4 The affair of the breaking up and sale of Napoleon's silver is described in Marchand, pp. 368–70; O'Meara, Vol. 1, pp. 122–3; Forsyth, Vol. 1, pp. 283–8; and Fournier La Touraille, p. 97.
5 Forsyth, Vol. 1, p. 287.
6 Marchand, p. 369.
7 *Ibid.*, p. 371; and O'Meara, Vol. 1, p. 138.
8 *Ibid.*, p. 372.
9 *Ibid.*, p. 373.
10 Rosebery, p. 77.
11 *Ibid.*
12 O'Meara, Vol. 1, pp. 157–62.
13 Forsyth, Vol. 2, p. 68.
14 The arrest and deportation of Las Cases are described in Marchand, pp. 382–92; O'Meara, Vol. 1, pp. 224–9; Forsyth, Vol. 2, p. 75; and Fournier La Touraille, pp. 104–8.
15 Marchand, p. 383.
16 Forsyth, Vol. 2, p. 75.
17 The full text of this letter is in Marchand, pp. 386–8.
18 This incident is described in Marchand, p. 389.
19 *Ibid.*, p. 392.
20 Mameluck Ali, p. 231.
21 Marchand, p. 398.
22 *Ibid.*, p. 428.
23 Forsyth, Vol. 2, p. 254.
24 Claude Ribbe, *Le Crime de Napoléon*, p. 76.
25 Bertrand, *Napoleon at St Helena, Memoirs of General Bertrand*, p. 69.

26 The subject of Napoleon and his wives and mistresses is covered comprehensively in Hibbert, *Napoleon, His Wives and Women*, and Castelot, *Napoléon et les Femmes*.

27 Roberts, p. 130.

28 Bertrand, pp. 124–5.

29 *Ibid.*, p. 125.

30 Hibbert, p. 263.

31 Warden, p. 126.

32 Ribbe, pp. 76–9.

33 J. David Markham, *Napoleon and Dr Verling on St Helena*, p. 94.

34 Hibbert, p. 263.

35 Markham, *Napoleon and Dr Verling*, pp. 59–60.

36 Bertrand, p. 218.

37 *Ibid.*, pp. 197–8.

38 Warden, p. 180.

39 Markham, *Napoleon and Dr Verling*, p. 47.

40 De Candé-Montholon, p. 149.

41 Bertrand, p. 127 and note 32 on p. 143.

42 Markham, *Napoleon and Dr Verling*, p. 33.

43 *Ibid.*, p. 47.

44 Marchand, p. 456.

45 Markham, *Napoleon and Dr Verling*, p. 98.

46 O'Meara, Vol. 1, p. 366.

47 There are full descriptions of Napoleon's gardening phase in Marchand, pp. 486–8; and Mameluck Ali, pp. 186–204.

48 Antommarchi, *Les Derniers Moments de Napoléon*, Vol. 1, p. 363.

49 O'Meara, Vol. 2, p. 463.

50 Forsyth, Vol. 2, pp. 209–10.

51 The seesaw incident is amusingly described by Bertrand, pp. 18–19; and by Mameluck Ali, p. 244.

Chapter Nine

1 Rosebery, p. 119.

2 Forsyth, Vol. 2, p. 50.

3 *Ibid.*, p. 129.

4 Fournier La Touraille, p. 75.

5 Copies of the exchanges between Lowe and Dr Verling are to be found in Chapter 10 of Markham, *Napoleon and Dr Verlingen on St Helena*.

6   *Ibid.*, p. 157.

7   Wilson, pp. 21–2.

8   *Ibid.*, p. 36.

9   *Ibid.*, p. 111.

10 Wilson, p. 11.

11 Marchand, pp. 400–1; and Fournier La Touraille, p. 112.

12 Forsyth, Vol. 2, p. 129.

13 The following account of the behaviour of Major Gorrequer and his relationship with Sir Hudson and Lady Lowe is based on the coded diaries of Gorrequer, *St Helena During Napoleon's Exile, Gorrequer's Diary*, deciphered by James Kemble and published in 1969.

14 Kemble, p. 25.

15 *Ibid.*, p. 123.

16 *Ibid.*, p. 158.

17 *Ibid.*, p. 267.

18 *Ibid.*, p. 79.

19 O'Meara, Vol. 1, p. 7.

20 Rosebery, p. 31.

21 Forsyth, Vol. 1, p. v of Preface.

22 Fournier La Touraille, pp. 95 and 98.

23 Marchand, p. 365.

24 O'Meara, Vol. 1, p. 267.

25 *Ibid.*, p. 292.

26 *Ibid.*, p. 186.

27 *Ibid.*, p. 136.

28 *Ibid.*, pp. 282–3.

29 *Ibid.*, p. 298.

30 The Lascelles and 66th regiment incident is described by O'Meara, Vol. 2, pp. 408–10.

31 *Ibid.*, p. 414.

32 *Ibid.*, p. 415.

33 *Ibid.* O'Meara's dismissal, including Hudson Lowe's letter informing Napoleon, is also covered in Marchand, pp. 434–5.

34 Markham, *Napoleon and Dr Verling*, p. 144.

35 Kemble, pp. 71–2.

36 The Breame and Hodson affair, together with the East India Company directors' letter to Hudson Lowe, are described in Chaplin, pp. 176–86.

37 *Ibid.*, pp. 233–4.

38 Ribbe, p. 85.

Chapter Ten

1 Marchand, p. 429.
2 The Rev. Boys' behaviour is described in detail in Chaplin, pp. 220–32.
3 Pocock, *Captain Marryat, Seaman, Writer and Adventurer*, pp. 79–80.
4 Forsyth, Vol. 2, p. 51.
5 Marchand, pp. 415–16.
6 *Ibid.*
7 Forsyth, Vol. 3, p. 154.
8 Marchand, pp. 519–20.
9 *Ibid.*, p. 518.
10 *Ibid.*
11 *Ibid.*, p. 522.
12 Bertrand, p. 149.
13 Forsyth, Vol. 2, pp. 213–14.
14 Mameluck Ali, pp. 244–5.
15 Rosebery, p. 143.
16 Marchand, pp. 474–5.
17 *Ibid.*, p. 476.
18 O'Meara, Vol. 2, p. 251.
19 *Ibid.*, pp. 236–7.
20 *Ibid.*, p. 407.
21 Marchand, pp. 450–2.
22 Antommarchi, Vol. 1, pp. 237–8.
23 *Ibid.*, p. 371.
24 Forsyth, Vol. 3, pp. 243–5. Mount Pleasant, with its wonderful vistas, still exists and is occupied by one of the island's leading families.
25 Antommarchi, Vol. 1, p. 387.
26 Mameluck Ali, p. 240.
27 The attendance of Dr Arnott from early April 1821 until Napoleon's death is described in detail by Marchand, p. 531 onwards and Bertrand, p. 134 onwards.
28 The affair of the book on Marlborough is referred to by Bertrand, p. 180 ff and Mameluck Ali, pp. 260–3, and also discussed in Dr Martin Howard's *Napoleon's Poisoned Chalice: The Emperor and his Doctors on St Helena*, pp. 201–2.
29 The dictation of the will is described by Marchand, p. 536 ff (the text of the will is given in full on pp. 598–613); Bertrand, pp. 180 ff; and Mameluck Ali, pp. 260–3.

30 Marchand, p. 611 and note 376, p. 730.

31 Roberts, pp. 242–3.

32 *Ibid.*, p. 243.

33 Bertrand, pp. 88–9.

34 The following description of Napoleon's last days and the treatment administered to him by his doctors is based largely on the detailed accounts in the memoirs cited above of Marchand, Bertrand and Antommarchi. There is also a full account in Forsyth, Vol. 3, p. 274 ff.

35 Marchand, p. 562.

36 Bertrand, p. 259.

37 Mameluck Ali, p. 270.

38 Bertrand, p. 181.

39 Antommarchi's report, under cover of a statement signed by Bertrand and Montholon, is set out on pp. 577–9 of Marchand, and in Antommarchi's own journal, Vol. 2, pp. 161–74. There is a briefer account in Bertrand, pp. 261–2.

40 *Qui a Tué Napoleon?* by Ben Weider and David Hapgood, 1982, and *Napoleon, Est il Mort Empoisonné?* by Weider, 1995.

41 Report in *Guardian*, 13 February 2008.

42 Lentz and Macé, *La Mort de Napoléon, Mythes, Légendes et Mystères*, p. 66.

43 Howard, p. 196.

Chapter Eleven

1 Lord Rosebery, p. 28.

2 *Ibid.*, p. 31.

3 *Ibid.*, p. 22.

4 *Ibid.*, p. 46.

5 *Ibid.*, p. 66.

6 Roberts, p. 236.

7 Forsyth, Vol. 2, p. 50.

8 Marchand, pp. 407–8; O'Meara, Vol. 2, p. 98; and Forsyth, Vol. 2, p. 145.

9 *Ibid.*, p. 406.

10 Bertrand, p. 264; and Forsyth, Vol. 3, p. 295.

11 Forsyth, Vol. 3, pp. 224–5.

12 O'Meara, Vol. 1, p. 101.

13 *Ibid.*, p. 122.

14 Harvey, *Cochrane, The Life and Exploits of a Fighting Captain*, p. 226.

15 Pocock, p. 80.
16 O'Meara, Vol. 1, p. 371.
17 Forsyth, Vol. 3, p. 288.
18 Antommarchi, Vol. 2, p. 180.
19 Forsyth, Vol. 3, p. 288.
20 Aristotle, *Poetics*, pp. 9–10.
21 Thompson, p. 120.
22 See, for example, *ibid.*, pp. 148–9 and 150–3.
23 *Ibid.*, p. 296.
24 O'Meara, Appendices to Vol. 3, pp. 481–3.
25 Pincemaille, *La Reine Hortense*, p. 297.
26 O'Meara, Vol. 1, p. 408.
27 Wilson, p. 159.
28 Forsyth, Vol. 2, p. 254.
29 Markham, *To Befriend an Emperor*, p. 187.

Epilogue

1 Marchand, pp. 592 ff.
2 Bertrand, p. 269.
3 Fournier La Touraille, p. 188.
4 Marchand, pp. 596–7.
5 De Candé-Montholon, p. 22.
6 The following account of the return of Napoleon's remains to Paris is based largely on the narrative in Gilbert Martineau's *Napoleon's Last Journey*.
7 *Ibid.*, p. 141.
8 *Ibid.*, p. 143.
9 Trollope, *Paris and the Parisians*, p. 9.
10 *Ibid.*, pp. 167–8.
11 Fournier La Touraille, p. 189.
12 *Ibid.*, p. 190; and Forsyth, Vol. 3, pp. 313–14.
13 Fournier La Touraille, p. 191.
14 There is a full account of Hudson Lowe's unsuccessful attempt to seek redress at law against O'Meara in Forsyth, Vol. 3, pp. 316 ff.
15 *Ibid.*, pp. 331–2.

SELECT
BIBLIOGRAPHY

~~~

Antommarchi, Francesco, *Les Derniers Moments de Napoléon* (2 Vols, Henry Cockburn, 1825)

Arnott, Dr Archibald, *An Account of the Last Illness and Decease and PM Appearance of Napoleon Bonaparte* (London, 1822)

Aristotle, *Poetics*, trans. Kenneth McLeish (Nick Hern Books, 2000)

Barbero, Alessandro, *The Battle: A History of the Battle of Waterloo* (Atlantic Books, 2006)

Bertrand, Count Henri Gratien, *Napoléon at St Helena, Memoirs of General Bertrand*, ed. Paul Fleuriot de Langle, trans. Frances Humey (Cassel, 1953)

Brisville, Jean-Claude, *La Dernière Salve* (Actes Sud, 1995)

Castelot, André, *Le Fils de l'Empereur* (Presses Pocket, 1960)

—— *Napoléon et les Femmes* (Perrin, 1998)

Chaplin, Arnold, *Napoleon's Captivity on St Helena, 1815–1821* (Savannah, 2002)

Chateaubriand, *Vie de Napoléon* (Editions de Fallois, 1999)

Chevalier, Bernard *et al.*, *Sainte Hélène, Ile de Mémoire* (Fayard, 2005)

Cordingly, David, *Billy Ruffian, the Bellerophon and the Downfall of Napoleon* (Bloomsbury, 2003)

—— *Cochrane, The Dauntless* (Bloomsbury, 2007)

Cronin, Vincent, *Napoleon* (History Book Club, 1971)

De Candé-Montholon, François, *Journal Secret d'Albine de Montholon, Maîtresse de Napoléon à Sainte Hélène* (Albine Michel, 2002)

De Perceval, Emile, *Napoléon à Bord de l'Epervier* (Collection Rediviva, 1998)

De Villepin, Dominique, *Le Soleil Noir de la Puissance, 1796–1807* (Perrin 2007)

Forsyth, William, *The Captivity of Napoleon at St Helena, from the Letters and Journals of Lieutenant-General Sir Hudson Lowe* (3 Vols, John Murray, 1853)

Fournier La Touraille, Jean-Pierre, *Hudson Lowe, Le Geôlier de Napoléon* (Perrin, 2006)

Fumaroli, Marc, *Chateaubriand, Vie de Napoléon,* (Editions de Fallois, 1999)

Gallo, Max, *Napoléon, L'Immortal de Sainte Hélène* (Editions Robert Laffont, 1997)

Gourgaud, Gaspard, *Le Retour des Cendres de l'Empereur Napoléon,* ed. Christophe Bourachot (Arlea, 2003)

Harvey, Robert, *Cochrane, The Life and Exploits of a Fighting Captain* (Robinson, 2000)

Hazareesingh, Sudhir, *The Legend of Napoleon* (Granta Books, 2004)

Hibbert, Christopher, *Napoleon, His Wives and Women* (Harper Collins, 2002)

Houssaye, Henry, *Waterloo 1815,* ed. Christian de Bartillat (Imprimerie Hérissey 1987)

Howard, Dr Martin, *Napoleon's Poisoned Chalice: The Emperor and his Doctors on St Helena* (The History Press, 2009)

Kauffmann, Jean-Paul, *La Chambre Noire de Longwood* (La Table Ronde, 1997)

Kemble, James, *St Helena During Napoleon's Exile, Gorrequer's Diary* (Heinemann, 1969)

Las Cases, Emmanuel, *Mémorial de Sainte-Hélène* (2 Vols, Editions de Seuil, 1968)

Latimer, Elizabeth Wormeley, *Talks of Napoleon at St Helena with General Baron Gourgaud* (McClury, 1903)

Lemaire, Thierry, *La Plume de l'Aigle, La Correspondance de Napoléon* (Scriptura Editions, 2004)

Lentz, Thierry, and Jacques Macé, *La Mort de Napoléon, Mythes, Légendes et Mystères* (Perrin, 2009)

Malraux, André, *Vie de Napoléon par Lui-Même* (Editions Gallimard, 1930)

Mameluck Ali, *Souvenirs sur l'Empereur Napoléon,* ed. Christophe Bourachot (Arlea, 2000)

Marchand, *Mémoires,* ed. Jean Bourguignon, (Tallandier, Bibliothèque Napoléonienne, 2003)

Markham, J. David, *Napoleon and Dr Verling on Saint Helena* (Pen and Sword, 2005)

—— *Napoleon's Road to Glory* (Brassey's, 2003)

—— *To Befriend an Emperor, Betsy Balcombe's Memoirs of Napoleon on St Helena* (Revenhall Books, 2005)

Martineau, Gilbert, *Napoleon's Last Journey,* trans. Frances Partridge (John Murray, 1976)

——— *La Vie Quotidienne à Sainte-Hélène au Temps de Napoléon* (Tallendier, Bibliothèque Napoléonienne, 2005)

McLynn, Frank, *Napoleon, A Biography* (Pimlico, 1997)

Moorehead, Alan, *Darwin and the Beagle*, (Hamish Hamilton, 1969)

Morgan, Matthew, *Wellington's Victories* (O'Mara Books Ltd, 2004)

Nofi, Albert, *The Waterloo Campaign* (Combined Publishing, 1993)

O'Meara, Barry E., *Napoleon in Exile: A Voice from St Helena* (2 Vols, Peter Eckler, 1823)

Pincemaille, Christophe, *La Reine Hortense, Mémoires* (Mercure de France, 2006)

——— *Napoléon et l'Ile d'Aix* (Geste Editions, 2008)

Pocock, Tom, *Captain Marryat, Seaman, Writer and Adventurer* (Chatham Publishing, 2000)

Ribbe, Claude, *Le Crime de Napoléon* (Privé, 2005)

Roberts, Andrew, *Napoleon and Wellington*, (Weidenfeld and Nicolson, 2001)

Rose, J.H., *The Life of Napoleon I* (Bell and Sons, 1924)

Rosebery, Lord, *Napoleon, The Last Phase* (Arthur L. Humphreys, 1900)

Roy-Henry, Bruno, *Napoléon, L'Enigme de l'Exhume de 1840* (L'Archipel, 2000)

Smith, Timothy Wilson, *Napoleon* (Haus Publishing, 2007)

Steiner, Sue and Robin Liston, *St Helena, Ascension and Tristan da Cunha* (Bradt Travel Guide, 2nd Edition, 2007)

Thompson, J.M., *Napoleon's Letters* (Prion, 1998)

Trollope, Fanny, *Paris and the Parisians* (Alan Sutton, 1985)

Tudoret, Patrick, *La Gloire et la Cendre, L'Ultime Victoire de l'Empereur* (La Table Ronde, 2008)

Tulard, Jean and Jourquin Jacques, *Itinéraire de Napoléon au Jour le Jour, 1796–1821* (Tallendier, Bibliothèque Napoléonienne, 2002)

Warden, William, *Letters Written on Board HMS The Northumberland and St Helena* (R. Ackermann, 1816)

Weider, Ben, *My Pilgrimage to St Helena* (International Napoleonic Society 2005)

——— *Napoléon, Est-il Mort Empoisonné?* (Pygmalion-Gérard Watelet, Paris 1999)

——— and David Hapgood, *Qui a Tué Napoléon?* (Robert Laffont, Paris 1994)

Wilson, Sir Arthur, *Lady Malcolm, A Diary of St Helena, 1816–17* (A.D. Innes, 1899)

PICTURE CREDITS

~~~

INDEX

~~~